CHANGING PATTERNS OF RELIGIOUS EDUCATION

CHANGING PATTERNS
OF
RELIGIOUS
EDUCATION

Edited by
Marvin J. Taylor

ABINGDON PRESS
Nashville

Library of Congress Cataloging in Publication Data

Main entry under title:
Changing patterns of religious education.
Bibliography: p.
Includes index.
1. Christian education—Addresses, essays, lectures.
I. Taylor, Marvin J., 1921–
BV1471.2.C47   1984   207   83-22400

ISBN 0-687-06046-X

Table 5.1 "Faith Stages by Aspects" (pp. 80-81) from *Stages of Faith: The Psychology of Human Development and the Quest for Meaning* by James W. Fowler. Copyright © 1981 by James W. Fowler. Reprinted by permission of Harper & Row, Publishers, Inc.

MANUFACTURED BY THE PARTHENON PRESS AT
NASHVILLE, TENNESSEE, UNITED STATES OF AMERICA

Contents

Introduction

This book is the sixth in a succession of introductory survey volumes published by Abingdon Press across more than half a century. The first was *Studies in Religious Education*, issued in 1931. Following the Second World War Philip H. Lotz edited *Orientation to Religious Education*, which appeared in 1950. Since that date I have served as editor for four additional volumes: *Religious Education: A Comprehensive Survey* (1960); *An Introduction to Christian Education* (1966); *Foundations for Christian Education in an Era of Change* (1976); and this collection. The goal through the years has been to provide persons interested in keeping abreast of religious education theory and practice, as well as college and seminary classes, with periodic overviews. This edition is dedicated to continuing this long line of service to clergy, lay religious education leaders, faculty, and students.

The discerning reader will note that in this series of volumes the titles have shifted from religious education to Christian education and then back again to religious education. This has not been merely accidental, and perhaps a word of explanation will be helpful. When the largely lay-led Sunday school traditions which characterized nineteenth-century educational practice became formalized and regularized into a professional "movement," it became known universally as "the religious education movement." There was no clear theological declaration in this title. It was simply a way of separating education which had *religious* purposes from general education of all varieties. It also reflected the fact that every religious body has educational ideals and programs, and this facilitated dialogue among them. Thus, the Religious Education Association could become "interfaith" (that is, Protestant, Catholic, and Jewish) from its early years. During and following World War II much criticism of the movement emerged. Influenced by America's belated discovery of Karl Barth, religious education was judged to be indefensibly liberal: that is, making entirely too little of its distinctively Christian heritage.

7

And for the next fifteen to twenty years *religious* tended to be replaced with *Christian,* and theological foundations were more central. While the importance of theology remains substantial, today this emphasis has nonetheless diminished, and the use of the more generic *religious* has become customary. Hence the reader would be quite mistaken if any *theological* inference is drawn from the title shift.

The format of the volumes has remained constant throughout the entire series. An editor plans the essays and solicits contributions from persons especially capable in the precise area of the chapter. In almost every instance, the contributors have written at much greater length elsewhere on these topics. That is the primary reason that this group of writers was selected. Their expertise will be apparent in the bibliographies and notes following the chapters. The purpose here has been to be oriented toward introduction and survey. Brief essays such as these could never be exhaustive. Many of the topics are so rich in resources that graduate programs in religious education have entire courses in virtually every one. To repeat: the goal here has been on introductory survey—the kind that will be useful for beginning courses in the field. The chapter references and the general bibliography at the end of the volume provide each reader with ready access to additional materials if a particular topic elicits interest and additional study is stimulated.

An examination of the table of contents will reveal the plan for the volume. Noting the fact that "mainline" Protestant, evangelical Protestant, and Roman Catholic educational patterns do have some parallel characteristics, contrasts among them have been established wherever possible. This did not prove possible in every instance, since some materials simply did not become available in a timely fashion. There are also some omissions which will be evident to the thoughtful reader. Higher education as a field of religious education does not appear, although it was included in earlier volumes. And the emphasis on non-North American education found in the 1976 book has not been repeated here. Nor has religious education in elementary and secondary schools been included, whether in public institutions or private Christian day schools. None of the religious education organizations are covered, nor are the entire subjects of organization and administration. The book obviously would be enhanced by the addition of those contributions. But an editor and a publisher must inevitably set some limits on a volume to make it feasible. The fields and topics covered represent those which we decided to include and which were available. Some readers may well wish that other choices had been made or that a larger volume had been projected. These selections appeared to be reasonable to us.

I am especially grateful to the twenty-one contributors whose work appears here. If the book proves to be useful, the credit is primarily theirs. In the midst of busy schedules and other obligations, they met deadlines and generally responded to my queries and overtures with enthusiasm and courtesy. I am deeply appreciative.

Marvin J. Taylor

CHAPTER 1

Theological Foundations for Religious Nurture

C. Ellis Nelson

The word *theology* is not in the Bible. The Bible contains statements of belief on almost every page; but the beliefs are stated in relation to specific life situations, or they are generalizations about a perennial life condition such as sin. These statements of belief are not gathered together in one place to form a complete system of thought about the Christian religion or about the faith of the Jews. The Apostle Paul's explanation of the role of faith, rather than law, in salvation in Romans 1–9, for example, is a strong comprehensive statement; but it is too brief to cover the whole subject of sin and salvation. Like other biblical writers, Paul was concerned with writing about God in relation to contemporary events and situations, rather than with composing a comprehensive theological system.

The word *theology* literally means "knowledge of God," and the inference is that theology is a system of doctrine or a well-worked-out statement of belief. It came into being when Christianity moved into the Greco-Roman world. At that time the first theological need was to identify the true beliefs of the new religion as distinct from heresy. One of the first widely accepted theological statements was the Apostles' Creed, thought to have been formulated against Marcion, who in the second century denied that the God of the Old Testament was the God of the New Testament. Another early theological need was that of adjusting Christian beliefs to Greek philosophy, which was prevalent among educated persons even in New Testament times (I Cor. 1:22). The Gospel of John reflects a philosophical outlook, as does the Nicene Creed (A.D. 325). There has always been a certain amount of tension between the Christian faith and any philosophy seeking to harmonize these beliefs within its system of thought. Tertullian (A.D. 160–220) formulated the problem with his famous question, "What has Athens to do with Jerusalem?" Many Christian

---

C. Ellis Nelson is President Emeritus of Louisville Presbyterian Seminary and Visiting Professor at Austin Presbyterian Theological Seminary.

theologians have answered that question by developing a theology with philosophical assumptions. Thomas Aquinas (1225–1274) used the philosophy of Aristotle, and in our day Paul Tillich has used the philosophies of Schelling and Kierkegaard.

The word *theology* is most commonly used to mean a systematic explanation of the Christian faith. This usage follows the definition offered by Anselm of Canterbury (1033–1109) in the subtitle to one of his books, *Faith Seeking Understanding*. This brilliant phrase, probably a paraphrase of ideas from Augustine, gives priority to faith; yet it is a kind of faith that has an internal compulsion to think about what it means to believe in God. This definition is widely accepted because all Christians have beliefs arising out of their heritage and religious experience. Thinking about beliefs so that they make sense out of contemporary life helps people become more secure in their religion.

The Role of Theology

For the purpose of this essay, the word *theology* will be used to mean a system of beliefs about God, humankind, nature, history, ethics, church, and related topics which have been formulated to help Christians understand their faith. However, theology is not just the content of faith: it is also an ongoing process, since a living faith must be related to modern knowledge and new discoveries. So the work of theology is never completed, and denominations and faith groups revise their doctrines from time to time to reflect changes in their understanding of faith.

Because Christian theology defines beliefs and often clarifies them in contrast to the beliefs of other religions or ideologies, theology has an apologetic function. This does not mean that modern theologians write in a forensic style, but it does mean that they make a case for Christianity which will stand up intellectually with contemporary knowledge. This process helps the faith of believers become more significant as they relate their faith to life around them.

Theologians and their work of finding meaning for life in the light of God's revelation play an indispensable role in the communication of faith. Educators, ministers, and lay leaders all need clarity about faith in order to communicate it correctly. Moreover, theologians—in formulating and explaining beliefs— will often prioritize beliefs, differentiating the essential from the less important and thus helping the church to use effectively the limited time available for instruction.

Limitations of Theology

Theology is an effort to love God with the mind; but we are expected to love God also with our heart, soul, and strength and to love our neighbor as ourself (Deut. 6:4-5 and Matt. 22:37-40). Individual theologians and the official theology of denominations recognize that the Christian religion is to be lived—not just thought about—because elements of faith, hope, love, prayer, and moral behavior involve the whole person. Moreover, the work and worship of a congregation involve more than thought, although theology should relate in a meaningful way to the whole life of the person or congregation. Theology affects practical, day-to-day life, but it is difficult to find an exact correlation. This difficulty arises, perhaps, because in our personal lives bodily instincts and selfish desires often overcome the rational choices of the mind. In church life our fears or our desires for security dictate decisions which do not always inculcate the love of neighbor we publicly profess. This human condition has been noticed since history was recorded. It is not a criticism of theology but a recognition that the rational, conscious work of the mind has limitations. In regard to the practical work of the church, the limitations of theology are as follows.

1. *Theology is one or two steps from experience.* John Macquarrie lists experience first as a formative source of theology.[1] We have experience before we reflect on it. This is true in our personal lives, for we have experiences of faith, love, and the symbols of religion (cross, communion, baptism) before the mind has developed to the stage of doing logical thinking at about the age of twelve to fourteen years. It is also true in our corporate lives, for things happen (wars, accidents, disease) before we think about the exact meaning of such events.

Experience, as such, as Jürgen Moltmann has pointed out, does not interest theologians very much unless they can generalize it to apply to the human condition or to conceptions of God.[2] These generalizing processes, necessary for theology, remove thought from life. This sets up a situation whereby ministers and educators who work with the experiences people are having may not easily be able to relate human events to the abstractions of theology. Unless some relation can be made between the experiences of ordinary people and theology which explains and illuminates experience, theology becomes esoteric.

2. *Theology is unable to provide a Christian answer to ethical questions.* If we examine the thought of theologians and the official creedal statements of major denominations, we will not find a Christian answer to specific ethical questions. Some Roman

Catholic theologians approve war; others sharing the same official theology are pacifists. The Presbyterian Church, U.S., has officially approved abortion under certain conditions while some Presbyterian theologians reject that position. The United Methodist Church has ordained ministers who are homosexuals, while the United Presbyterian Church U.S.A. has voted not to do so.

The issue is not whether theology is concerned with ethics—it is. The issue is how to relate theology to specific ethical matters. Several proposals have been made. John Bennett has suggested a "middle axiom," by which he means guidance that is "more concrete than a universal ethical principle and less specific than a program that includes legislation and political strategy."[3]

Paul Lehmann and Stanley Hauerwas have developed the idea that the living community—in practical terms, the congregation and, perhaps, the denomination—through wrestling with an ethical issue will be able to generate a Christian solution to practical problems.[4] This view has much to commend it, but the process will not guarantee a solution; and, indeed, the two writers, insofar as they take positions on issues, are not of a common mind. However, this stance of expecting the community of believers to take responsibility for making ethical decisions and monitoring those decisions in the light of subsequent experience is an excellent way to work back and forth between human experience and theology in order to form decisions which are firm enough to help people with the problems that they must do something about.

3. *Probably the limitation that is most distressing in our day is the inability of theology to establish a common authority for faith.* This is more a commentary on our modern world than a negative judgment about theology. The history of the problem is too long and complicated to document in this brief essay; but the Enlightenment (starting about the beginning of the eighteenth century) developed ideas such as the autonomy of the individual, the doctrine of progress, the preeminence of reason, the right of individuals to happiness—all of which were unsettling to the traditional views. This century was followed by great scientific discoveries and the mind-shaking theories of Charles Darwin, Sigmund Freud, Karl Marx, and Albert Einstein, just to mention major thought systems that are still shaping our common life.

Authority for the Christian faith until the Enlightenment was the Bible and church tradition, but since that time it has, for many theologians, shifted to other sources. Now we have some who start with human experience and build an empirical theology (Henry Nelson Wieman), and some who begin with the process metaphysics of Alfred North Whitehead (John Cobb and Daniel

Day Williams), the phenomenology of Heidegger (John Macquarrie and Karl Rahner), dialectical philosophy (Karl Barth), class struggle based on Karl Marx (Gustavo Gutiérrez), or history (Gordon E. Kaufman). These and other sources of authority give the resulting theologies significant differences in beliefs about God, humankind, and the church.[5] In North America today the theology that claims to have a common authority is evangelicalism. The claim might be a correct assessment about the authority they place in the Bible; yet within evangelicalism there are significant differences of belief about Christ, the work of the Holy Spirit, and the ethical requirements of faith.

4. *Theology does not lead directly to educational practice or methods.* Educational methods are based on experience and experimentation and, as such, have an independent rationale. For example, Trinitarians and Unitarians both use visual aids because they are effective. Process theologians as well as Barthians use small-group discussions because experience has shown that an informal, nonthreatening environment in which people can ask questions or seek clarification of ideas is a better educational practice than large lecture groups where student participation is at a minimum. One might make a case for the indirect relationship between theology and educational methods. That is, a theological system has a character as well as a content, and the character can have significant influence on educational practice. For example, liberal theology flourished in America between World War I and World War II. That theology, well summarized by Shelton Smith, was related to the pragmatism of John Dewey as well as to the spirit of the Enlightenment.[6] It fostered informal methods and gave special attention to teaching methods which would encourage individuals to develop their own personal abilities and to relate everyday experiences to worship and religious faith. The laboratory school at Union Theological Seminary in New York, which later became part of the Sunday school of Riverside Church when it was built in the late 1920s, was a thoroughgoing effort to unite liberal theology with educational methods. But we must not conclude that educational methods, as methods, are the natural corollary of liberal theology. The methods and procedures used in the Union Theological Seminary laboratory school could be—and probably are—used in orthodox or evangelical churches.

Theology in Education

If there is no direct relationship between theology and educational methods, of what use is theology in Christian education? The answer is that education is more than methods. Education is a process by which more mature people nurture, care for, and lead less experienced people. Most planned Christian education is conducted by adults for children and youth, or by adults who have special skills and knowledge for other adults who are less knowledgeable or are untrained in those special areas. But we must not forget that in congregations people have a variety of informal relationships. In these associations people instruct each other, provide guidance in problematic life situations, and, above all, emphathize with each other in joys and sorrows. Christian nurture is all of these things—it is a sharing of one's faith in the midst of life. The form of sharing in the classroom is planned and in conversation it is unplanned; but in both forms it is a deliberate explanation and passing on of what one person believes to be true about God and God's will for the world and its people. In this sense, all people who make a confession of faith in Jesus Christ are both theologians and educators. That is why we should speak of the *laos*—the people of God—as working together to learn the meaning of faith.

As a practical matter, however, from biblical times some people have been selected to devote some, if not all, of their time to communicating the faith. Today ministers, priests, teachers in church school, and lay leaders are designated to educate. Let us focus attention on the use of theology by those who have a special interest in transmitting an understanding of faith to others.

The Educator as a Theologian

Ministers and educators are theologians because they interpret the faith as they share it. The only issue is the adequacy of their theology and the way they function as theologians. The adequacy of an educator as a theologian is to be judged on the same basis as one would judge the adequacy of a theologian's theology.

The way the educator functions as a theologian is extremely important. If educators think of theology as doctrine to be memorized or learned only in terms of "this is what Christians believe," then theology is a "given"—something that comes to an individual and should be accepted. This makes it dispensable or of marginal value. The educator will then use bits and pieces of doctrine as they fit whatever he or she is doing.

If the educator recognizes that he or she is a theologian, then the situation changes drastically. The educator realizes that he or she has a personal stake in theology—it is not something one must accept but a thought process in which one must engage. What comes from theologians or from church doctrine is generalization about experience and, if true, it will match the person's experience. The "if true" is a crucial phrase, for we are obliged as theologians to test preformulated doctrines. In the testing of our experience, we make the doctrines our own or modify them to conform to our understanding of God.

This appears to make the individual the measure of theological truth when, in fact, church theology is built up over a long period of time and has authority because many people have subscribed to it. There is no way around this dilemma. The individual is, in the final analysis, accountable to God for his or her beliefs; to lessen that obligation would be to avoid the hard work of thinking about faith. Preformulated theology is a set of statements about God, Christ, sin, and so on. It will remain a set of statements until a person understands them and relates them to the specific events in his or her life. The educator must help do the relating in order that theology illuminate life and death.

Educators' first concern about theology is that they have an adequate theology so that they may explain their faith in God to other people. Having a theology does not mean that one has completed an assignment—it means that one has obtained certainty enough to offer his or her beliefs to others. It also means that the educator should exhibit in his or her person characteristics of one who thinks about faith. That means the educator continues to learn, to read, to consult theologians, and to be open to the leading of God's Spirit. The hardest part of this personal quest for meaning is integration. Because theology is mental, there is always the temptation to keep it segregated in the conscious part of the mind rather than to relate our theological insight to our conduct.

Educators who are living examples of persons struggling for faith in order to find meaning in life are a great inspiration to their students. Educators who refuse to think about faith and simply retail preformulated statements about what people thought in former times are stunting the spiritual life of their students.

Educators Must Sponsor Theological Inquiry

As already stated, the act of preaching or teaching is an interpretation of religion, and the person doing so has a theological position. But taking a position is not the same thing as thinking about one's religion. Thinking about it requires some knowledge of what others have thought and what the biblical writers say about the subject and an effort to relate thought and life in an environment where views can be expressed, examined, and questioned. The process takes time—a matter of months or maybe years. Since theological statements are about beliefs, they are as close as words can come to what we build our life around. This condition gives belief statements their power, but by the same token they are not easily changed.

Both Calvin and Luther said it was not enough to know doctrine. One must have the experience to which the doctrine relates.[7] Some people can readily relate their sin and guilt to the doctrine of forgiveness but have difficulty with the doctrine of creation. And doctrines about special providence, immortality, and evil are difficult for almost everyone. But unless educators sponsor some form of continuing discussion about these matters, they fail to help people develop the critical intelligence necessary to cope with life.

Perhaps educators shy away from sponsoring theological inquiry among adults and older youth because they are afraid they will not come to the right theological answer. This fear is not well founded. There are already several theological points of view among people in any class. A careful discussion over a period of time will not produce more dissonance; it may, in fact, help dislodge superficial ideas or infantile wishes and replace them with a more adequate theological affirmation. We should not be too dismayed with theological diversity, for there is a certain amount of it in the Bible. Jesus is described differently by each of the four biographers in the New Testament, even though they all agreed he was the Son of God. And the argument between the Judaizers and the Paul-Peter party is documented in Acts 15. What we learn from all of this is that disputation carried on among people who are earnestly seeking the truth about God and God's will for believers is an old and useful method for arriving at truth.

Fostering the Formation of Ethical Norms

Earlier in this essay it was noted that one could not move by deductive reasoning from a theological position to a solution of a practical ethical issue on which all Christians would agree. This was cited as a limitation of theology, and several of the ways of getting around this limitation were given. This limitation does not lessen the importance of theology for ethics; it just alerts us to the complications of making ethical judgments.

Theological systems of denominations as well as individual theologians include ethics because ethical conduct is a concomitant of belief. But these ethics are stated in general principles, whereas ethical decisions are always concrete and are always related to changing human conditions. Culture and its mores change. This is particularly true in Western and industrial societies where science and technology are well advanced. For example, oil refineries and electrical generating plants operate continuously. They cannot be shut down. So the ancient rule of not working on the Sabbath cannot be followed. The development of life-support systems in medicine has created new problems about the meaning of death, and computer science now produces new problems about confidentiality of information. Moreover, the particular human situation in one ethical situation may differ significantly from another, making general rules difficult to apply.

Does this mean that, because new social conditions arise and new factors continue to change the human situation, theology has little to say about concrete ethical problems? No. It means that theology is essential as a starting place, and the human situation is the stopping place. In between, the church must work through the issues in the mood of prayer in order to have an ethical position that honors both. The church in this instance means the church as it exists—not an ideal church that exists only in the mind. The church is made up of people who come from the world where they are actually making the decisions about medical ethics, moral business practices, or personnel practices. They know the realities of the life situation, but they have no safe place—literally, no sanctuary—where they can think about and work through the issues in an environment that is concerned for the welfare of all people and characterized by the values of honesty, compassion, and a sense of justice. The congregation and the denomination of which it is a part are the places where Christian ethics must be formulated for practical issues.

The formulation of Christian ethics is a process that continues as long as there are changes in our society. But the process needs to be deliberately sponsored; the participants need to be self-conscious about their goals; and the data for discussion need to be carefully selected. The congregation is the basic unit for such discussions. There people have an ongoing relationship, so that over a period of time they can explore and perhaps formulate an ethical standard for a practical issue. The beliefs of the people form the basis of their association, but beliefs are not fully understood until they are used in response to real life situations. The process requires theology. Church leaders fostering the process of ethical norming will find that it educates the whole person because all that a person is and believes is involved in practical ethical conduct.

Hermeneutics

According to Gerhard Ebeling, never before the eighteenth century did a theologian have to consider history as a problem.[8] Prior to that time, theologians thought critically about history and were concerned to have accurate historical documents. They used history and the Bible as a databank from which to draw ideas and doctrines and on which to base their theological theses. Then in the eighteenth century a group of intellectuals emerged out of the Enlightenment who by the use of reason questioned many Christian beliefs. Historical, textual, and literary critical methods were developed which required theologians to examine data—especially the books of the Bible—by a process that had its own presupposition: in the Old Testament earlier accounts were more primitive and less reliable, whereas in the New Testament earlier accounts were considered more important and later accounts less satisfying. Authority for the spiritual life was weakened as reason and research scholarship became the basis for judging the value of the biblical record.

During the past hundred or more years in which this critical biblical scholarship has been influential in denominations, leaders have experienced considerable communication difficulty. The introduction of critical methods frightens many laypeople who sense that the truth of the Bible is being diluted. Yet to avoid the method was to be blind to data from archaeology and history. Liberal churches accepted much modern scholarship, conservative ones resisted this scholarship, and an uneasy truce was enacted in the mainline denominations. For many people—laypersons as well as ministers—the Bible became a puzzle from the past rather than a source of inspiration and help. Today theologians are developing new ways of thinking about biblical interpretation which encourage all of the technical scholarship needed to establish the text and honor the historical context while, at the same time, identifying and respecting the theology that formed it. Called "canonical criticism," this method goes a long way toward providing a hermeneutic that is usable in congregational life. This method helps us see that the canon (that is, the books that were approved for inclusion in the Bible) is a process related to the ongoing life of a believing community.[9] Many of the books of the Bible were edited by the believing community over a period of time. This editing is a theological process required by changing situations.

The practical import of this position is that the situation of individuals in the congregation and of the church in the community is the place where God works today with creative redemption. What we believe about God, formed from a study about what God did in biblical times, is what we transmit to our congregations as we attempt to live by the guidance of God's Spirit.

Curriculum

Theology is reasoning about faith. The result is indispensable for educators or others who have a responsibility for preparing study materials. The first problem in preparing such materials is identification of the goal. Theological reflection is necessary for that purpose. The second problem is selection of materials to be studied, and theology helps sort out the essential from the less important. The third problem is method of study, and theology offers some help. It is indicated in the section on "limitations" that theology did not lead to methods, but theology has a role in thinking through the issues involved. Reason, as the tool of theology, should be used to judge the adequacy of methods. For example, group process methods are so dynamic and interesting that educators tend to think almost any discussion is good and group-designed goals are desirable. But theological analysis helps us realize that authority is not in the group but in allegiance to Christ—indeed, the group can at times be demonic unless we judge group activity by Christian standards.

The fourth problem in curriculum is evaluation, and theology operates here also. Teachers need to know whether goals are being reached and whether the materials and methods are adequate. Since theology helps select these elements of curriculum, it will also help evaluate them. The techniques used in evaluation—data-gathering—come from the social sciences. But when the data have been assembled, our theology informs our judgment as to how well we have achieved our purpose. In some theological outlooks, the acquisition of materials by memory is a good, measurable educational result. In other theological outlooks, all objective data will be placed in a subordinate position while looking for manifestation of affective behavior. However, in every case one's theology guides the process of curriculum evaluation.

A Look Ahead

Each ongoing Christian tradition has an official theology written in creeds or in sermons and denominational publications. This theology is used to train ministers, professors, and other leaders who in turn explain and defend it. Such theology gives an interpretation of the Bible, a world view, ethical standards, and a philosophy of life that includes explanations of evil, death, and common life situations. The result is guidance for worship, sermons, and church school classes. This official theology changes slowly, but it changes as new conditions require new explanations. Many times the changes occur in individuals and congregations before they are finally adopted by the whole denomination.

Individual theologians are free to speculate about the meaning of faith in relation to ideas or changing human conditions. The work of individual theologians is absorbed by the denominations when it has stood the test of criticism and experience. So to look ahead is to look around at what individual theologians are writing today for the edification of Christians.

In the realm of speculative theology, that is, schools of thought which are attempting to develop theology around a philosophy or human condition, there are four that are well established.

The *phenomenological* approach to theology is a description of human experience in such a way as to remove "as far as possible, concealments, distortions, and whatever else might prevent us from seeing the phenomenon as it actually gives itself."[10]

Process theology uses the philosophy of Alfred North Whitehead to affirm that what is actual is in process and that God is active within the process. This approach to theology assumes a modern scientific view of the world and attempts to fit Scripture and tradition into that frame of reference.[11]

Liberation theology starts with a group or class of people who have been oppressed or exploited and relates their suffering and hope to the Christian faith. The idea that God is concerned for poor, disenfranchised, or powerless people is being applied to women, blacks, and ethnic groups.[12]

The *historical* approach is difficult to characterize except that the writers take the historical tradition of the Christian faith with utmost seriousness and desire to interpret the faith so that it will provide guidance for us in our present historical situation.[13]

The pluralism of our present theologies distresses many people who look to theology to provide certainty. Educationally speaking, pluralism may be a good thing: we are forced to see that theology is not certainty but a thought process which must be fostered in order to clarify beliefs.

Notes

1. John Macquarrie, *Principles of Christian Theology* (New York: Charles Scribner's Sons, 2d ed., 1977), 5.
2. Jürgen Moltmann, *Experiences of God* (Philadelphia: Fortress Press, 1980), 55.
3. John C. Bennett, *Christian Ethics and Social Policy* (New York: Charles Scribner's Sons, 1946), 77.
4. Paul L. Lehmann, *Ethics in a Christian Context* (New York: Harper & Brothers, 1963). Stanley Hauerwas, *A Community of Character* (Notre Dame, Ind.: University of Notre Dame Press, 1981).
5. John Macquarrie, *Twentieth Century Religious Thought* (London: S.C.M. Press, 2d rev. ed., 1981).
6. H. Shelton Smith, *Faith and Nurture* (New York: Charles Scribner's Sons, 1941).
7. John E. Smith, *The Analogy of Experience* (New York: Harper & Row, 1973), 28.
8. Gerhard Ebeling, *Word and Faith* (Philadelphia: Fortress Press, 1963), 364.
9. James A. Sanders, "The Bible as Canon," *The Christian Century*, 2 December 1981, 1250-55.

10. Macquarrie, *Principles of Christian Theology*. See also Karl Rahner, *Foundations of Christian Faith* (New York: The Seabury Press, 1978) and Paul Ricoeur, *Essays on Biblical Interpretation* (Philadelphia: Fortress Press, 1980).
11. John B. Cobb, Jr. and David Roy Griffin, *Process Theology: An Introductory Exposition* (Philadelphia: The Westminster Press, 1976). See also Ewert Cousins, ed., *Process Theology* (New York: Newman Press, 1971) and Daniel Day Williams, *The Spirit and Forms of Love* (New York: Harper & Row, 1968).
12. Gayraud S. Wilmore and James H. Cone, *Black Theology: A Documentary History* (Maryknoll, N.Y.: Orbis Books, 1979). See also Gustavo Gutiérrez, *A Theology of Liberation* (Maryknoll, N.Y.: Orbis Books, 1973) and Rosemary Radford Reuther, *New Women, New Earth: Sexist Ideologies and Human Liberation* (New York: The Seabury Press, 1975).
13. Helmut Thielicke, *The Evangelical Faith*, vol. 1 (Grand Rapids: Wm. B. Eerdmans Publishing Co., 1974). See also Jürgen Moltmann, *The Trinity and the Kingdom* (San Francisco: Harper & Row, 1981); Gordon D. Kaufman, *Systematic Theology* (New York: Charles Scribner's Sons, 1968); and David Tracy, *The Analogical Imagination: Christian Theology and the Culture of Pluralism* (New York: Crossroad, 1981).

CHAPTER 2

Protestant Philosophies of Religious Education

D. Campbell Wyckoff

Half a century ago the philosophy of religious education was a lively discipline. Debates centered around John Dewey and his position. Since he worked out his philosophy around the issues and problems of education, others were led to concentrate on educational thought, even if their philosophical stances differed. Interest spilled over into religious education. Dewey himself considered what he called "the religious"[1]—a serious process of valuing and commitment—to be an important human phenomenon. His followers in the churches felt encouraged to philosophize about the religious educational process.

While Dewey was lecturing and writing at Columbia University and William Heard Kilpatrick was interpreting him across the street at Teachers College, the other end of town was being heard from in the person of Herman Harrell Horne, professor of philosophy and history of education at New York University's Washington Square campus at the foot of Fifth Avenue. Horne was an idealist of Hegelian stripe and at the same time a devout Protestant with keen concern for the church's educational program. Horne spent a great deal of his time teaching in the leadership training schools of the area, out of the conviction that the church's educational leaders needed the best philosophical grounding possible for their practical work with children, youth, and adults.

The focus of the debate was so clear that one of Horne's most popular books, *The Democratic Philosophy of Education*, consisted of a section-by-section critical commentary on Dewey's *Democracy and Education*.[2] Horne wrote constructively on the philosophy of education, critically on the contemporary educational scene, and popularly for church leaders.[3] He was one of the first, if not the first, to lecture to the public from the classroom by radio. His efforts brought into being the Department of Religious Education

D. Campbell Wyckoff is the Thomas W. Synnott Professor of Christian Education Emeritus at Princeton Theological Seminary.

in New York University's School of Education, although he was never a member of that department.

Horne's greatest influence, however, was probably in the graduate classroom. Teaching in a leadership school, he was incisive and dramatic. Teaching undergraduates, he tended to be pedantic. But his graduate seminars gave off the same sort of intellectual sparks as a Socratic dialogue. He and his students worked at the problems of philosophy within a kind of grid, the axes of which were the categories of metaphysics, epistemology, logic, and axiology (education was an axiological matter) and four philosophical positions: idealism, realism, pragmatism, and naturalism. Horne made few disciples for his idealist views, but he made good educational philosophers by insisting on rigorous philosophical argument conducted in the framework of intellec- tually productive dialogue. At the same time, he pushed for educational implications, and, since many of his students were religious educators, the philosophy of religious education devel- oped markedly under his influence.

For all the books that Horne wrote, he never published his own philosophy of religious education. *The Philosophy of Christian Education* is inadequate to represent either his method or the substance of his thought. J. Donald Butler, one of his students, took on the task of writing the book that Horne never wrote. *Four Philosophies and Their Practice in Education and Religion*[4] is the way Horne thought and worked. Butler's four philosophies are those with which Horne dealt, and the implications drawn for education and religion were in the idealist tradition that Horne espoused.

Science and Social Responsibility

The question of the day, however, was how in a scientific age one could speak about the things of religion. A tradition had grown up around Edwin Diller Starbuck, William James, and George Albert Coe, which translated religious experience and thought into psychological categories. From this new discipline of psychology of religion, religious education was approached in terms of human development and the dynamics of personality, motivation, and learning. The application of firm results from scientific psychologi- cal investigation in the classroom made it less imperative to philosophize about education.

Coe represented social interests as well. Dewey had awakened the educator's social conscience, while Walter Rauschenbusch and the social gospel movement, building as Dewey did on the humanitarian movements of the nineteenth century, had forced social responsibility and social action into the church's consciousness. Coe used both the psychology of religion and the awakened social consciousness to reorient religious education to a social viewpoint. In *A Social Theory of Religious Education*, he saw the following components as comprising theory:

1. An indication of the *kind of society* that is regarded as desirable.
2. A conception of the *original nature* of children.
3. A conception of the *sorts of individual experience* that will most surely and economically produce in such children the kind of sociality that is desired.
4. A statement of at least the more general *standards and tests* by which one may judge the degree to which these sorts of experience are being provided by any educational institution or process.[5]

Coe also had a strong sense of personalistic idealism, most clearly expressed in *What Is Christian Education?* His creative personality-principle centered in his belief in the infinite worth of persons. "To value personality . . . is to value self-activity in all persons. If persons are of final worth, then every particular instance of self-activity has within it something of unimpeachable validity."[6] His definition of Christian education was in the same personalistic terms: "It is the systematic, critical examination and reconstruction of relations between persons, guided by Jesus' assumption that persons are of infinite worth, and by the hypothesis of the existence of God, the Great Valuer of Persons."[7] In Coe's position on religious education, the sciences of religion, a local and global sense of social responsibility, and a philosophy of personalistic idealism were joined. Horne denied that Coe was a philosopher, and Dewey repudiated him as a disciple, but the scientific, social, and personalistic theory that he gave to religious education in the 1920s did have quite definite philosophical roots, even if it was not worked out in a recognizable philosophical style.

But the question of how one could speak about religion in a scientific age was a philosophical one and could not be dealt with adequately by psychologists of religion, thinkers with social ills primarily in mind, or by personalistic idealists. It was at the University of Chicago that the problem was dealt with most radically by Henry Nelson Wieman and by the religious educators William Clayton Bower and Ernest John Chave. Wieman was a philosopher of religion who throve in the midst of advanced biblical critical thought, the scientific study of religion, and the emerging process philosophy of Alfred North Whitehead—a dynamic philosophical position that came to be represented at

Chicago by Charles Hartshorne. Wieman did not hesitate to describe God as "the supreme creative event," or to define religion as "devotion to supreme value." He did not flinch at a "normative psychology of religion," the norms being derived from the philosophy of religion developed in terms of "theistic naturalism." It was this normative psychology of religion that served as the bridge between theistic naturalism and religious education. Philosophy of religious education in this mode held that

all *education* is the process of sharing effectively certain selected parts of the accumulated culture of society. *Secular education* carries on the process in such ways that the individual is enabled to organize his behavior progressively to the end of fulfilling his function in society. The social function of the individual is that of appreciating and promoting the highest known values of his culture and of seeking ever higher ones, for the sake of human fulfillment. *Religious education* carries on the process in such ways that the individual will develop loyalty to the absolutely supreme and inclusive value which is beyond all values known or conceivable through the present resources of society. This supreme and inclusive value is progressively apprehended through a sequence of specific objectives of loyalty. The individual integrates all his living about each highest specific objective as it emerges, but always with an outreach toward that highest Uncomprehended.[8]

In Bower, the philosophy of religious education was developed around the concept of creative experience. In Chave, on the other hand, the strictly scientific side came through most clearly.

Philosophical Bases for Religious Education

In weighing the developments of the pre-Barthian period, it must not be forgotten that American religious education was heir to a philosophy of education that had developed with strong and integral concern for the religious element. Comenius's empiricism and Rousseau's romanticism had combined in Pestalozzi in the conviction that education was nurtured in the community of Christian love, with primary concern for the pupil and for the atmosphere in which the pupil was to learn and grow. Froebel, learning from Pestalozzi, made that concern for the individual and the atmosphere real in the institution of the kindergarten. Herbart, also learning from Pestalozzi, saw the task of the school as that of the self-actualization of the learner within a pervasive and progressive Christian culture. These same themes, but in secularized form, appeared in Dewey.

Note the strong thread of romanticism in the theme of the self-actualization of the individual in a community, home, school, and world that embody Christian truth and value. American theology, in the person of Horace Bushnell, took on that romantic cast and made it in many ways definitive for religious education. The influence is from the German romantics through Coleridge to Bushnell. Coleridge bridged Kant's chasm between reason (God's side) and understanding (the human side) by means of imagination. The use of the language of imagination enabled the human to grasp the divine through an imaging that could not be achieved through the ordinary processes of the understanding. Coleridge constructed a kind of manual to help persons develop the type of imagination that was equal to the task.[9] Bushnell mastered those methods and embodied them in his writing and preaching. When it came to the politically volatile question of Christian education, he brought these ways to the treatment of the subject in *Christian Nurture*.[10] In that volume, which religious education in America considers its cornerstone, the romantic element entered our philosophy of religious education and has stayed.

In the United States, however, the mainstream of religious education, when not strictly catechetical, was modeled on the educational philosophy of the medieval university. In the medieval university, education was developed as a series of interrelated disciplines that encompassed human knowledge and concerns—the arts and sciences, medicine, law, and theology. Theology was regnant, but, from the time of Aquinas on, it took full account of philosophical questions. Thus religion and philosophy acted as coordinate norms for the development of the educational enterprise. Carried over into American higher education under church auspices, this tradition of philosophy of education (and the philosophy of the curriculum) was dominant and unquestioned.

While Christian higher education proceeded along relatively traditional lines (and in many cases still does), parish education was more dominantly influenced by the romantic movement and the science of education.

The Theological Challenge

The reception of Karl Barth's thought in North America changed the situation drastically. Barth's was a biblical theology, in which the categories were strictly theological and the substance and method derived strictly from the study of the Scriptures. One did not discuss metaphysics, epistemology (especially not epistemology!), logic, or axiology. One dealt with church dogmatics.

Furthermore, there was no traffic with the sciences of religion. "Religion" itself was an illegitimate offspring of the secular mind. Thus philosophy and theology were polarized. Under Barthian influence, philosophy of religious education ceased to thrive, and theology became the dominant discipline of concern to Protestant church educators.

The first evidences of this change were to be found in the challenges of the curriculum of Christian education. The International Council of Religious Education in its remarkably nondefensive "Study of Christian Education" sought to reconcile the differences between Christian educators of the psychological-social type and the theologians working under Barth's influence. The crucial point was curriculum, where they concluded:

The purpose of the curriculum of Christian education is to confront individuals with the eternal gospel and to nurture within them a life of faith, hope, and love, in keeping with the gospel. The organizing principle of the curriculum, from the viewpoint of the Christian gospel, is to be found in the changing needs and experiences of the individual as these include his relation to (1) God, as revealed in Jesus Christ; (2) his fellow men and human society; (3) his place in the work of the world; (4) the Christian fellowship, the church; (5) the continuous process of history, viewed as a carrier of the divine purpose and revealer of the moral law; (6) the universe in all its wonder and complexity.[11]

The new theological stance was also evident in such curricula as *Christian Faith and Life* and the *Covenant Life Curriculum*. The essential position of *Christian Faith and Life* was:

There is no true knowledge of God and no true understanding of any aspect of human life except as it is revealed in Jesus Christ. But that truth cannot reach the world in its need—it cannot reach even good Church members in their need—unless there are persons in whom Christ so lives that through them he can make himself known to others. Such persons are in the highest sense teachers, communicating by word and by action not merely a system of ideas or code of conduct but the very life which has become theirs in Christ. Perhaps it would be truer, however, to say that it is communicated through them than that they communicate it, for, whatever man may do and however convincing his testimony to Christ, it is only the working of God's Spirit in and through the teaching that can make Christ known as Lord and can unfold the infinite riches of life in fellowship with God.[12]

The *Covenant Life Curriculum* was based on the idea that

the educational work of the Christian church finds its motive in the fact that God has revealed himself, finds its message in the revelation itself, and uses methods that are consistent with that revelation of God and his will.

. . . God enters into covenant with his people, giving them a foundation of security out of which grows freedom to respond in maturity to the will of God. The covenant community . . . issues his invitation to men to be joined in covenant relationships with him through Jesus Christ.[13]

Several theologians whose interest turned to religious education worked out rather systematic approaches to its thought and practice. In 1950, Randolph Crump Miller maintained that

the clue to Christian education is the rediscovery of a relevant theology which will bridge the gap between content and method, providing the background and perspective of Christian truth by which the best methods and content will be used as tools to bring the learners into the right relationship with the living God who is revealed to us in Jesus Christ, using the guidance of parents and the fellowship of life in the Church as the environment in which Christian nurture will take place.[14]

Sensing a basic change in orientation for religious education thought, Miller maintained, "The new task is to make theology relevant, realizing that the goal of Christian education is Christian truth, that truth may be acquired only through the interpretation of experience, and that we become Christians only as we use truth to place ourselves in commitment to the living God revealed to us in Jesus Christ and through the fellowship of the Church."[15]

James D. Smart, a Canadian pastor and theologian, had early read and digested Karl Barth's work. The opportunity to edit the *Christian Faith and Life Curriculum* (the "new curriculum" of the Presbyterian Church in the U.S.A.) in the mid-1940s focused his attention on questions of Christian education. In 1954, he voiced a theological emphasis even more radical than that of Miller:

Christian education . . . must bring the entire discipline of theology to bear upon the educational problem, and, in its exploration of what it means for the Church to be an effective educational agency in the service of the Word, it must not only be ready to learn from those who are investigating the fields of educational psychology and technique from a secular point of view but must conduct its own careful researches in the light of its own objects and aims. . . . The Christian educator has thus to be on guard lest, in taking over supposedly scientific conclusions from the secular educator, he take over also, unconsciously, certain unacknowledged, non-Christian or even anti-Christian assumptions, which the secular educator did not deduce from his observations but brought to them from some other source.[16]

While Smart might tolerate guidance from "educational psychology and technique" after it had been checked to assure its freedom from non-Christian values, it is clear that he would not be expected to utilize philosophical insights, much less be informed by any philosophy of education as such.

Closely associated with the development of *United Church Curriculum*, the theologian Roger L. Shinn, in his detailed explanation of that curriculum and its theological and educational bases, saw at the heart of the matter

a way of Christian education that gets at its job by introducing persons into the life and mission of the community of Christian faith. It finds that life to be a pilgrimage in which persons are continuously meeting God, their neighbors, and themselves. Within that pilgrimage church and home have decisive roles. Organized programs, study themes, books and audio-visual equipment, and teaching skills influence the experience. Above all, persons share with other persons in the process of a continuous dialogue between biblical faith and contemporary life.[17]

The use of the figures "pilgrimage" and "dialogue," in juxtaposition with biblical faith, contemporary life, and the life and mission of the community of Christian faith, kept theology at the heart of the enterprise but opened the way for a dynamic conception of religious education as a function of a living and breathing church in vital contact with its world.

Among theologians, Nels F. S. Ferré probably gives closest attention to education. Having done doctoral work under Alfred North Whitehead at Harvard, he developed a keen interest in the sciences and philosophy in their illuminating interplay when attempting to understand the dynamics of human becoming in the context of the created order. Sustained by a vital biblical faith, he adds a concern for understanding God's relationship, particularly but not exclusively as creator, to human becoming. As his studies in systematic theology matured and were published, he inevitably turned his interest to education.

The first arena of his educational probing is higher education. In *Christian Faith and Higher Education*[18] he develops in effect a full theology of education. Identifying the school primarily as a "community of seeing," he maintains that it cannot become effective without the integrity of relationship to the "community of feeling" and the "community of doing." But theologically all three communities are grounded in the "community of being," and only the community of being as a whole can generate creative changes. Thus all education is religious education through and through. Very specifically, the more these creative changes "are lighted and led by the Spirit, the more satisfactory they are." The central question is, "How can vertical transcendence, God's will, most fully gear into our most relevant horizontal transcendence, the momentum of education?"[19]

Ferré sees God's purpose in creation as pedagogical; God's method in creative process being to teach by indirect means and vicariousness, which implies, for instance, extensive use of the case study method, in which integral aspects of real life are analyzed and dealt with constructively. Beyond this, every discipline of higher education has its place in contributing to the community of seeing and must be dealt with in the context of the hierarchy of the other three communities.

In *A Theology for Christian Education*, [20] Ferré turns to the whole arena of religious education, works through a full practical theological methodology for Christian education, and proceeds to the development of a trinitarian treatment, issue by issue, rooted again in the perspective of God as Educator: "All of creation is a pedagogical process for learning to know God's will and to live it. The only need and purpose we know for creation is for God thus to teach through it."[21]

Paul Tillich's philosophical theology provides a vital point of contact for religious educators and philosophers of education. It was interest in Tillich, for instance, that drew John H. Westerhoff into theology in the first place. The interest for philosophers is a dual one—in Tillich's methodology and in the substance of his thought. His method of correlation puts philosophical questions (philosophical rather than theological categories)—primarily those of ontology—to theology, so that the result is theological answers (the substance of his thought) couched to a great extent in philosophical terms. His motivation is his conviction that the modern world no longer asks its basic questions in theological ways, but rather uses philosophical categories to probe life and its meaning. Yet, he holds, theology has otherwise unavailable insights that are needed in the exploration of meaning.

Among philosophers of education, Philip H. Phenix has made most extensive use of Tillich. Thus, addressing the general educational world rather than religious educators in particular, Phenix is able to entitle one of his books *Education and the Worship of God*, describing it as

offered as a contribution to the continuing discussion of the complex problems of dealing with religion responsibly and maturely in the school curriculum. Its central thesis is that the concerns of faith are chiefly manifest in the regular subjects of study and not solely or primarily in specifically religious studies or devotional exercises. Its most distinctive contribution is that it deals with the religious perspectives implicit in the study of several of the standard academic disciplines. At the same time, the use of traditional religious ideas and practices in opening up the deeper meanings of the ostensibly secular studies is illustrated.[22]

The use of the term *worship* is a case in point: "Worship is the offering of devotion to God. A person worships whenever he reverently contemplates and dedicates himself to the being in whom (or in which) he ultimately puts his trust and confidence. Worship is not confined to those who are traditional theists."[23]

Perhaps the most extreme example of Phenix's Tillichian method is found in a chapter called "Practicing the Presence of God":

Religion consists in "practicing the presence of God." . . . Since faith is one's total life commitment, it manifests itself in everything one does. The worship and service of God are not limited to conventionally holy occasions but take place chiefly in the conduct of apparently secular affairs, including those of teaching and learning. . . . From the standpoint of faith, each discipline reveals different aspects of ultimate reality and evokes a distinctive set of reverential responses.[24]

Theologians interested in education have thus ranged from those who rather strictly avoid any tinge of secular thought (which means maintaining distance from philosophies of education) to those who openly encourage bilingualism. In between are a few who approach a theology of education on theology's own terms but do so creatively and without fear of the critical use of philosophical insights.

Contemporary Philosophies and Religious Education

Yesterday's four regnant philosophies of education have today been joined by existentialism, phenomenology, process philosophy (in the form of process theology at times), and linguistic analysis. Has this enrichment of the field of philosophy resulted in any new vitality for philosophy of religious education?

Looking first at the four traditional philosophies, it is noteworthy that no religious educator today is working primarily in either an idealist or a realist mode. In the case of the other two, there is a marginal but noticeable influence on religious education thought. There are traces of naturalism, for instance, in the thought of John H. Peatling, and of pragmatism in the thought of James W. Fowler. Both, interestingly, have a primary base in religious research.

Peatling's thought is very difficult to unravel. Some of his sources are unusual, as are his language and style. While he uses a great deal of traditional biblical and theological material, however, his scientific commitments are more far-reaching than one is at first led to believe, and occasionally they verge on naturalism. He sees education as open-ended and future oriented. Necessarily, because "education is a strange process of open-ended coping; it cannot ignore the present state of knowledge or the possibility of future expansion." Religious education is "a subset of education. . . . Like education itself, religious education is a strange process of open-ended coping." It has an essential element of tentativeness, without which it would lapse into socialization.[25] Such arguments lead to his plea that religious education become a psychological science.

The pragmatic element in Fowler's thought is again marginal, but visible. It lodges in his generic use of "faith." Faith is a universal human experience, and may thus be investigated within any human context. The "stages of faith" are hypothesized to be generalizable across cultures and religious groups. Although he cautions against uncritical constructive use of his research findings, the inevitable temptation is to put them to use "as is" in religious education and particularly in curriculum. (Since curriculum is by nature a sequential phenomenon, any stage theory presents the same temptation.) Were this to be done, the particularity of the Christian faith (or any other faith) would be compromised, and the result would be a generic religious education. A generic religious education is a possibility as an academic discipline; it is not possible as a practical reality. At the same time, the pragmatic element can be a help in fostering communication among religious groups in a pluralistic society.[26]

Turning to the newer philosophical positions, the work of James E. Loder may be seen to contain strong existential elements. But it must be noted immediately that he does his work in philosophy of religious education on an interdisciplinary basis. His clue is that particular human phenomena are addressed not by one, but by several disciplines. An aspect of human experience, a particular type of experience, will open up to the understanding only if it is pursued by means of a quest that involves all the appropriate disciplines in a focused way. The method probably had its inception in his conviction that Kierkegaard and Freud were necessary for getting at what he called "religious pathology" (the misuse of religious experience, or its failure to come to the point of "the leap of faith") and allowing the Christian faith to address it redemptively.[27]

While generally avoiding the "existentialist" label, Loder has probed Kierkegaard passionately and followed through faithfully and discriminatingly on every lead that his investigation has suggested to him, seeking all the data that might be sifted to uncover the dynamics inherent in the processes of being and becoming religious. Since these dynamics inevitably undergird religious education, his program has been one of identifying and studying the most integral of religious themes. He has come to the position that "there are certain generic structures embedded in raw, i.e., uninterpreted, human experience that give shape to language and thought, to self-understanding, to the ordering of personal, interpersonal, and intergroup relationships, to the formation of hierarchies of value and symbol systems, including the disciplines we use to study these phenomena."[28] He suggests the theme of "transformation" as appropriate "for not all, but certain of the foundation disciplines most germane to Christian education."[29]

Early on, Loder discovered and described in detail a creative process of conflict resolution that is fundamental to a variety of human changes, from learning to conversion.[30] Further probing through the years has sharpened his grasp of the dynamics of what he now calls "convictional experiences" and the integral relationship in convictional experiences of the workings of the human spirit and the Holy Spirit.[31]

J. Gordon Chamberlin has become so interested in phenomenology that his work has turned entirely in that direction. He was introduced to modern phenomenology during a sabbatical leave in Latin America and saw in it "a distinctive view that would be broad and inclusive and would focus attention upon the essential character of the social phenomenon—education."[32] Analyzing the particular functions of philosophy of education, he cites the following: description of the persons to whom educational activities may be directed; indication of the appropriate intentions for those participating and the reasons for such objectives; identification of assumptions about how the persons involved learn the things intended; indication of the appropriate responsibility of a teacher in helping students learn the matters intended; identification of the appropriate structures and processes that educators can employ to aid the person involved in reaching the objectives intended; and relation of the patterns and objectives of educational activities to the rest of the lives of those involved.[33]

At this point carefully avoiding premature attention to religious education, Chamberlin's aim was to analyze and define education itself. In his more recent book, *The Educating Act: A Phenomenological View*, he continues the investigation but begins the approach to religious education by introducing into the study detailed biographical material from persons whose lives exemplify a marked religious quality.[34]

Charles F. Melchert works consistently and self-consciously within the methods of linguistic analysis. Since he has not yet published a book, his work is difficult to gather and assess, but the key piece appears to be his article "What Is Religious Education?" Analysis in his method always means meticulous examination of the elements and nuances of each word being used, the criterion being that meanings must be public, nonarbitrary, and necessary components of the word under investigation. Here he pulls apart the words *education* (and *helping* and *understanding*) and *religion* (and *awe*). The analysis completed, he is in a position to argue the differences among authorities, and to conclude that "religious education . . . will entail helping others to understand in the ways appropriate to religion . . . such ways including not only the traditional academic and intellectual pursuits, but also the more experiential, ineffable and self-transcending ways of understanding appropriate to and characteristic of religion and the religious."[35]

Philosophy, Theology, Theory

Clearly, some religious education thinking today has primary rootage in philosophical interests, including narrative theology, a theology of play and wonder, liberation theology, Third World theology, black theology, feminist theology, and ecumenical theology. Some recent systematicians (David Tracy, for instance) have included practical theology in their work, providing a base for theological understandings of religious education. The work of "catechesis" is currently being revitalized in Protestantism by John H. Westerhoff.[36] The rest of serious Protestant thought in religious education is usually termed *theory*, and is usually a process of identifying key issues in religious education practice, and seeking informed guidance on them.[37]

Looking Ahead

The questions that emerge in connection with the philosophy of religious education, constituting something of an agenda for its near future, may be stated as follows:

How are philosophy, theology, catechesis, and theory to be assessed as approaches to the understanding and guidance of the religious education enterprise?

Is a philosophical method still an option for productive thinking in the field of religious education?

If a theoretical approach is taken, what specific role is philosophy to play in it?

Is the term *philosophy* to be redefined to include any fundamental systematic thinking about religious education, whether it is strictly philosophical in character or not?

If philosophy is to figure prominently in religious education thinking, in what philosophical direction does promise lie?

Notes

1. See John Dewey, *A Common Faith* (New Haven: Yale University Press, 1934).
2. John Dewey, *Democracy and Education* (New York: Macmillan, 1916).
3. Horne was a prolific writer, and, while most of his writings are pertinent, only a few of them are cited here. His own *Philosophy of Education* was published by Macmillan in 1904. The commentary on Dewey was published by Macmillan in 1932. *Jesus the Master Teacher* (New York: Association Press, 1920) was his most popular book, and is still in print under the title *The Teaching Techniques of Jesus* (Grand Rapids: Kregel Publications, 1971). *The Philosophy of Christian Education* was published by Fleming H. Revell Co. in 1937.
4. J. Donald Butler, *Four Philosophies and Their Practice in Education and Religion* (New York: Harper & Brothers, 1951; 3d ed., 1968).
5. George Albert Coe, *A Social Theory of Religious Education* (New York: Charles Scribner's Sons, 1917), 9.
6. George Albert Coe, *What Is Christian Education?* (New York: Charles Scribner's Sons, 1929), 63.
7. Ibid., 296.
8. Henry Nelson Wieman and Regina Westcott-Wieman, *Normative Psychology of Religion* (New York: Thomas Y. Crowell Co., 1935), 461.
9. Samuel T. Coleridge, *Aids to Reflection* (Burlington, Vt.: Chauncey Goodrich, 1840).
10. The most recent edition of *Christian Nurture* was published in 1979 by Baker Book House, Grand Rapids, with an introduction by John M. Mulder. It uses the text of the 1861 edition.
11. Paul H. Vieth, *The Church and Christian Education* (St. Louis: The Bethany Press, 1947), 145-46.
12. *Basic Principles, Christian Faith and Life* (Philadelphia: Board of Christian Education of the Presbyterian Church in the U.S.A., 1947), 4.
13. *Christian Education Within the Covenant Community—the Church* (Richmond, Va.: Board of Christian Education, Presbyterian Church, U.S., 1958), 4.
14. Randolph Crump Miller, *The Clue to Christian Education* (New York: Charles Scribner's Sons, 1950), 15.
15. Ibid., 17. Miller's interest in new theological possibilities has not diminished. He has published interpretations of religious education from the perspectives of biblical theology, "American theology," and the more philosophically oriented linguistic analysis and process theology. His current interest is almost entirely in process theology.
16. James D. Smart, *The Teaching Ministry of the Church* (Philadelphia: The Westminster Press, 1954), 41-42.
17. Roger L. Shinn, *The Educational Mission of Our Church* (Philadelphia: United Church Press, 1962), 114.

18. Nels F. S. Ferré, *Christian Faith and Higher Education* (New York: Harper & Brothers, 1954).
19. Ibid., 116.
20. Nels F. S. Ferré, *A Theology for Christian Education* (Philadelphia: The Westminster Press, 1967).
21. Ibid., 210.
22. Philip H. Phenix, *Education and the Worship of God* (Philadelphia: The Westminster Press, 1966), 10.
23. Ibid., 20-21.
24. Ibid., 162.
25. John H. Peatling, *Religious Education in a Psychological Key* (Birmingham, Ala.: Religious Education Press, 1981), 135-36.
26. James W. Fowler, *Stages of Faith: The Psychology of Human Development and the Quest for Meaning* (San Francisco: Harper & Row, 1981).
27. See James E. Loder, *Religious Pathology and Christian Faith* (Philadelphia: The Westminster Press, 1966).
28. James E. Loder, "Transformation in Religious Education," *Religious Education*, March-April 1981, 205.
29. Ibid., 206.
30. See Loder, *Religious Pathology and Christian Faith*.
31. See James E. Loder, *The Transforming Moment* (San Francisco: Harper & Row, 1981).
32. J. Gordon Chamberlin, *Toward a Phenomenology of Education* (Philadelphia: The Westminster Press, 1969), 10.
33. Ibid., 149-51.
34. J. Gordon Chamberlin, *The Educating Act: A Phenomenological View* (Washington, D.C.: University Press of America, 1981).
35. Charles F. Melchert, "What Is Religious Education?" *The Living Light*, 14, 3 (1977): 352. See also "Understanding and Religious Education," in *Process and Relationship*, ed. Iris V. Cully and Kendig Brubaker Cully (Birmingham, Ala.: Religious Education Press, 1978), 41-48, and "Understanding as a Purpose of Religious Education," *Religious Education*, March-April 1981, 178-86, together with a response by Craig Dykstra in the same issue, 187-94.
36. See O. C. Edwards, Jr. and John H. Westerhoff III, eds., *A Faithful Church: Issues in the History of Catechesis* (Wilton, Conn.: Morehouse-Barlow Company, 1981).
37. See Jack L. Seymour and Donald E. Miller, eds., *Contemporary Approaches to Christian Education* (Nashville: Abingdon Press, 1982). An introductory chapter summarizes the present situation and suggests a method for assessing various proposals. Subsequent chapters review those proposals. The final chapter provides clues to evaluation of the proposals and suggests agenda for the future.

Bibliography

Butler, J. Donald. *Four Philosophies and Their Practice in Education and Religion*. Rev. ed. New York: Harper & Brothers, 1951; 3d ed., 1968. A systematic exposition of the philosophies of naturalism, idealism, realism, and pragmatism, together with their implications for education and religion. Contains an invaluable "vocabulary of philosophy." Concludes with a statement on building a philosophy of education and an outline of the author's own philosophy.

Chamberlin, J. Gordon. *The Educating Act: A Phenomenological View*. Washington, D.C.: University Press of America, 1981. The author's studies of education from a phenomenological point of view have led him to an analysis of the educational act as intervention, expecting help, developing aims for oneself, the educational occasion as integral life experience, and helping-learning as an intersubjective relationship. Educational outcomes he sees in terms of resolution of conflicting authority claims, engaging in the full range of experiences in coming-to-understand, and the undertaking of appropriate action.

Manheimer, Ronald J. *Kierkegaard as Educator*. Berkeley: University of California Press, 1977.

Interprets Kierkegaard's writings as a rather consistent attempt consciously to engage in self-education ("Kierkegaard regarded his authorship as his own education"). The emphases are on interpretations of the Socratic educator ("the authorship, taken as Kierkegaard's dialectic of education, remains poised at the threshold where the Socratic and Christian meet"), *Either/Or* as a drama of education, and education as the communication of possibility. A foundational book of permanent value for the serious religious educator.

Phenix, Philip H. *Education and the Worship of God*. Philadelphia: The Westminster Press, 1966.

Religious aspects of public education. "Its central thesis is that the concerns of faith are chiefly manifest in the regular subjects of study. . . . Deals specifically with the religious perspectives implicit in the study of several of the standard academic disciplines": language, science, art, ethics, and history. Discusses the basic stance of the religious person in the secular school.

Rood, Wayne R. *Understanding Christian Education*. Nashville: Abingdon Press, 1970.

Organizes a wealth of historical, philosophical, and theological material around four key figures: Horace Bushnell, John Dewey, George Albert Coe, and Maria Montessori. A concluding chapter spells out the author's own position analytically, critically, and comparatively.

Seymour, Jack L., and Donald E. Miller, eds. *Contemporary Approaches to Christian Education*. Nashville: Abingdon Press, 1982.

A serious and detailed assessment of the state of Christian education theory. The options explored are religious instruction, nurture in the faith community, spiritual development (working through Piaget, Kohlberg, and Fowler), a liberation approach that takes account of the North American situation, and a hermeneutic approach that roots in narrative and involves the dialectic of self with tradition and community.

Smith, David L. *Symbolism and Growth: The Religious Thought of Horace Bushnell*. Chico, Calif.: Scholars Press, 1981.

Bushnell's thought is "modeled on a theory of the power of symbolic expressions, linguistic and otherwise, to facilitate human moral growth." Bushnell's writings are reviewed, with an especially pertinent treatment of the theologian as educator, finding that "Bushnell believed that theology, properly conceived, could play a role in restoring human receptivity to God's self-communication."

CHAPTER 3

Philosophies of Religious Education Among Roman Catholics

Gabriel Moran

The purpose of this essay is to address the question, What is the underlying structure of ideas that gives unity and distinctiveness to Roman Catholic writing on religious education? The reader may wonder why I assume that there *is* any unifying structure of ideas. I can only reply that if I am asked to write on Roman Catholic (as contrasted to Protestant, Jewish, or Hindu) philosophies of education, I am bound to ask about the common assumptions, personal convictions, and institutional loyalties that describe the group. What I discover may not be a perfectly unified set of ideas that would deserve the title "philosophy of religious education." I would hope at least to discover some philosophical ideas that link disparate positions within Roman Catholicism today.

The diversity among Roman Catholic writers can be puzzling to an outside observer. Indeed, many Roman Catholics find the diversity within their church to be a puzzle or something worse. The variety of opinions and approaches is nowhere more evident than in the educational area. In the first half of this essay I will claim that the diversity is even greater than is usually assumed. I will then propose in the second half that there is a unity in this writing built around the meaning of the word *religious.*

In the first part I will cite examples of Roman Catholic writing on religious education. I am mainly interested in illustrating the diversity rather than trying to classify writers according to my own typology. In all cases I have to infer a "philosophy of religious education" because that category as such does not appear in this literature.

Previous Essays in This Series

An appropriate place to begin is with the essays by Roman Catholic writers in the previous collections of this series (see the

Gabriel Moran is Associate Professor of Religious Education, New York University.

introduction): Gerard Sloyan's in 1960, Neil McCluskey's in 1966, and James Michael Lee's in 1976.[1] The reader should note that in each of those essays the author was making the Roman Catholic statement in a Protestant collection. In each case the author had to attempt a sweeping survey of the Roman Catholic Church's past and present. My essay is not comparable in scope because there are other Roman Catholics in this book to tell other parts of the story.

The essays by Sloyan, McCluskey, and Lee illustrate what I said about the striking diversity. Each of the essays has its own value, but any reader of the three together would wonder whether the essays are on the same topic. The essays are entitled "Roman Catholic Religious Education"; "Religious Education in the Roman Catholic Church"; and "Roman Catholic Religious Education," but it is not immediately evident that there is a common referent of meaning.

The diversity can be partly accounted for by two factors. One is the personalities, interests, and convictions of the respective writers. Each wrote from his own strength and emphasized what seemed to him the most important threads of development. The second factor is that the Roman Catholic Church in these last two decades has been going through a period of extraordinary change. Sloyan on the eve of Vatican II, McCluskey at the conclusion of the council, and Lee a decade later reflect a rapidly changing scene within Roman Catholicism. These two factors are significant but not fully explanatory of the diversity.

Gerard Sloyan's 1960 essay begins with a definition of religious education as "the unfolding of the terms of God's gift freely given—life—and of the response of free acceptance to that gift" (p. 396). Sloyan takes the reader through patristic and medieval periods and follows with special attention to the post-Reformation period and to the biblical-liturgical renewal in the contemporary period. The essay then shifts to the Catholic schools of the United States and impressive statistics indicating the success of those schools.

Sloyan did note that the church schools could not keep pace with the constantly increasing Catholic population. He ended the essay by suggesting that a crisis of religious education in Roman Catholicism had great ecumenical possibilities. Very few people at the time perceived what was beginning to happen in this area. For some years Gerard Sloyan was almost alone in channeling into the United States the catechetical renewal that was occurring in European and missionary countries.

By the time of Neil McCluskey's essay in 1966, millions of U.S. Catholics knew about biblical, liturgical, catechetical, and ecumenical movements. McCluskey's essay is almost exclusively concerned with the origins of a separate school system and the question of whether that school system should be perpetuated. Nowhere in the essay is there a definition or even direct reflection on religious education. McCluskey seems to assume that we know what religious education is; the question is where is it best carried out.

Neil McCluskey was responding to several events that defined the issue at that moment. The Second Vatican Council was the most obvious influence, one that pervaded all Catholic church life. Closer to home, the crisis of the schools that Sloyan had foreseen suddenly emerged. Another set of events influencing McCluskey was the U.S. Supreme Court's decisions on prayer in the public school. The Court decisions opened a new context for discussing the relation between the Roman Catholic Church and public schooling.

By the time of James Michael Lee's 1976 essay, the single focus of McCluskey's essay had disappeared. In a sense "the Catholic school" had been replaced by several kinds of Catholic school. Lee comments briefly on the situation of Catholic schools. He then proceeds to the claim that religious education has emerged or is emerging as a distinct field. While this field does not exclude "the religion lessons in the Catholic school" it is a "single, unitary enterprise, irrespective of the setting in which it occurs" (p. 250).

From the 1960s to the present, Lee has seen the choice as one between religious education as a "messenger boy of theology" and as a "mode of social science." Lee describes himself in the essay as "the founder and chief proponent of the social science approach to religious education" (p. 253). Lee's definition of religious education is "the process by which religious behavior is facilitated" (p. 253).

Other Illustrations of Diversity

Boston College has sponsored a series of symposia, the first of which is published under the title *Foundations of Religious Education*.[2] The four Roman Catholic speakers were asked to address the question of foundations of religious education. The titles of the papers are indicative of their diversity: "Key Issues in the Development of a Workable Foundation for Religious Instruction" (James Lee), "Christian Education for Freedom:

A 'Shared Praxis' Approach" (Thomas Groome), "Socialization as a Model for Catechetics" (Berard Marthaler). The fourth paper, by me, has the less revealing title of "Where Now, What Next?"

Each of the participants in the symposium began with the term *religious education* but quickly expressed reservations about the term itself. For Groome, religious education was thought to be too global; hence the need is to be specifically Christian if one wishes to start from a union of theory and practice. For Lee, "the word *education* means the broad process whereby a person learns something"; what interests Lee is the more specific issue of instruction. For Marthaler, religious education needs a particular "model" that he finds in the idea of socialization; hence his main interest is catechetics, by which he means religious education as a socialization process. In my own essay, I resist what I take to be a church meaning of religious education; for advocating a more comprehensive meaning of religious education, I deal with the relation of church and nonchurch as well as proposing a model of education.

The word *model* that shows up in my own essay and is highlighted in Marthaler's essay is a common way today of describing diversity. Many commentators would probably say that Groome, Lee, Marthaler, and Moran present four models of religious education. Although that explanation seems to offer clarity, I suspect that the language of models obscures the issue here. The language of models already presupposes an agreement about what is to be modeled. Very few, if any, Roman Catholic writers have offered a set of models for religious education. Lee's religious instruction and Groome's Christian education are alternatives to religious education. Marthaler in his essay proposes a "socialization model," but he does not attempt to name the other models that might be possible. In another place Marthaler does try to name models of catechetics, a venture that is quite different from models of religious education.[3] There probably is sufficient agreement within the Roman Catholic Church that a thing exists called catechetics. People can then disagree about how to shape or model that reality.

The problem I am trying to expose here is that the disagreement is more profound than if there were several models of religious education or differing theories of religious education. Because *religious education* is such a weak or limited term to most writers, they quickly move away from it to a more specialized language with which they theorize, philosophize, or construct a coherent set of ideas and practices. The language of models has become the standard liberal way of allowing or explaining diversity. That language of models assumes some fundamental agreements, including the acceptance of a technical language born from twentieth-century sciences. The language of models is itself only one way of speaking and is not very helpful in the most profound disagreements.

As a further exposition of diversity I cite one other study, *An Invitation to Religious Education* by Harold Burgess.[4] This book speaks of "theoretical approaches" rather than models; it proposes "to engage in a descriptive analytic study of the theorizing of representative religious educationists concerning some fundamental units of religious education" (p. 9). The author devises a category system with six questions asked about each theoretical approach (aim, content, teacher, student, environment, evaluation). The limitations in talking about models of religious education are also dramatically illustrated by Burgess's theoretical approaches. However, I should acknowledge that Burgess undertook an ambitious project in trying to classify both Catholic and Protestant writers. Few other writers have made any systematic attempts.[5]

The basic problem with Burgess's approaches is the *what* that they approach. *Religious education* is in the title and throughout the book but all the problems with the term in Catholic and Protestant history are never examined. The book's first footnote reads: "The decision to employ the term 'religious education' rather than 'Christian education' or 'catechetics' represents an effort to use as broad a term as possible. No particular nuance is intended" (p. 16). With "no particular nuance" *religious education* turns out to be a vague term whose actual reference is Protestant history with the addition of some Catholic representatives. Not surprisingly, no Jewish writer represents a theoretical approach to religious education. In fact, the first three of the four approaches are essentially historical periods of recent Protestant history. The fourth approach is James Michael Lee's religious instruction as a mode of social science. In the book's final footnote, Burgess ponders whether the first three approaches might be specific variations within a generic approach.

The weakness of the fourfold classification is revealed by the presence (or absence) of the Catholic authors. The first approach of "traditional theological" includes such Roman Catholic writers as Josef Jungmann and Johannes Hofinger. These men actually were revolutionary forces in the Roman Catholic Church. A Protestant writer can mistake talk about the Bible and liturgy as merely traditional, whereas the Bible in the context of liturgical and social justice concerns has been at the center of Catholic church renewal. In that regard there is a striking absence of Catholic writers in the "social-culture approach." That fact indicates not a lack of concern about social issues by Roman Catholic writers but the limitations of the book's criteria.

In the third approach ("contemporary theological") I find myself teamed with several Protestant theologians, including James Smart. I can only say I find the association amusing; I am not sure Smart would have been similarly amused. Our positions were antithetical on most things, particularly the meaning of revelation that Burgess threads throughout the chapter. The problem lies in the assumption that someone using the category of revelation must be working in the same vein as Barthian or post-Barthian theology. At least some of my Catholic colleagues understand my intention to use revelation as a religious category but not a category governed by Christian theology.[6] Burgess's fourth approach ("social-science") is a clear and concise exposition of James Michael Lee's work. The difficulty remains of relating what Lee does to other writers in the Roman Catholic Church.

Having set out the wide range of writers and the difficulty of classifying them, I turn to the other side of my topic: What unites them or at least creates a coherent pattern? My task is to find some underlying philosophy or philosophies that would make intelligible the variety of positions. I will refer to the first half of this essay for illustrations and add references to other people, especially women who are prominent in this area (Maria Harris, Gloria Durka, Joanmarie Smith, Mary Boys, Suzanne Toton).[7]

The Religious Bond

What unites Catholic theorists on religious education is a positive attitude toward the religious. That statement may seem banal or even tautological, but the attitude toward the religious generally distinguishes Catholic from Protestant writing. If there were a clearly distinct and fully functioning field of religious education, then the centrality of the category of the religious for anyone working in that field could probably be assumed. Because the field is not fully existent in Roman Catholicism, Protestantism, Judaism, Islam, or elsewhere, an author's attitude toward the religious has to be inferred.

Catholic and Protestant writers generally move away from the term *religious education*, but they do not necessarily move in the same way. Writers who never use the term *religious education*, or use it with "no particular nuance," still have a relation to what the Western world calls religion. Catholic and Protestant differences on this point go back centuries. In most ecumenically oriented meetings today we try to avoid harsh contrasts; it is widely presumed that liberal Catholics are closer to liberal Protestants than to conservative Catholics. While I have no desire to go back to old stereotypes and to pit Protestant against Catholic, I think there may be value in searching for a difference of attitude that still divides us. I leave it to the Protestant reader to draw the contrasts here while I try to show a connection among Catholic writers.

I said that Roman Catholic writers generally move away from the term *religious education* as the name of their endeavor. However, what they shift toward is "being religious" in a more concrete way. Roman Catholic writers generally associate a positive meaning with the adjective *religious* and even the noun *religion*. Two notes go along with religion whether or not the speaker is fully conscious of them. Religion in an older meaning has always included the external and behavioral. Religion in the modern world always implies some plurality and comparison.

Religious Education and Behavior

Roman Catholic religious education is never far removed from a concern with external behavior. Within that concern there is a spectrum of "philosophies" about behavior. An outside observer in the modern world is liable to dismiss all such concern as legalistic, parochial, or merely traditional. For the religious person *to do* the right thing is crucial. Behavior has a value of its own; it is not reducible, for example, to an "expression of faith." Religion must be practiced even when there is no feeling of spontaneity. On this point, as on several others, Catholic writing is often closer in sentiment to Jewish writing than to Protestant writing.

If one keeps this concern with external practice in view, the wide range of Catholic writing falls along a spectrum. Conservatives and liberals alike deal with law, liturgical prayer, and the institution called the church. By "law" Catholics can refer to an elaborate code of canons requiring an army of experts or to the law written into the universe and visible to anyone. By "liturgy" one can mean fulfilling the Sunday obligation to attend Mass or pouring animal blood on government computer cards. By "institutional concern" one can mean preserving holy mother church from criticism or communal experiments for the sake of radical social change.

I would now like to test my first note against several authors. I pointed out that the 1960 essay by Gerard Sloyan and the 1976 essay by James Michael Lee have identical titles but seem to be on different topics. However, Sloyan's definition of religious education quoted above ("the unfolding of the terms of God's gift . . .") goes on to stress that religious education is concerned with an "objective element, sacred truth." Indeed, that concern runs throughout Sloyan's treatment of the catechetical movement and the schools. Lee's definition of religious education ("the process by which religious behavior is facilitated") is everywhere evident in its concern for religion as an external behavior. Sloyan and Lee differ, but they differ about a common topic.

For another unity in contrast, consider the Groome and Marthaler essays in *Foundations of Religious Education*. Marthaler's socialization model and Groome's shared praxis seem to be disparate languages. What unites them is a concern with religion as an external and institutionalized reality. Neither essay focuses on the inner attitude of the individual. Both authors are practical minded in the sense of wanting to change personal behavior and institutional structures.

I would like to note here another strand of Roman Catholic writing, represented by Maria Harris. Her main themes of aesthetics, feminism, and professionalization may seem to have little to do with the concerns of the men who have been cited.[8] Consider, however, her consciously positive attitude toward the word *religious*, and her writing can be seen as a powerful critique of external forms. Harris is one of a growing tide of women in the church who are patiently but insistently saying that the forms for women must change: the language, imagery, and institutional roles. Her concern with the aesthetic in religious education is attention to external behavior in the widest sense, that is, the design of environment to bring about human change without violence to the nonhuman world. Her aesthetic concern strikes a responsive chord with many women.[9]

The Roman Catholic philosophic spectrum on this point concerning behavior runs from a learning of doctrine and receiving of sacraments to a biblically and liturgically inspired attempt to shape new communal settings. Because for Roman Catholics the Bible is almost always seen within an institutional setting, Protestants may mistake the intent of Catholics who emphasize the Bible, whether Jungmann in the past or Mary Boys today. Protestants may also miss the fact that Roman Catholics such as

Lee or Moran who seldom quote the Bible are usually presupposing a biblical-liturgical-church reality.

Religion as Comparative

I turn now to the second note of the word *religion*, namely, pluralism and comparison. One thing that was wrong with the term *comparative religion* was its redundancy. It is of the nature of the modern meaning of religion to be a comparative term. This meaning, which can be dated from about the eighteenth century, has some continuity with the note of external behavior. When modern scientific and historical studies made apparent the many conceptions of the gods and the many ways of life, the word *religion* was the available word to make comparisons. In the ancient world there might have been true religion and false religion. In the modern world there are Jewish, Hindu, Muslim, and Christian religions. By attending to what exists in practice, one can suspend judgment about a configuration being good or bad, true or false. Some religious practices (for example, human sacrifice) may be judged bad or false religion. But a statement such as "Hinduism is a false religon" may not have any intelligible meaning, because Hinduism is such a complex term, and criteria for comparing religions are still in early development. One way in which people try to avoid the whole problem is to use *religion* as a word to describe other people. Hindus and Muslims can play this game as well as Christians. We have the way, the truth, the life; other people have religion.

My claim is that Roman Catholic writers on religious education do keep religion as a central and positive category. The result is that they incorporate the elements of pluralism and comparison. Roman Catholics are generally comfortable with saying that Catholicism is their religion, one of the religions of the world. For the more reactionary part of the church, the Catholic religion is ultimately the right one. Even here there might be admission that Catholics could learn much by studying other religions. By attending to external practice, it is obvious that some lines of continuity can be drawn from Roman Catholic practice on one side to Buddhist contemplative communities, Hindu goddess figures, and Jewish Sabbath ritual on the other side.

In the liberal wing of the Roman Catholic Church, there is also concern for the one true religion. These people could even use the same formula: ultimately the Catholic religion is the only true one. Here, however, the writers would wish to insist on a distinction between the Catholic religion still being born in the world and the current ecclesiastical form of Roman Catholicism. For this part of the Roman Catholic Church, a dialogue with others is not only admissible but is essential to the existence and meaning of religious education. The dialogue, it should be noted, is not with "world religions" but with other religions of the world.

The attitude that "one religion is as good as another" is foreign to nearly all Catholics. Some Roman Catholics think that everyone should join the true church that exists; others think that everyone should join the universal religion as it is coming to be. The most liberal Roman Catholic is likely to maintain a firm relation to the institution and thereby to a tension between the existing shape of the Roman Catholic Church and the universal or catholic religion. The terms *liberal* and *conservative*, borrowed from the post-Enlightenment period, can be quite misleading when applied to Roman Catholic writers.

I offer once more a test of authors cited. I would claim that they all deal with religion as a pluralism within a set of realities demanding comparison. Consider Gerard Sloyan's 1960 essay that began with a definition of religious education as "the unfolding of the terms of God's gift freely given—life—and of the response of free acceptance to that gift." What may not be noticed is that there is no Roman Catholic or Christian parochialism to that description. The body of the essay is appropriately concerned with the intramural history and situation of the Roman Catholic Church, but his context is truly religious. He makes no assumption that the Roman Catholic Church is the one true religion. In fact, his definition would invite Jews or Muslims to describe how God's gift of life is unfolded in their responses.

A common theme among Roman Catholic writers is a need for dialogue with Jews. The concern goes beyond an advocacy of acquaintance with the Old Testament. Writers like Harris, Boys, and Moran constantly refer to accepting the Hebrew Bible with its own autonomy and dialoguing with the contemporary Jewish community so as to establish a field of religious education. Other writers may not highlight Jewish relations but they do assume religious cooperation in struggles for justice (for example, Suzanne Toton) or they assume, like James Michael Lee, a social science approach that is explicitly comparative from the start.

The spectrum of Roman Catholic writing on this point runs from the inculcation of the saving truth in the one true religion to a dialogue on the meaning of religion itself. As I have warned, that is not always what is described as conservative to liberal. An ideology of liberal Catholicism can be inculcated as the saving truth. On the other end, a traditional set of Roman Catholic practices can be part of an openness to and dialogue with religions beyond the church. For example, the liturgical renewal built around the new Rite of Christian Initiation for Adults can be part of a dialogue with the present community, the past, and the nonchurch world.[10] Jungmann's work from the 1930s and Sloyan's work in the 1950s thus retain a pertinence in the church of the 1980s.

Conclusion: Educational Implications

I have concentrated on the religious part of religious education. I can make some return to the category of religious education by suggesting educational implications of the above. If one accepts religion as central and positive in one's thinking, then certain educational practices are likely to follow. I note two educational correlations with the two notes of religion described above.

Schooling

Catholic religious education, especially in the United States, has always had a strong basis in schools. I do not just mean courses in Christian doctrine but schools that (1) form a child's behavior in accordance with Catholic practice, and (2) teach religion as a visible reality that can be intelligently grasped. When Georgetown was founded as the first Catholic school in 1791, it was open to people of all religions. The school reserved the right to regulate conduct; the parents decided whether the child would receive religious instruction.[11]

In Sloyan's 1960 essay he raised doubts about the future of Catholic schools (or, as they are still called, Catholic education), but he strongly praised their reality: "There is the insistence in Catholic education that the individual has special obligations to his fellows in a racially, economically and politically diverse society. In the religious sphere positive bigotry is nonexistent in the Catholic school" (pp. 406-7). To the extent that an institution deserves the name *Catholic school* it teaches religion, and it is aware of religion's interaction with institutional structures. It is conscious that religion's part in external behavior can slide into narrowness and bigotry.

The two large studies by Andrew Greeley provided evidence that Catholic schools were doing with some success what Sloyan said they did.[12] The question became whether the degree of success of existing schools justified the astronomical costs, and that for no more than half the children. Greeley regularly lambasts people in religious education who, he claims, thought an hour's weekly instruction would duplicate a Catholic school's effects. Actually, Roman Catholic writers in religious education not only don't attack Catholic schools, but they visualize a Catholic school as an excellent setting for religious education. Lee's 1976 essay, no less than McCluskey's and Sloyan's, is formed in the image of the Catholic school. Lee's religious instruction is supposedly for diverse settings, but his modes of religious education (religious instruction, religious guidance, administration of religious education) bear the stamp of the school.

The difference among Roman Catholic writers has been concerned with how best to reach all of the children and also the adults. The Catholic school—or rather several kinds of Catholic school—is part of almost everyone's thinking. A school that cut across society's segregations (including age) would have wide support. Some authors (Marthaler, Harris, Moran) have stressed the nonschooling parts of education. But the philosophies differ on how to situate schooling, not whether it has a central role. When the school does its part to shape behavior, then other settings such as family and liturgical celebration can be formative of personal and institutional life.

Religion in Dialogue with Education

My final point is that if religion is accepted as a term of comparison, then it can become a central educational category. A dialogue is thereby called for between the modern meaning of education and a truly catholic religion. What many Roman Catholic writers are trying to do is dialogue across religious lines within an educational setting. The modern school that wishes "to teach religion" cannot just proselytize in Christianity or Islam; neither should it just explain away Christianity or Islam. A real confronting of religion and education creates a delicate tension for which no one has certain answers.

In Roman Catholicism the long experience with the schools, combined with the claim to be *the* catholic religion, heightens the tension: how to maintain the integrity of both the religious and the educational. Roman Catholic writers to varying degrees allow an autonomy to the word *education*—including the modern emphasis on critical self-reflection. There is a real danger here, as any loyal and practicing devotee of religion knows. Nonetheless, Roman Catholic philosophies of religious education can be understood only if one is aware of the dialogue which creates the meaning of religious education. Thus, Groome can describe his shared praxis as a "group process of critical reflection in the light of the Christian

Story and Vision on present action" (p. 22). Lee, as we have seen, actually treats religious education as a mode of social science. Harris, Boys, Toton, and other writers cited vary in the kinds of critical tools they emphasize. Nonetheless, each allows that religion in education means comparing, criticizing, and perhaps altering the meaning of one's own religion.

Let me cite one example for contrast. The opening sentence of Lewis Sherrill's fine book *The Rise of Christian Education* is: "To reach the deepest understanding of Christian education, whether in history or at present, one must begin with Christianity and proceed thence to education."[13] That may indeed be the way to understand Christian education, but it is also the reason why so many Roman Catholic writers insist they are in religious education rather than Christian education. The first is not just wider than the second. In religious education, the education is a partner in dialogue, not a consequence or a coda; and the religious partner is full of ambiguity and uncertain conclusion. Various forms of Christianity are the outcome of religious education. Of course, much of the literature from ecclesiastical offices does presume we must first agree on what Christianity is (or more likely what the true teachings of the church are) before we can move to education. Most Roman Catholic writers in religious education resist this presumption, not out of disloyalty but in the name of a wider church and a truer catholicism.

No one knows for sure if this tension of religion and education can be maintained. Many people within and beyond the church think that modernity is slowly swallowing the Roman Catholic Church. A healthy church of the future probably depends on such things as: (1) involving adults in educationally effective ways, (2) stimulating more interreligious dialogue in which the deeper roots of Catholicism are uncovered, and (3) shaping the communal, liturgical, political life of the church so as to make possible a powerful Christian witness. I think there is more agreement among Roman Catholic writers than the intramural battles often suggest. We differ about the effectiveness of instruments, and we differ along a double spectrum concerning the notes of religion. We agree in trying to establish a pattern that would be truly religious and effectively educational.

Notes

1. Marvin J. Taylor, ed., *Religious Education* (Nashville: Abingdon Press, 1960); Marvin J. Taylor, ed., *An Introduction to Christian Education* (Nashville:

Abingdon Press, 1966); Marvin J. Taylor, ed., *Foundations for Christian Education in an Era of Change* (Nashville: Abingdon Press, 1976).

2. Padraic O'Hare, ed., *Foundations of Religious Education* (New York: Paulist Press, 1978).

3. Berard Marthaler, "Towards a Revisionist Model in Catechetics: Reflections on David Tracy's Blessed Rage for Order," *Living Light* 13 (Fall 1976): 458-69.

4. Harold Burgess, *An Invitation to Religious Education* (Mishawaka, Ind.: Religious Education Press, 1975).

5. One of the few books that is equally ambitious is Didier-Jacques Piveteau and J. T. Dillon, *Resurgence of Religious Instruction* (Birmingham, Ala.: Religious Education Press, 1977). This book's analysis of Catholic writers is generally more accurate than that of Burgess. However, what the two Catholic authors do is attach Protestant writers to a Roman Catholic history.

6. See Gabriel Moran, "From Obstacle to Modest Contributor: Theology in Religious Education," in *Religious Education and Theology*, ed. Norma Thompson (Birmingham, Ala.: Religious Education Press, 1982), 42-70.

7. Maria Harris, *Portrait of Youth Ministry* (New York: Paulist Press, 1981); Gloria Durka and Joanmarie Smith, *Modeling God* (New York: Paulist Press, 1976); Mary Boys, *Biblical Interpretation in Religious Education* (Birmingham, Ala.: Religious Education Press, 1980); Suzanne Toton, *World Hunger* (Maryknoll, N. Y.: Orbis Books, 1982).

8. See Maria Harris, "DRE's in the U.S.: The First Twenty Years," *Living Light* 17 (Fall 1980): 250-59; "Women and Church Ministries," *P.A.C.E.*, no. 7 (1976); "Religious Education and the Aesthetic," *Andover Newton Quarterly* 17 (November 1976): 125-32.

9. See Gloria Durka and Joanmarie Smith, eds., *Aesthetic Dimensions of Religious Education* (New York: Paulist Press, 1979).

10. See William Reedy, ed., *Becoming a Catholic Christian* (New York: William H. Sadlier, 1979).

11. John Tracy Ellis, *American Catholicism*, 2d ed., rev. (Chicago: University of Chicago Press, 1969), 54.

12. Andrew Greeley and Peter Rossi, *The Education of Catholic Americans* (Chicago: Aldine Publishing Co., 1966); Andrew Greeley and William McCready, *Catholic Schools in a Declining Church* (Mission, Kan.: Sheed Andrews & McMeel, 1976).

13. Lewis Sherrill, *The Rise of Christian Education* (New York: Macmillan, 1944), 1.

CHAPTER 4

Evangelical Philosophies of Religious Education

Warren S. Benson

Is There an Evangelical Philosophy of Religious Education?

As there is no one Protestant philosophy or one liberal philosophy, so there is no one evangelical philosophy of Christian education. Yet all of these philosophies have certain commonalities which enable the theories within each to be subsumed under a generic rubric. As such there is an evangelical philosophy of Christian education.

The commonalities or foundation stones of an evangelical philosophy are theological. The deity of Jesus Christ and the authority of Scripture are the touchstones of evangelical[1] theology. To the evangelical, an authoritative Bible answers with certitude the two questions upon which a philosophy of education should be constructed: What is humankind? What is his or her purpose?

Education within evangelicalism is an interesting blend. Throughout this century evangelicals have been extremely eclectic. They have been reactive and action oriented rather than polemical and theoretical. Their concern for numerical growth and the vigor of an individual's Christian experience often has superseded a reflectively developed philosophy of education. This was not a studied intentionality. Rather it progressed quite naturally from the historical context in which evangelicalism found itself.

The Sunday school conventions of the late 1800s and the early 1900s brought a vitality and a collegiality that affected much of American Protestantism. The conventions, in the hands of gifted laymen such as B. F. Jacobs, John Wanamaker, and H. J. Heinz, had a marked influence on the Sunday school. Sydney Ahlstrom has remarked that "revivals and revivalists would come and go,

Warren S. Benson is Associate Dean of Academic Affairs and Professor of Christian Education at Trinity Evangelical Divinity School.

but the Sunday schools remained as a stabilizing force in the churches. . . . They attracted dedicated leaders of great ability . . . and the Sunday schools did produce a pious and knowledgeable laity on a scale unequaled anywhere in Christendom."[2] As the conventions grew, the lay leadership of the movement tended to resort to amateur promotional techniques to perpetuate their growth. This frustrated the small but growing corps of professional elite in religious education. Slowly their influence was felt, and the volunteers began to transfer the leadership to these trained specialists.[3]

With the formation of the Religious Education Association in 1903, and certainly by the founding of the International Council of Religious Education in 1922, two vital developments had emerged. First, laymen were submitting to the order of that day, namely, that specialists including professors of Christian education and local church directors of Christian education[4] should take over the major leadership roles. Second, and in part as a result of the first, the leadership of the movement was shifting toward the theological left. Robert Lynn and Elliott Wright state:

By 1930, however, the old-style volunteers had been eased out of seats on top-level boards supposedly directing Sunday school affairs. The full-time professional was clearly in charge and the volunteers were treated, perhaps unconsciously, as potential trainees, the beneficiaries of the experts' guidance. Local teachers-laymen resented the apparent condescension from on high.[5]

Theological Winds

As the laity lost control of the leadership, the professionals and institutions that had trained them gained the ascendancy. During the 1920s and 1930s, these religious educators leaned more heavily toward theological liberalism. The emphasis on the conversion experience was becoming the province of evangelical churches and institutions. In the northern tier of the United States and Canada a diminishing number of colleges, seminaries, foundations, and publishing houses remained in evangelical hands. The devastating theological controversy of that period left few competent leaders and writers within the ranks of evangelical Christian education. The social action of the liberals was perceived as being synonymous with their social gospel message. Kenneth S. Kantzer has said:

In its early years, fundamentalism shaped its identity in opposition to liberalism. Evangelicalism, as its spiritual child, has not yet freed itself from this warping. In spite of its strong emphasis on *sola Scriptura* (the Bible alone), it still reflects its heritage of one-sided opposition to liberalism. Surely this alone explains the deep-seated evangelical suspicion of social action as it identifies it with the social gospel.[6]

In the late 1930s new theological winds began to blow. The impact of Karl Barth, Reinhold Niebuhr, and the neo-orthodoxy they championed was momentous. At that time dialogue was a more reasonable option between evangelical and neo-orthodox thinkers. However, neither group moved toward the other. Had a move been attempted, the evangelical wall of suspicion probably would have cut off any significant interaction.

It should be noted that strong pockets of evangelical educational philosophers could be found among both the Reformed and the Arminian-Wesleyan denominations. The Southern Baptists, Christian Reformed, Church of the Nazarene, and a vanguard of other educators, some of whom were in mainline churches, contributed to the intellectual leadership of evangelical Christian education through the 1930s and early 1940s.

Philosophical Winds

It is impossible for any educational philosophy to dissociate itself from the societal context in which it is formed. Early in the twentieth century the awesome impact of John Dewey was felt in every aspect of American education. The specters of Rousseau, Pestalozzi, Froebel, and even Herbart could be seen in Dewey. Yet Dewey was distinctly his own person. His influence on evangelicalism was evident as well.

Burgess has said:

John Dewey's philosophical doctrines and progressive educational proposals may be counted among the most significant factors which have given form to the social-cultural theoretical approach to religious education. His philosophical redefinition of knowledge and learning, though totally antithetical to the traditional concepts of religious education . . . became a theoretical fundamental of the social-cultural position.[7]

Dewey took issue with those who held to absolute truth and who inculcated that truth with certitude. The celebrated philosopher-educator's antisupernaturalism and his inadequate views of metaphysics and human nature prompted evangelicals to shy away from him. However, without equivocating their position on the authority of Scripture, there has been an epistemological shift among some evangelicals toward a more active, experiential, and relational way of knowing to which Dewey was so heavily committed. The evangelical is sometimes perceived as assuming that education is to be equated with depositing accumulated data. Paulo Freire identifies this as "the banking concept of education,"[8] and Dewey designated it as "the funded capital of civilization."[9]

Evangelical Lawrence O. Richards suggests that Bible teaching and experience are inseparable components in the teaching-learning process.

The implications of the biblical and behavioral science data are far-reaching. For a person to "be" a Christian, in the fullest biblical sense, his identity and perceptions of reality need to be rooted in participation in a community which is committed to give living expression to God's revealed perception of reality. It is simply impossible to communicate a biblical faith in a schoolized way, with stress on cognitive structures, unless that setting is simply one facet of the life of a committed community in which the learner participates fully.[10]

Teaching across the street from Dewey at Columbia University's Teachers College was George Albert Coe (1862–1951), considered by many to be the finest theoretician in Protestant religious education during the first half of this century.[11] However, Smart finds in Coe "a rather thin doctrine of divine immanence, a belief in the naturalness of Christian growth, a blissful confidence in the goodness of man, and a Unitarian conception of Jesus Christ."[12]

Evangelicals argue that the Bible critiques experience and provides the cognitive structures of faith. Coe argued precisely the reverse; namely, that religious education creates theology. Wayne R. Rood states:

Though his theology is technically implicit, Coe is explicit enough about it. Theology is implicit because it is projected from the religious experience of men. . . . [He] specifically denies any effort to construct a theological system, and makes no apology for the unorthodox nature of his theological conclusions.[13]

Coe utilized the insights of Dewey in religious education. "Dewey's notion that education is the participation of the individual in the social consciousness of the race and that it is grounded in the reconstruction of experience (which in turn is to lead to social reconstruction) are central themes in Coe's understanding of Christian religious education."[14] Coe's lack of a biblical base and his interpretation of experience were unacceptable to evangelicals.

Historical Developments Within Evangelicalism

The American Sunday School Union (now American Missionary Fellowship) was founded in 1817 and flourishes to the present, particularly in rural areas. Standard Publishing Company began in 1866. It became the literature house for the evangelical wing of the Christian churches and the Churches of Christ. David C. Cook started a curriculum publishing company in 1875 that remains strong to the present. J. M. Price founded the School of Religious Education at Southwestern Baptist Theologial Seminary in 1915, the second institution of its kind, that now numbers fifteen hundred in enrollment. In 1921 Frank E. Gaebelein began the Stony Brook School, a secondary preparatory school that has been a model for Christian schools. By 1933 Henrietta Mears, director of Christian education at First Presbyterian Church of Hollywood, California, was writing her own Sunday school curriculum materials that eventuated into Gospel Light Publications. In the same year Clarence Benson and his Moody Bible Institute students were writing curriculum that became Scripture Press Publications.

The National Association of Evangelicals, founded in 1942,[15] developed the National Sunday School Association three years later. Although the NSSA terminated operations in 1976, the local area associations they spawned have remained healthy. The National Association of Professors of Christian Education brings together many professors of colleges, Bible colleges, and theological seminaries for intellectual stimulation and professional growth. Currently the Sunday school board of the Southern Baptist Convention employs over one thousand people who produce materials for their own churches and many other Baptist and non-Baptist constituencies. But the development of a great depth level in a movement can come about only with the growth of individual members. There are several representative evangelical educators of the last forty years who have shaped the contemporary scene.

Frank E. Gaebelein

In 1953, Frank E. Gaebelein delivered the Griffith Thomas Lectures at Dallas Theological Seminary. As *The Pattern of God's Truth* (Chicago: Moody Press, 1968) they were destined to have a profound effect on many evangelicals who were grappling with the problems of integrating the truth of various disciplines with Scripture. Currently Nicholas P. Wolterstorff, Arthur F. Holmes, Kenneth O. Gangel, and Ronald A. Chadwick are writing on the integrational problem.[16]

That all truth is God's truth wherever it be found was a claim of the early church. This is a statement about God's understanding of truth, not man's. It does not mean that all truth is contained in the Bible or deducible from what we find there. Gaebelein, as a Renaissance man, embraced these concepts and utilized them in the integrational task. He preserved a unique place for the Word of God.

No other book can compare in educating power with the Bible. Let no Christian educator ever apologize to the sophisticated of the educational world for giving the Bible the highest place. To take as the center of the curriculum the one book among all other great books to which alone the superlative "greatest" can without challenge be uniquely applied—this is neither narrow nor naive. Rather it is simply good judgment to center on the best rather than the second best.[17]

The aggressive and growing Christian school movement looked to Gaebelein because of his erudition and his approach to the teaching of content. Programmed learning, which one segment of this movement has followed to a fault, is foreign to Gaebelein's methodology. On the other hand, the emphasis on socialization by Lawrence O. Richards and John H. Westerhoff III also is at variance with his position. Burgess is correct in stating that Gaebelein "places a high priority on the verbal teaching of the scriptures and upon the pulpit as a functional center of Christian religious education."[18] But to posture him as being insensitive to the cruciality of immediate learning outcomes is to overstate the case.[19]

Kenneth O. Gangel

People such as Rebecca Price, her protegé Howard G. Hendricks, and former Gordon-Conwell professor Charles Schauffele have had distinguished careers in the field of education but have not written on the philosophy of education. Nevertheless, the influence of these teachers and the hundreds of their graduates in Christian education ministries attests to their superb contribution. Kenneth Gangel has written widely. Although the bulk of this literary investment has been of a popular nature, his substantive work is worthy of consideration.

"The most important thing about education is to learn what God has said."[20] Since there is a God, and that God has spoken in history, understanding what God has said in both special and natural (general) revelation becomes the core of the curriculum. God's revelation forms the frame of reference for everything we learn. Rationalism posits that man alone is responsible for the creation and certification of truth. Herein Gangel draws a careful distinction between revelationism and rationalism. Because Scripture portrays an experienceable reality, the truth of Scripture can be validated by our own experience and that of others. This is not to say that the "truth" of the Bible "depends on our experience." Rather, we would expect a correlation between what Scripture teaches about reality and our experience.

The foundational philosophic construct for education is metaphysics—an understanding of ultimate reality that rests in God. Gangel quotes James W. Sire in a statement of his educational philosophy.

Christian theism is primarily dependent on its concept of God, for theism holds that everything stems from Him. He is He Who Is. Thus theism has a basis for metaphysics. Since He Who Is also has a worthy character and is thus the Worthy One, theism has a basis for ethics. Since He Who Is is also He Who Knows, theism has a basis for epistemology. In other words, theism is a complete world view.[21]

Gangel, following in the tradition of Gaebelein, has spoken at length regarding the principles and process of integrating faith and learning. He suggests six principles:

1. A commitment to the authority of the Bible.
2. A recognition of the contemporaneity of the Bible and the Holy Spirit.
3. A clear understanding of the nature, source, discovery, and dissemination of truth.
4. The integrative process is based on designing a curriculum which is totally constructed on the centrality of special revelation.
5. A demand for the development of a Christian world and life view.
6. Bibliocentric education is to extend to all areas of student life.[22]

Still writing within the context of Christian higher education, he, like Gaebelein, calls for every teacher to be at least an amateur theologian. However, the integration of truth is not to be confused with chapel or classroom devotions. Gangel further charges teachers to work at achieving a balance between open-mindedness and unchallengeable doctrine.

In a published lecture entitled "Developing a Philosophy of Teaching: Conditioning or Indoctrination?" he quotes Arthur F. Holmes regarding the dangers of indoctrination.

I think of the indoctrinator as the dogmatist for whom all issues are settled and all truth known and, as a result, all creative scholarship erodes away. He is the legalist who, enforcing things as they are, forgets that faith, like love, cannot be forced, but rather rises as the free response of the mind to that revelation of truth, an enlightened mind that has been freed from the shackles of opinion and prejudice. The indoctrinator has a ready made set of answers for every question. He mass produces organizational men who, given the right stimuli, recite appropriate sentences and respond with appropriate behavior patterns. But when his students meet new problems or start to think for themselves, they have neither the answers nor the developed intellectual powers to work them out. Having learned neither the true meaning nor the use of academic freedom, they either remain shackled by fear or else become disillusioned libertines, the campus cynics whose loyalty is to themselves rather than to the Truth.[23]

Nor can the teacher be a libertine who espouses the idea "no truth can be more true than another" and that all truth stands on the same level in an uncritical relativism. Gangel admits that believing in absolute truth "might also produce some indoctrination," but he challenges the pedagogue to fairness and objectivity in handling the ideas and concepts of others.

Findley B. Edge

Edge has written for both the layman and the serious student. His *Teaching for Results* (Nashville: Broadman Press, 1956) and *Helping the Teacher* (Nashville: Broadman Press, 1959) have provided excellent tools for teaching the Bible. Many evangelicals have been influenced philosophically by Edge's *Quest for Vitality in Religion* (Nashville: Broadman Press, 1963) and *Greening of the Church* (Waco, Tex.: Word, 1971). In an autobiographical sketch entitled "A Search for Authenticity,"[24] Edge describes his own pilgrimage as an educational philosopher.

As a student, Edge was greatly affected by Gaines S. Dobbins. During those years he was plagued by the question of authenticity in church life and the tangential problems of experiential religion and the church's seemingly inevitable bent toward institutionalism. In passing on the belief and value system from one generation to the next, the inner dynamic seemed to be lost, and the needs of society failed to be addressed.

However, other interests arose in Edge's teaching career at Southern Baptist Theological Seminary. Reading Horace Bushnell and studying with Ernest Ligon motivated him to emphasize the family as the central context for teaching. Postdoctoral work at Yale Divinity School with Randolph Crump Miller convinced him that "one's philosophy of Christian education ought to grow out of one's theology." But his disillusionment with the church and the problem of institutionalism continued to frustrate him. "It was an existential reality."

Edge developed what he calls "an experiential philosophy of Christian education." *Quest*, subtitled *A Theological Approach to*

Religious Education, states his case. First, "the essence of God's call is a call to mission," to the Lordship of Christ in all of life. Second, that mission includes not only personal salvation, but also the healing of people in their human and social brokenness.[25] Third, the priesthood of believers affirms not only the direct access each Christian has to God, but also that each is a minister and accountable to God to fulfill that ministry. The layperson is not to pay a professional staff member to execute his or her responsibility. The church is to initiate approaches for implementation that allow the laity to utilize their spiritual gifts and get involved in the action. Then institutionalism is more likely to be eliminated and the dynamic of the faith retained. Edge provided some of the careful thinking which the renewal movement needed in his *Greening of the Church.* He related renewal concepts to traditional churches with viable steps for implementation.

Lois E. Le Bar

Writing and lecturing often are viewed as the media by which to affect the greatest number of people. Two persons who influenced the thinking of Lois Le Bar were Rebecca Price and Clarence Benson. Benson, a pioneer among evangelical educators, was a prolific writer. Price, on the other hand, wrote very little but influenced many through her teaching at Wheaton College. Later she joined the faculty at the founding of Fuller Theological Seminary in 1947. Both Price and Le Bar received training in inductive Bible study at Biblical Seminary. It stamped Le Bar methodologically and philosophically.

This penchant for the study of Scripture provided a rich resource for building Lois Le Bar's philosophy of education. She evaluates religious education theories and practices from a biblical perspective. Yet her *Education That Is Christian* (1958, revised only slightly in 1981) and *Focus on People in Church Education* (1968), as well as chapters written for anthologies, give evidence of an openness to many of the concepts of the socialization model.

Bible teaching can overemphasize KNOWING at the expense of FEELING and DOING. Teachers can mistakenly assume that knowing will automatically lead to the corresponding feeling and doing. But that is contrary to Scripture. . . . Feelings are the energizers, the natural mainsprings of action.

Some teachers act as if the first and great commandment were expressed as knowing all the facts of Scripture rather than in terms of loving. Loving is the essential link between knowing and doing. . . . We are not wasting time when we cultivate attitudes and work on emotional problems.[26]

Le Bar accentuates educating the whole person and employing nonformal approaches. In her judgment evangelicals have a major problem due to the tendency to equate authoritarian methodology with an authoritative message. Emphasis should be placed on people learning rather than on teachers teaching. "Initially, in teaching, the continuity of experience is more important than continuity of content. . . . Later in the process . . . truth becomes organized systematically in doctrine and theology."[27]

Burgess capsulizes Le Bar's philosophy of method and curriculum as follows:

Since Jesus did not use stereotyped methods Le Bar concludes that the "scriptural method" is not a stereotyped method. She develops a curriculum plan for teaching religion in which the Word of God, both living (Christ) and written (the Bible), is at the center. The appropriate teaching method for this curriculum makes use of such concepts as pupil needs, life situations, personal experiences, and most especially, the Holy Spirit.[28]

Ted W. Ward

The professor of adult education and former Director of Michigan State University's Institute for Research in Human Learning has profoundly affected evangelical Christian education. Ted W. Ward delights in rearranging neatly devised categories, as his phrase "Christian education is neither"[29] indicates. Contemporary secular society in the Western world has been influenced by rationalism with its rootage in Hellenistic philosophy. Ward scores evangelical Christian education for its reflection of this viewpoint.

During most of its history, the New Testament church has drawn its values and metaphors of education more from Aristotelian Greek thought than from the authentic background of Christian philosophy: Hebrew culture. Praxis forces us back to a biblical valuing of knowledge as that which is acted on. The Hellenistic satisfaction with static contents of the mind is embedded in Christian education. But it is challenged by a whole-person concern for truth-in-action much closer to Jesus' own claim that truth was not defined apart from its incarnation.[30]

The Christian outcome of education would not be that of the Greek-like satisfaction with its clarified concepts. The central purpose of education and of life is biblical concern for obedience—acting on truth. Christianity cannot be defined apart from knowing and doing. Ward is critical of the church's two most common metaphors of education—filling a container and the manufacturing process.

One of the key problems in both of these concepts of education is their rooting in a tabula rasa view of childhood. Worse yet, this view of the learner as an empty slate to be written on by "those who know" is even applied to the teaching of adults.

> The learner is more acted on than active . . . this orientation demeans the image of God shared in each person and it encourages a passive receptivity, ultimately lacking in creativity and skills of education.[31]

Ward's teaching responsibilities in curriculum research and international education and his former administrative role as codirector of the Values Development Education Program at Michigan State have accelerated his involvement in theological education by extension (TEE) and moral development seminars. As a consultant to TEE, he has pleaded for integrative seminars which would provide the connecting link between cognitive input (of compulsive programmed instruction people) and the "practical service tasks." A concern for technique and technology should not eclipse the cruciality of reason and faith. He also identifies the reduction of teaching and learning to "a set of commonplaces" and an overemphasis on technology as two of the problems which church education faces.

Ward is critical of theological education in a number of areas but cites as one of the "grave ills" the compartmentalization of Christian education into a distinct field isolated from ministerial service. In local church education he identifies the home as the center of biblical Christian education and chides us for being "preoccupied with children at the expense of adult nurture and especially of parent development." As a developmentalist Ward has defined learning as follows:

> Learning is not seen as acquiring or internalizing ideas from the environment or other people, but it is seen to be a result of attempting to construct a meaningful understanding of one's experience in one's environment. . . . Learning is seen as a process of successive mental constructions. Knowledge is not acquired or internalized from the environment or people in the environment, it is a product of restructuring or reinvention by the individual. The learner is active in transforming what is perceived into structures that help him or her more adequately organize and make sense of experience.[32]

Ward's sometimes strident critiques are accepted because of his deep commitment to the church and his contribution to the education of people who serve in Christian ministry roles on the domestic and international scenes.

Lawrence O. Richards

Lawrence Richards is the most prolific contemporary evangelical philosopher of Christian education. In the summer of 1967 Richards, his colleagues in the Department of Christian Education at Wheaton College, Mary and Lois Le Bar, and a group of students and alumni gathered at the college's camp facilities near Eagle River, Wisconsin. They endeavored to take a fresh look at the total ministry of the church, and he wrote the results of their dialogue in *United Evangelical Action*.[33] Although he had been writing previously for Scripture Press Publications, this series launched Richards as a national name in evangelicalism.

Richards was calling for change, at times radical change. Renewalists such as Elton Trueblood, Robert Raines, Keith Miller, Findley Edge, and Bruce Larson were being read with interest. In his graduate work at Garrett-Evangelical Seminary and Northwestern University, he was reading in educational and social psychology. A Phi Beta Kappa graduate in philosophy at Michigan, he was steeped in Scripture at Dallas Seminary where at that time four years of Greek, three years of Hebrew, and four years of English Bible were required.

In his *New Face for the Church*[34] Richards gave full expression to the central ideas of these articles. Three of the ideas were: (1) the major deliberations of church leaders focus on problems of organization rather than those of people, (2) status is ascribed on the basis of performance and frequency of involvement, and (3) Christians see themselves in terms of their organizational role rather than as fellow ministers with the clergy. He challenged churches to open up their traditional forms to new patterns of community and group life, leadership styles, social concern, and the establishment of the home as the nurture center of Christian education.

Richards continued to write the Christian education column in *United Evangelical Action*, while his friend Elmer Towns became the Sunday school columnist for *Christian Life* magazine. Towns, currently dean of Liberty Baptist Seminary, started to collect data on Sunday school attendance across North America which eventuated in the writing of *The Ten Largest Sunday Schools*.[35] Richards and Towns attended the same seminary, subscribed to a high view of Scripture, but moved to opposite poles philosophically. The key words for Richards are *nurture* and *relationships;* Towns emphasizes *evangelism* and *aggressive leadership*. They have been followed by different constituencies, though the clarity of the distinctions is breaking down. While fundamentalists have adhered to the philosophy of church life and growth espoused by Towns, many evangelicals have embraced the vitality of Richards's concepts. A large percentage remains on Richards's side of the continuum in an attempt to employ the best of both philosophies, while continuing to be opposed to the autocratic leadership styles often used by fundamentalists. That which separates these two ecclesiologically based viewpoints is not a question of church size necessarily, but rather the perception of the nature of the church, worship, organizational and leadership styles, and the way in which individual and corporate spiritual and numerical growth takes place.

In Richards's *Creative Bible Teaching*,[36] he discusses the nature of revelation, the authority of Scripture, and his commitment to excellence in teaching praxis with the various age levels. He also shares some of his disillusionment with those who are preoccupied with method and fail to teach for life change.

We [evangelicals] see the Word of God as revealed, as true information from God. And so it is. But we tend to see it as information ONLY. We neglect the personal dimension. . . . When the Bible is understood and taught as information in which we meet God, when our goal in teaching and reading is to be responsive to the One who speaks to us, then we move beyond information and beyond law into the realm of personal relationship. And it is only this—personal relationship with God—that can transform. . . . There must be response . . . and response is of faith.[37]

Eleven years after the appearance of Richards's *Youth Ministry: Its Renewal in the Church*,[38] the book remains in current use. Blending the fresh thinking of social learning theory and adolescent psychology with his own renewal stance, he gives a biblical dimension to the concepts of modeling and self-identity. Being a theoretician rather than a practitioner, he wisely wedded his theories to the programming perspective of gifted youth ministers in the churches and para-church ministries in the examples and illustrations cited in the text.

A Theology of Christian Education[39] is Richards's most important work to date. While not a theology in the classical sense of the term, it is a substantial renewal ecclesiology of church life. Taking a clue from Randolph Crump Miller, Richards says that "ecclesiology must be the source of our educational understanding and that Christian education is truly a theological discipline."[40] He insists that the goal of Christian education is not to be an educational system that produces content knowledge but rather a supplier of what is needed for the process of growth. He takes a whole-person approach that keeps in balance the life of persons both in their individual and corporate identities.

Christian education is concerned with life, and with the growth of eternal life within the human personality, toward likeness to the God who gives it. Christian education is concerned with the progressive transformation of the believer toward the character, values, motives, attitudes, and understanding of God Himself.[41]

Christian education then can never deal with individual life alone. Christian education has to concern itself with the processes within the body which nurture corporate and individual growth in Christ. Any Christian education approach which focuses on either the individual or the group in exclusion of the other is bound to fall short.[42]

Charles M. Sell has stated that the issue regarding "schoolization," that is, the prevailing structured educational program of the church, and socialization is the most crucial discussion in contemporary Christian education philosophy.[43] Socialization has been defined as "the process of being inducted into the ethos, which in turn produces our self identity."[44] C. Ellis Nelson, John H. Westerhoff III, and Wayne R. Rood have ably defended the socialization viewpoint, and Lawrence Richards has laid an evangelical foundation for it.

Perry G. Downs is correct when he says that "Richards began to shift away from the more formal approach presented in *Creative Bible Teaching*"[45] and changed to a thoroughgoing socialization posture in *A Theology of Christian Education*. For him, "the critical location for Bible teaching is not the classroom but rather the household,"[46] though the classroom is not excluded. Writing in 1982, Richards continues his criticism of the "schoolization" approach.

Schoolized approaches associated with secular and religious education may be counterproductive when our goal is viewed in terms of life. It is theology, and not educational philosophy, which must rule Christian education.

Theology points us to the landmark truths that are to be taught, warns us against a transmissive approach that would treat Scripture as information, and suggests that learning processes must be found to communicate the Christian revelation as an unveiling of reality.

It is simply impossible to communicate a biblical faith in a schoolized way, with stress on cognitive structures, unless that setting is simply one facet of the life of a committed community in which the learner participates fully.[47]

Although Richards has moved philosophically, he has not equivocated on his stance regarding the authority of Scripture. Richards accepts the socialization position[48] and issues a call to the church. "Strikingly, the challenge of guiding the community of faith toward shared experience of revealed reality is not the province solely of the Christian educator. It is instead the heart of an adequate concept of ministry, and thus a mission shared by all congregational leaders."[49]

A Theology of Church Leadership[50] and *A Theology of Personal Ministry*[51] have added considerably to Richards's already substantial writings on the church and Christian education. *Church Leadership* has struck a vibrant chord for the importance of servant leadership and the disavowal of an overdependence on the management process as perceived by groups such as the American Management Association. In doing so he tends to overstate the case and presents a leadership model which approaches laissez-faire.[52] *Personal Ministry* encourages and gives direction to Christians desiring to maximize their service inside and outside the gatherings of the people of God. Building relationships and equipping persons continue to be crucial concepts to him. Richards attempts to present a more balanced style of leadership when he says:

The biblical pattern is not chaotic or laissez-faire. Leaders have definite responsibilities to carry out. But the leader's role is different from the role of the leader in the secular model. Strong leadership means working with a brother or sister to pray through his or her vision. Servant leadership means spending time to train or show how a ministry may be carried out. All the leader surrenders in the biblical approach is any claim of a right to control or make decisions for us. Christ is the head of the church, and His will is discovered by the laos as the Spirit acts as God's voice to them.[53]

The Power of the Publishers

The publishers of Christian education materials have had an important role in shaping the philosophy of contemporary Christian education. The Lutheran Church—Missouri Synod and the Southern Baptists are of sufficient size to have developed multifaceted publishing houses. Most evangelicals are quite dependent on the nondenominational publishing houses for both curriculum materials and books. Mainline denominations and the two aforementioned fellowships often have the leverage of loyalty with their constituencies. This enables them to develop curriculum designed for people's actual needs rather than their perceived needs. An example would be the creating of intergenerational or discovery-oriented curriculum.

Evangelical independent publishing houses must read their market carefully. If they are to show a profit, they must produce materials for which there is sufficient demand. Their continuance is based on that reality. Therefore, at times they are hesitant to publish certain materials which are needed but for which the people have little perceived interest. This influences their publication of scholarly materials as well. For instance, popular volumes sell in far greater quantities than substantive works. Currently this problem is diminishing because evangelical publishers have a profitable enterprise. But the necessity of producing the creative and the profound is carefully weighed. Family-owned companies respond from different criteria than denominationally controlled houses. Both have considerable power in determining the direction of the entire Christian education ministry, including educational philosophy.

A New Day?

A growing cluster of evangelical philosophers are joining people like Gangel, Ward, and Richards. The challenge of John H. Westerhoff, James H. Fowler, Mary C. Boys, James Michael Lee, James E. Loder, and their colleagues Sara P. Little, D. Campbell Wyckoff, Randolph Crump Miller, and C. Ellis Nelson brings fresh stimulation and impetus to evangelical Christian education. However, philosophers who employ a biblical base and attempt to interact with those data have greater credibility with evangelicals. As our Christian education comes of age, there is a growing vanguard of competent philosophers.

The following are representative of those who are writing in the field. Among Southern Baptists are Jack D. Terry, Daniel Aleshire, Bruce P. Powers, LeRoy Ford, and William A. Smith. The writers within the Reformed tradition come from a distinguished history philosophically. Current leaders are Nicholas P. Wolterstorff, N. H. Beversluis, Norman De Jong, Norman E. Harper, and Arthur F. Holmes. From the Christian church movement are Eleanor Daniel, Christine Templar, and Charles R. Gresham. Donald M. Joy, Catherine Stonehouse, J. W. McCant, A. Elwood Sanner, A. F. Harper, Harold William Burgess, and F. Franklyn Wise work within Wesleyan Christian education. Ruth Beechick, Charles M. Sell, Ronald A. Chadwick, Roberta R. Hestenes,

Elmer L. Towns, Neal F. McBride, and Clifford V. Anderson represent a broad spectrum of evangelical communions and groups.

The evangelical is often accused of certain rigidities, and some of the criticism is justified. There are foundational doctrines that give evangelicalism its distinctiveness. One of these is the conviction that humankind is fallen and in Jesus Christ resides our only hope. Incipient universalism is unacceptable. Through redemption the marred *imago Dei* is in the process of being restored, and meaningless existence is radically righted.

Although evangelical Christian education is advancing, its progress is hindered by a provincialism that is being shed ever so slowly. But in its emergence it must not lose its soul. It has been won at too great a cost.

Future Concerns

Some emerging problems needing study and research are:

What schools of thought may be most contributory in developing an evangelical philosophy of education? Is philosophical method still to be taken seriously?

Assuming the given of the authority of Scripture, what implications does that carry for the concept of academic freedom?

How may the strengths of nonformal as well as formal learning be maximized in church settings?

What philosophical constructs should be used in critiquing diverse learning styles?

In curriculum construction, how may we design for the development of roles and relationships without diminishing the biblical data?

Notes

1. Evangelicals would concur with the definition given by Carl F. H. Henry: "Evangelical Christians are thus marked by their devotion to the sure Word of the Bible: they are committed to the inspired Scriptures as the divine rule of faith and practice. They affirm the fundamental doctrines of the Gospel, including the incarnation and virgin birth of Christ, His sinless life, substitutionary atonement, and bodily resurrection as the ground of God's forgiveness of sinners, justification by faith alone, and the spiritual regeneration of all who trust in the redemptive work of Jesus Christ." "Evangelical," in *The New International Dictionary of the Christian Church*, rev. ed., ed. J. D. Douglas (Grand Rapids: The Zondervan Corp., 1978), 358-59.
2. Sydney E. Ahlstrom, *A Religious History of the American People* (New Haven: Yale University Press, 1972), 742.
3. For a discussion of this transfer of leadership see Robert W. Lynn and Elliott Wright's *The Big Little School*, rev. ed. (Nashville: Abingdon Press, 1980), 120-29. It is the judgment of this writer that generally when agencies such as the Sunday

school become professionally led rather than lay led, a biblical principle (Eph. 4:11-16) is being thwarted, and weakness rather than strength is the consequence. Professionals are to train others to do the work of the ministry.

4. Most evangelicals employ the term *Christian education* in decided preference over *religious education*. Southern Baptists use the term *religious education* to denote local church education ministry and *Christian education* for their higher educational enterprises.

5. Lynn and Wright, *The Big Little School*, 127.

6. Kenneth S. Kantzer, "Evangelicalism: Midcourse Self-appraisal," *Christianity Today* 27, no. 1 (7 January 1983): 10.

7. Harold William Burgess, *An Invitation to Religious Education* (Mishawaka, Ind.: Religious Education Press, 1975), 62.

8. Paulo Freire, *Pedagogy of the Oppressed* (New York: The Seabury Press, 1970), 58ff.

9. John Dewey, "My Pedagogic Creed," in *Basic Writings in Christian Education*, ed. Kendig Brubaker Cully (Philadelphia: The Westminster Press, 1960), 312.

10. Lawrence O. Richards, "Experiencing Reality Together: Toward the Impossible Dream," in *Religious Education and Theology*, ed. Norma H. Thompson (Birmingham, Ala.: Religious Education Press, 1982), 215. Not all evangelicals agree with Richards's socialization position. See below for discussion.

11. Thomas H. Groome, *Christian Religious Education: Sharing Our Story and Vision* (San Francisco: Harper & Row, 1980), 117.

12. James D. Smart, *The Teaching Ministry of the Church* (Philadelphia: The Westminster Press, 1954), 58.

13. Wayne R. Rood, *Understanding Christian Education* (Nashville: Abingdon Press, 1970), 200.

14. Groome, *Christian Religious Education*, 117.

15. Neither the Southern Baptists nor the Lutheran Church—Missouri Synod became part of the National Association of Evangelicals. Southern denominations such as the Free-Will Baptists and the Church of God, Cleveland, Tennessee, and a number of local churches of a variety of communions did join. This is mentioned as it assists in clarifying why the Southern Baptist Convention and some other conservative southern denominations had limited influence on the development of Christian education in the East, North, Far West, and Canada. This has changed as Southern Baptists have moved north.

16. See Wolterstorff's *Reason Within the Bounds of Religion* (Grand Rapids: Wm. B. Eerdmans Publishing Co., 1976) and *Educating for Responsible Action* (Grand Rapids: Wm. B. Eerdmans Publishing Co., 1980); Holmes's *Faith Seeks Understanding* (Grand Rapids: Wm. B. Eerdmans Publishing Co., 1971) and *All Truth Is God's Truth* (Downers Grove, Ill.: Inter Varsity Press, 1983); Gangel's four articles in *Bibliotheca Sacra* 135, nos. 537-40 (1978); and Chadwick's *Teaching and Learning: An Integrated Approach to Christian Education* (Old Tappan, N.J.: Fleming H. Revell Co., 1982).

17. Frank E. Gaebelein, *A Varied Harvest* (Grand Rapids: Wm. B. Eerdmans Publishing Co., 1967), 41.

18. Burgess, *An Invitation to Religious Education*, 27.

19. Ibid., 51.

20. Kenneth O. Gangel, "Christian Higher Education at the End of the Twentieth Century," *Bibliotheca Sacra* 135, no. 538 (April-June 1978): 103.

21. James W. Sire, *The Universe Next Door* (Downers Grove, Ill.: Inter Varsity Press, 1976), 42.

22. Gangel, "Christian Higher Education at the End of the Twentieth Century," 100-5.

23. Arthur F. Holmes, "Academic Freedom in the Christian College," *Bulletin of Wheaton College* (February 1964), 2. Reprinted by permission from the February 1964 *Bulletin of Wheaton College*.

24. Findley B. Edge, "A Search for Authenticity," in *Modern Masters of Religious*

Education, ed. James Michael Lee (Birmingham, Ala.: Religious Education Press, 1983).

25. See Findley B. Edge, *The Greening of the Church* (Waco, Tex.: Word, 1971), chaps. 3 and 4.

26. Lois E. Le Bar, "Planning for Teaching," in *Introduction to Biblical Christian Education*, ed. Werner C. Graendorf (Chicago: Moody Press, 1981), 168, 170.

27. Lois E. Le Bar, "Curriculum," in *An Introduction to Christian Education*, ed. J. Edward Hakes (Chicago: Moody Press, 1964), 91-92.

28. Burgess, *An Invitation to Religious Education*, 47.

29. Not educational because it fails to have a foundation in human development and instruction; not Christian because it is based on mass programs that tend to divide and isolate families . . . and reduce the whole marvelous matter of redemption and growing in grace to a series of "informational chunks" which are to be dumped on people at just the right moments in life.

30. Ted W. Ward, "Biblical Metaphors of Purpose—Part I," *Bibliotheca Sacra* 139, no. 554 (April-June 1982): 109.

31. Ted W. Ward, "Evaluating Metaphors of Education—Part III," *Bibliotheca Sacra* 139, no. 556 (October-December 1982): 294-95.

32. Ted Ward and Rodney McKean, "Six Models of Teaching for Moral Development," *Christian Education Journal* 3, no. 2 (1983): 25.

33. Lawrence O. Richards wrote a series of articles in the August, September, October, November 1967 issues and the Fall and Winter 1968 issues of *United Evangelical Action*. The magazine is published by the National Association of Evangelicals.

34. Lawrence O. Richards, *A New Face for the Church* (Grand Rapids: The Zondervan Corp., 1970).

35. Elmer Towns, *The Ten Largest Sunday Schools* (Grand Rapids: Baker Book House, 1969).

36. Lawrence O. Richards, *Creative Bible Teaching* (Chicago: Moody Press, 1970).

37. Ibid., 57, 58.

38. Lawrence O. Richards, *Youth Ministry: Its Renewal in the Church* (Grand Rapids: The Zondervan Corp., 1972).

39. Lawrence O. Richards, *A Theology of Christian Education* (Grand Rapids: The Zondervan Corp., 1975).

40. Ibid., introduction.

41. Ibid., 22.

42. Ibid., 16.

43. Charles M. Sell, *Family Ministry* (Grand Rapids: The Zondervan Corp., 1981), 82.

44. Groome, *Christian Religious Education*, 110.

45. Perry G. Downs, "Christian Nurture: A Comparison of Horace Bushnell and Lawrence O. Richards," *Trinity Journal* 3 NS, no. 2 (Fall 1982): 208. See Downs's "Christian Nurture: A Comparative Analysis of the Theories of Horace Bushnell and Lawrence O. Richards," unpublished doctoral dissertation at New York University, 1982.

46. Richards, *A Theology of Christian Education*, 193.

47. Richards, "Experiencing Reality Together," 210, 211, 215.

48. See Groome, *Christian Religious Education*, 109-31, for a very helpful, and in this writer's judgment, a successful attempt at evaluating the strengths and weaknesses of *socialization* and *education* (Groome's terms) and a call for both, not either/or. "Christian religious education needs the context of a Christian faith community, and such a community needs a critical educational activity that is more than another agency of socialization," 126. Groome seems to have achieved the balanced perspective on this issue which is so crucial. As Charles R. Foster has said in his brief refutation of John Westerhoff's disillusionment with the Sunday school, "I believe that a 'school' in some form is still important in the transmission of values, beliefs, and practices from one

generation to the next." In Jack L. Seymour and Donald E. Miller, *Contemporary Approaches to Christian Education* (Nashville: Abingdon Press, 1982), 169. This author would make an even stronger case for the validity of the school or formal approaches within the socialization process.

49. Richards, "Experiencing Reality Together," 215.
50. Lawrence O. Richards, *A Theology of Church Leadership* (Grand Rapids: The Zondervan Corp., 1980).
51. Lawrence O. Richards *A Theology of Personal Ministry* (Grand Rapids: The Zondervan Corp., 1981).
52. Richards, *A Theology of Church Leadership*, chaps. 7 and 8.
53. Richards, *A Theology of Personal Ministry*, 298.

Bibliography

Burgess, Harold William. *An Introduction to Religious Education.* Mishawaka, Ind.: Religious Education Press, 1975.
A balanced and skillful presentation of religious educators using the paradigms of the traditional theological (Gaebelein, Hofinger); social-culture (Coe, Bower); contemporary theological (Miller, Moran); and the social science approach (Lee). Helpful introduction to these schools of thought and how they intersect with each other. Names cited are only representative except in the social science approach.

Byrne, H. W. *A Christian Approach to Education.* 2d ed. Milford, Mich.: Mott Media, 1977.
A systematic statement of education from an evangelical viewpoint. Deals with foundations, the implications of a theistic philosophy for the educative process, and the integration of that perspective with the areas of biblical studies, social sciences, natural sciences, the humanities, and communicative skills. Originally written in 1961 and it bears that time frame.

Chadwick, Ronald A. *Teaching and Learning: An Integrated Approach to Christian Education.* Old Tappan, N.J.: Fleming H. Revell Co., 1982.
The volume deals with the four questions of what, why, how of Christian education and where are we going? Presents the basic issues in constructing a philosophy of education. It takes the very thorough work of Byrne forward in the area of integration. Slanted to the Christian day-school teacher and administrator.

Gaebelein, Frank E. *Christian Education in a Democracy.* New York: Oxford University Press, 1951.
A book of permanent value to evangelicals because of its timing in the development of contemporary Christian education. Crucial foundation stones were laid upon which the present generation is attempting to build in the areas of Christian elementary, secondary, and higher education. Insightful perspective on public school education and the church as educator.

Gangel, Kenneth O., and Warren S. Benson. *Christian Education: Its History and Philosophy.* Chicago: Moody Press, 1983.
A chronological flow of historical and educational thought. Its focus is cultural-biographical, discussing each philosophy in its particular socio-historical setting. Gives attention to significant individuals and their influence on the life of the church. Emphasizes the early church and nineteenth century.

Joy, Donald M., ed. *Moral Development Foundations: Judeo-Christian Alternatives to Piaget/Kohlberg*. Nashville: Abingdon Press, 1983.

Barry Chazan, Mary Elizabeth Moore, Paul J. Philibert, Stephen A. Schmidt, Ted Ward, Craig Dykstra, Doug Sholl, Samuel F. Rowen, and the editor are the essayists. Strongly committed to a theistic position, each in his or her own theological framework grapples with moral developmental structures and principles of Piaget and Kohlberg. These "confessions" describe how they work in research and theoretical settings. Read with Lawrence Kohlberg's *The Philosophy of Moral Development* (New York: Harper & Row, 1981).

Sell, Charles M. *Family Ministry: The Enrichment of Family Life Through the Church*. Grand Rapids: The Zondervan Corp., 1981.

The family paradigm has become prominent in establishing a philosophy of church ministry. Foundational source for this thrust. Presents a theological base for the home covering marriage and family themes, parent and marital training programs, and intergenerational learning. Solid interaction with questions regarding singles, divorced, and one-parent families.

Wolterstorff, Nicholas P. *Educating for Responsible Action*. Grand Rapids: Wm. B. Eerdmans Publishing Co., 1980.

Philosophy professor at Calvin College challenges the uncritical acceptance of secular and authoritarian approaches in the areas of modeling, discipline, moral development, values clarification, and using taxonomies in teaching.

CHAPTER 5

Faith Development Issues and Religious Nurture

Craig Dykstra

In order to carry out the fundamental tasks of religious nurture and religious education, we depend upon some conception of the religious life. The task of religious nurture is to bring people into a way of living and being. We need to have some clarity about what the qualities and characteristics of that way of living and being are. Our conception of the religious life provides the basic clues for what we hope for through the nurturing process. Our aims and goals as educators are governed by it. What we think a mature Christian is provides the basic image at the heart of our expectations for life in religious community and for the kinds of people we will eventually become. Our conception of the religious life also shapes what we expect will happen along the way. It is an anticipation of the contours of a journey. We all know that human beings grow and change and become what they were not. A conception of the religious life includes some hunches about its turning points and transitions. Thus our conception of the religious life tells us not only what we are to become, but also what we are at the beginning and what we must go through to become what we are to be.

The Christian tradition has developed a number of approaches to providing a conception of the Christian life over the course of its history. One is the tradition of the virtues. The New Testament provides several catalogs of the Christian virtues. These were expanded in later theological formulations which often included theological, moral, natural, supernatural, and other virtues. The tradition of the virtues is a long one, and there are contemporary versions. An alternative approach is the tradition of spiritual discipline. A reaction to the tradition of the virtues, which in the medieval church had become controlled by an authoritarian hierarchy and increasingly schematized, the mystical way of

Craig Dykstra is Associate Professor of Christian Education at Louisville Presbyterian Seminary.

spiritual discipline sought to nurture a way of life characterized by immediate and personal relationship to God. From Meister Eckhardt and Julian of Norwich in the fourteenth century, through Ignatius of Loyola and Thomas a Kempis, to the contemporary emphasis on spiritual direction, this tradition emphasizes the personal pilgrimage dimension of Christian life. More heavily ethical in tone but still akin to the tradition of spiritual discipline were the Puritan expressions of the religious life articulated in literary works such as John Bunyan's *Pilgrim's Progress* and Milton's *Paradise Lost*. All of these are examples of attempts to provide a picture of the Christian life which could guide Christian living and religious nurture.

The contemporary work on "faith development" is a part of the search for a conception of the religious life, and it appeals to us as religious educators because it attempts to fulfill an ancient need in a new time. Two aspects of the current situation make faith development theory something different from its precursors, however. One is the rise of pluralism, and the other is the advent of psychology as a social science. Contemporary faith development theory is influenced by both.

The earlier conceptions of the Christian life were largely theological expressions, adopted by churches and societies in which there was widespread theological agreement. Since the Enlightenment, and even more so in the twentieth century, the plurality of religious visions has become increasingly apparent and the parochial nature of particular conceptions has come under intense criticism. This plurality has precipitated a crisis in theology itself which culminates in a theological inability to describe a common conception of the Christian life.[1] This problem is exacerbated by increasing awareness of and attention to world religions in a global context.

The rise of pluralism parallels the rise of the discipline of developmental psychology. During the early decades of the twentieth century, the powerful voices of Sigmund Freud and Carl Jung began to be heard. A bit later, still another major psychologist, Jean Piaget, published books of lasting significance. Psychology as a science was in full bloom—and the side of it that studied the growth and development of the human personality has taken center stage for many religious educators as they seek to rethink the question of religious nurture and reconstruct a conception of the religious life in which to ground that nurture. Developmental psychology has become a significant conversation partner—at times, perhaps, overwhelming theology in contemporary religious education theory.

Psychological Approaches to Human Development

It is possible to distinguish two major approaches to the psychology of human development. One we may call the life-cycle approach; the other is the structural-developmental approach.[2]

The life-cycle approach has its deepest roots in the psychodynamic tradition. Freud, Jung, and Erik Erikson are foundational figures here. The life-cycle approach suggests that there are important turning points in every person's life in which crucial issues need to be faced and through which new capacities for human functioning emerge.

Freud concentrated on the psychosexual development of the child. As the child's body develops organically, said Freud, particular zones of the body become sequentially central for organizing the child's relationships to others and to the self, and hence for the developing personality. He believed that he could explain many religious phenomena (in addition to psychological pathologies) by searching for their roots in the way fundamental human energies and aspirations were channeled during these transformations.

Erikson built on Freud's work to develop a theory of "the eight ages of man" which covered the life-span from early infancy to old age. Concentrating more on the social environment (though never abandoning Freud's biological base), Erikson described eight "crises" or turning points which emerge during every person's life—crises which follow a schedule related closely to a person's age. How we deal with these crises in our lives provides the content of our own conception of the nature of human life. Because Erikson described human development in this way, his theory was quickly appropriated and widely used by religious educators as a description of the human journey and the issues in human life with which religion must deal in order to be humanly significant.

Jung's work is less widely used by religious educators, but is nonetheless important. Two dimensions of his thought are most noteworthy: his concept of *individuation* and his discussions of the role of symbols in human development. *Individuation* is Jung's key word for describing human maturity. It means becoming the unique individual person that one can be through a process of differentiating and integrating all the various and complex parts of the self into a conscious, balanced whole. In healthy development, all the facets of the personality, including the unconscious, are encountered and have an opportunity to be expressed without unbalancing or repressing other facets. Individuation is heavily influenced by what happens during childhood and adolescence, but it is only accomplished during the third stage of life—middle age, after thirty-five or forty. An important way to individuation is through the analysis of symbols—the symbols that appear in one's dreams and fantasies, in one's language, and in the culture which lives on in tradition and in our collective unconscious. Jung held that some of our most profound symbols were born in the early Christian era and that a deep exploration of them would lead to a richer, more mature life.

A more recent representative of the life-cycle approach is Daniel Levinson. Like Jung, Levinson is more interested in adulthood than in childhood. But like Erikson, Levinson charts out a series of specific eras in the adult male life cycle.[3] Each era involves the process of constructing what Levinson calls the individual life structure. Levinson finds a regular pattern, highly related to age, in which people move through distinct periods of building, living in, then tearing down and rebuilding life structures. The periods between the ages of 17 and 22, 40 and 45, and 60 and 65 seem to be predictably turbulent because they are transition periods during which life structures are being torn down. The widespread notion of a "mid-life crisis" can be attributed to Levinson's work and the writings of his popularizers.

Structural-developmental theories of human development differ from life-cycle theories in several important respects. They do not speak of ages and eras of human development. They speak of stages. And though life-cycle theorists often use the word *stage*, structuralists have something more specific in mind. Structuralists believe that human development is governed by the sequential emergence of new "structures." A structure is a patterned process for organizing experience that is built into the human organism. These structures have formal, describable properties that consti-tute the internal rules of human functioning. A new stage is the advent of a new structure. Our structures determine the limits by which we are bound in our capacities to respond to our environments. New stages are descriptions of new and more complex internal capacities for dealing with experience. Structural development is closely linked to age, especially early in life; but structural development may stop at any point, even though we go on experiencing and aging. Thus a forty-five-year-old might have the same mental structures as a ten-year-old and therefore be similarly limited in the *way* he or she processes experience, even though the contexts and issues of the adult's experience are different.

The founder of structural developmentalism is the Swiss psychologist Jean Piaget. He argued that children move through a series of structural changes (stages) in which new capacities for performing intellectual "operations" in their environment emerge. Piaget claimed that the development of cognitive structures is the most important determiner of the way we organize social relations and understand and use rules and other social codes, including religious symbols and meanings. Other psychologists since Piaget have appropriated his basic insights and have applied them to a vast array of human processes. One of the most important of these for understanding the impact of structural developmentalism on contemporary faith development theory is Lawrence Kohlberg.

Kohlberg expanded some of Piaget's earlier work on the effect of cognitive structural development on children's understanding and use of moral rules, and he developed a six-stage theory of moral development. According to Kohlberg, a person's cognitive structural stage limits and directs the way he or she deals with situations of moral conflict. Kohlberg's significance for faith development theory lies in the way he has brought structural developmental theory to bear on an issue so central to religious concerns—the ways we think about and live out our moral lives.

Current Work on Faith Development[4]

The most widely known recent contribution to faith development theory is probably that of James W. Fowler. Fowler's theory makes use of many insights from the life-cycle theorists, but it is most heavily dependent upon the structural developmentalists. Central to the structuralist understanding of development is the view that the structuring process is both internal and external. In the interaction between self and world, not only are the self's basic patterns of thinking structured; the environment to which the self is related is also structured. The developmental process is at the same time a process of forming a self and an experienced world. This central structural insight rang true to Fowler and corresponded with an understanding of "faith" that had come from his theological studies of Paul Tillich, H. Richard Niebuhr, and others.

For Fowler, faith is not something which some people have while others do not. Rather, it is an *activity* in which everyone, by virtue of being human, is involved. It is the activity of making meaning; interpreting one's fundamental human experience; composing an understanding of one's ultimate world; and shaping one's self and one's beliefs, attitudes, and values in relation to that world.

There are, of course, differences in faith. One kind of difference is commonly recognized: differences among people's explicit beliefs, organizing images, central symbols, ethical rules, and community practices. Sometimes these variances are institutionalized in religious traditions and communities; other times they are not. In any case, they are the factors that distinguish Christians and Moslems, theists and atheists, "believers" and "nonbelievers." Another kind of difference is more subtle, however; it is not just that the "contents" of our ideas and values differ, but that our *ways* of valuing and believing and construing are based on different fundamental patterns of operation. These are structural-developmental differences.

Following Piaget and Kohlberg, Fowler describes these developmental differences in terms of stages. At each stage, one's faith is governed by a different set of unconscious operational rules or laws. The governing pattern gives to one's faith a distinctive shape that is similar to that of others at the same stage, whether the content of that faith is Christian or non-Christian, religious or nonreligious. As we develop, these unconscious rules change in a predictable way. One pattern leads to the next in a sequence which does not vary among individuals. Also the later patterns are more complex, comprehensive, and integrated; and thus are more mature.

Fowler describes six faith stages and gives them the following names: intuitive-projective faith, mythic-literal faith, synthetic-conventional faith, individuative-reflective faith, conjunctive faith, and universalizing faith. Fowler argues that each stage can be formally described in terms of seven aspects. The following table arranges the stages according to these aspects.

Fowler claims that the pilgrimage of faith can be better understood if we have his stages of faith and the ideas that lie behind them in mind. He believes that development through these stages is good and ought to be fostered. But he also recognizes that our "faith operations" are not the only significant factor. The character of our faith also depends upon what he calls its contents; that is, what we value and prize most, what particular "images of power" we hold and align ourselves with, and what "master stories" we learn from and live by.[5] Both the operations and the

5.1 Faith Stages by Aspects[6]

ASPECT:	A. Form Of Logic (Piaget)	B. Perspective Taking (Selman)	C. Form of Moral Judgment (Kohlberg)	D. Bounds of Social Awareness	E. Locus of Authority	F. Form of World Coherence	G. Symbolic Function
STAGE:							
I	Preoperational	Rudimentary empathy (egocentric)	Punishment-reward	Family, primal others	Attachment/dependence relationships. Size, power, visible symbols of authority	Episodic	Magical-Numinous
II	Concrete Operational	Simple perspective taking	Instrumental hedonism (Reciprocal fairness)	"Those like us" (in familial, ethnic, racial, class and religious terms)	Incumbents of authority roles, salience increased by personal relatedness	Narrative-Dramatic	One-dimensional; literal
III	Early Formal Operations	Mutual interpersonal	Interpersonal expectations and concordance	Composite of groups in which one has interpersonal relationships	Consensus of valued groups and in personally worthy representatives of belief-value traditions	Tacit system, felt meanings symbolically mediated, globally held	Symbols multi-dimensional; evocative power inheres in symbol

IV	Formal Operations (Dichotomizing)	Mutual, with self-selected group or class—(societal)	Societal perspective, Reflective relativism or class-biased universalism	Ideologically compatible communities with congruence to self-chosen norms and insights	One's own judgment as informed by a self-ratified ideological perspective. Authorities and norms must be congruent with this.	Explicit system, conceptually mediated, clarity about boundaries and inner connections of system	Symbols separated from symbolized. Translated (reduced) to ideations. Evocative power inheres in *meaning* conveyed by symbols
V	Formal Operations (Dialectical)	Mutual with groups, classes and traditions "other" than one's own	Prior to society, Principled higher law (universal and critical)	Extends beyond class norms and interests. Disciplined ideological vulnerability to "truths" and "claims" of outgroups and other traditions	Dialectical joining of judgment-experience processes with reflective claims of others and of various expressions of cumulative human wisdom	Multisystemic symbolic and conceptual mediation	Postcritical rejoining of irreducible symbolic power and ideational meaning. Evocative power inherent in the reality in and beyond symbol *and* in the power of unconscious processes in the self
VI	Formal Operations (Synthetic)	Mutual, with the commonwealth of being	Loyalty to being	Identification with the species. Transnarcissistic love of being	In a personal judgment informed by the experiences and truths of previous stages, purified of egoic striving, and linked by disciplined intuition to the principle of being	Unitive actuality felt and participated unity of "One beyond the many"	Evocative power of symbols actualized through unification of reality mediated by symbols and the self

contents of faith can and usually do change throughout our lives, and different combinations of these changes lead to various kinds of transformations.[7] Tracing and understanding these changes is even more complex than "stage transitions" alone, but we cannot ignore them and their interrelations.

Despite Fowler's acknowledgment of the significance of the contents of faith, he has frequently been criticized for not paying enough attention to their formation and development. He has also been criticized for inadequate attention to what happens during the earliest years of life. The work of Ana-Maria Rizzuto, a psychiatrist in the Freudian school, focuses precisely on these points. Her book, *The Birth of the Living God*, is a study of "the possible origins of the individual's private representation of God and its subsequent elaborations. It is also a study of the relation existing in the secret chambers of the human heart between that God and the person who believes in him during the vicissitudes of the life-cycle."[8]

Rizzuto is not a theologian and makes no claims concerning the existence or nature of God. Her concern is the images or representations of God that are formed in people. She argues that virtually everyone (at least in Western society) has some such representation, and that its content and a person's relationship to it combine as a fundamental determinant of personality, self-perception, and the ways in which one relates to the world. The earliest sources of this representation are rooted in memory traces established in our earliest years in emotionally profound relationships to the ones who brought us into being. Among the most important are the eye-contact relationships that develop in the context of feeding. The image of the mother's face is crucial.[9] As the child grows, many other experiences with the mother, father, and other caretakers also become grist for the child's imaginal mill. The child organizes his or her experience "through fantasies and creative reshaping of perceptions and representations"[10] which create an internal world inhabited by powerful pictures of the self, parents, and a variety of "invisible, nonexperiential character[s]"[11]—including God. In normal development, these other invisible characters disappear. But not God. Why? First, the reality of God is reinforced by the beliefs of the Western child's culture, while the others are all rejected. Second, the child has a psychological need for "parental company" in his or her internal world, and God is the invisible character in the child's imaginal world that has the most parental qualities.

All this is accomplished, says Rizzuto, by the age of five or six. Thus, as she puts it, "all children arrive at the house of God with their own God under their arm."[12] Educators, pastors, and other figures will contribute something to the shaping of a person's God representation, but its basic contours are already formed before formal religious education begins. Through the course of our lives, however, we experience a series of crises or turning points. One of two things can happen then. First, one can cease to believe in one's childhood God. One's God representation is set aside because it is not adequately meaningful or helpful in dealing with the crisis. The representation is not changed but is merely disbelieved and ignored—perhaps to appear again at the point of another crisis. The second possibility is that a revision of one's God representation will be required. For many people, a life crisis is also a religious crisis. In order for people to maintain belief in God during a fundamental re-imaging of themselves, their worlds, and their lives, their God must be transformed as well.

Transformations of self and the God representation are not easy, however. According to Rizzuto, stage transitions of the type Fowler describes do not suffice. "It is only," she says, "the subjective modification of the emotional experience in one's private world with God as a felt reality, and therefore of oneself in relation to God, that permits a change in the characteristics consciously or unconsciously attributed to God."[13] Furthermore, for many, personal struggles which involve God representations are often immense struggles of striving to adapt developmentally while being bonded to a God representation which cannot be allowed to change. Some people may thus "be loaded with an anachronistic and restrictive God, an indicator of unresolved developmental issues."[14]

A third significant contemporary contribution to this area of study is provided by James E. Loder.[15] Loder's work is not primarily focused on faith development but does concern the relationship between faith and human development. Working as a practical theologian, Loder makes use of both psycho-dynamic and structural-developmental sources. His main concern, however, is to use their insights without collapsing faith into psychological categories. He claims that we live in a four-dimensional world. Psychological theories, he argues, tend to deal only with the two dimensions of "self" and "lived world." But two other dimensions, which he calls "the void" and "the Holy," are just as real. According to Loder, faith must be understood in relation to all four.

Loder's basic theme is transformation, not development. For Loder, development, psychologically understood, is one kind of transformation. But the transformations most significant for faith are "existential transformations" in which the self's drive to sustain itself in existence through development is relativized by an encounter with the Divine Presence. In this context, human development, in and of itself, is seen to trace a history of increasing alienation from the grounds of our existence—an alienation which itself must be negated in "convictional experience" by the power of "the Spirit." Given the context of conviction (or faith), human development is freed *from* the compulsion to protect and enlarge the self and is freed *for* "sacrificial love." Furthermore, conviction may make possible reversals of arrested development and even leaps ahead which by-pass some stages to resolve issues in other than the "normal" sequence. Faith for Loder, then, is not primarily a developmental phenomenon but a new context for development which may be precipitated in part by development's own deficiencies.

Issues in Faith Development

The work of Fowler, Rizzuto, and Loder is not, of course, the only material available on how faith develops. But they are major representatives of the studies being carried out today. A close look at them raises a number of important questions about what faith development means. I shall raise two here.

First, what is faith? Fowler focuses on the activity of making meaning, and he identifies that with faith. Rizzuto, for all her differences from Fowler in method, also concentrates on making meaning as it is centered in our representations of God. There is no doubt that we create images of God and of our ultimate environments, that these change and develop, and that these dynamics are related to faith. But do these dimensions exhaust the meaning of faith? If there is such a reality as God who is not simply the result of our own meaning-structuring activity, how is the activity of such a God related to what the developmental theorists describe? Is it primarily through the transformation of development, as Loder claims? Or does such a solution discount too much the creative activity of God within development?

Fowler says that faith is universal and Rizzuto that everyone has a God representation (though not every adult believes in his or her God). Biblically, however, faith seems rather exceptional. What differences in the meaning of faith might be involved here?

Furthermore, what is the relation between the general developmental structures and dynamics which the theorists describe and the particular religious faiths? Is Christian faith one version of a general phenomenon, or does it, as Loder seems to argue, have its own unique structures and dynamics? If the latter, would Christian faith development be something radically different from what a study of general structures of human awareness reveals?

Second, what is the significance of developmental stages? For the life-cycle theorists, including Rizzuto, the various predictable turning points in the life cycle become pregnant occasions and opportunities for the reworking of one's fundamental values, images, beliefs, trusts, and loyalties. But these crises may bring us either to abandon or to reconstruct our God representation. Whatever the relation between faith and our representations of God, life-cycle crises do not necessarily prompt growth in faith.

Structuralists tend to see it differently. Fowler, for example, tends to identify movement up the stages with maturing in faith. Stage 6 (universalizing faith), in a sense, is a description for him of what mature faith means. But should we take his stage hierarchy as an outline of the religious pilgrimage and his highest stages as our image of religious maturity? If so, does this mean that no one who has not developed formal operational intelligence can be mature in faith? Are the seven aspects of faith which he elaborates the only or the most important ones? We may even ask, as Loder seems to, whether faith is a developmental phenomenon at all. There is no doubt that faith grows and changes. And there is no doubt that we develop a variety of capacities at different levels for thinking, role-taking, and creating and using symbols. But whether the development of certain structures and representations is the same thing as growth in faith depends upon what *faith* means.

Implications for Religious Nurture

Religious educators have been paying a great deal of attention to faith development theory. The reason, I believe, is the hope that it can provide a portrait of the religious life that will clarify the appropriate aims of religious nurture and identify the major stages and turning points in the religious journey. If the questions that I have raised about contemporary faith development theory have any substance, then we can probably conclude that faith development theory does not yet satisfy that hope. Current theory describes important dimensions of the religious life, but it does not define the purposes and goals of religious nurture for any particular faith or even necessarily chart out the major turning points. All this is still a matter of intense debate.

Nevertheless, these theories have important contributions to make on several issues of perennial concern to religious educators. First, they provide significant help on the issue of readiness. What capacities for thinking and imaging will people at various ages be likely to have? What fundamental issues are they likely to be concerned with? What can they assimilate, and how is this assimilation most likely to take place? These are all important questions which developmental theories help to answer.

Second, and related to readiness, these theories help us understand one another better. They provide concepts that allow us to stand more easily in another person's place and see things the way he or she does. They help us know some reasons why other people say things the way they do and react as they do. They help us see what might be going on when others "misunderstand" what we are saying or interpret experiences differently from the way we do. Knowing these things, and knowing why, can facilitate the process of communication in teaching and nurture.

Third, there are hints here about the kinds of methods that are likely to be most fruitful for religious education. If faith is deeply connected with images that arise in interpersonal relationships, the most effective teaching methods will be highly interactive and personal. They will be experiential, relational methods rather than transmissive ones. And they will be methods which attempt to make connections between the images and experiences in people's lives.

Finally, it is becoming more and more clear that the religious nurture that forms people's faith does not come primarily in formal educational contexts. All the work in faith development theory confirms this. Our faith is formed in our primary communities through day-to-day interactions with the people who surround us. As people responsible for religious nurture, we can now be even more aware that the growth in faith of those we nurture is shaped by the quality and character of our own faith and the faith that is alive in our communities.

Notes

1. It is widely thought that this left Christian education without fundamental bearings. See Sara Little, "Theology in Religious Education," in *Foundations for Christian Education in an Era of Change*, ed. Marvin J. Taylor (Nashville: Abingdon Press, 1976), chap. 3.
2. See James E. Loder, "Developmental Foundations for Christian Education" in *Foundations for Christian Education in an Era of Change*, chap. 5, for more extensive

treatment of the major figures and ideas in these two approaches which Loder labels "Psychodynamic Views" and "Structuralism."

3. Levinson's book is deliberately entitled *Seasons of a Man's Life* (New York: Alfred A. Knopf, 1978) because he bases his conclusions on the study of a limited population of forty adult *men* between the ages of thirty-five and forty-five. It should also be noted that Levinson makes no cross-cultural claims for his conclusions.

4. A survey of the current work in faith development theory should not blind us to the important contributions made by psychology to theories of Christian nurture during the early years of the twentieth century. A whole field called "the psychology of religion" developed in response both to the empirical psychology of William James and Edwin D. Starbuck and the psycho-dynamic work of the Freudian tradition. This, when combined with the liberal theology that was predominant in America until the Second World War, generated a plethora of volumes on religious experience and the role of mature religious sentiments in mental health and proper human development. The religious education movement was itself heavily psychological in orientation, and the work of George Albert Coe, William Clayton Bower, Ernest J. Chave, Ernest M. Ligon, and, later, Lewis J. Sherrill must not be forgotten as early attempts to provide theories of faith development. Current work is, however, a kind of second renaissance after the dissolution of a neo-orthodox theology which found little room for trust of human religious experience or progressive religious development.

5. James W. Fowler, *Stages of Faith* (San Francisco: Harper & Row, 1981), 276-81.

6. Ibid., 244-45.

7. Ibid., 281-91.

8. Ana-Maria Rizzuto, *The Birth of the Living God* (Chicago: University of Chicago Press, 1979), 3.

9. See Ana-Maria Rizzuto, "The Psychological Foundations of Belief in God" in *Toward Moral and Religious Maturity*, Christiane Brusselmans, convenor (Morristown, N.J.: Silver Burdett Co., 1980), 128, where Rizzuto says, "I propose that the maternal face is the first traceable component of the child's relation with his mother that becomes integrated into the representation of God."

10. Rizzuto, *Birth of the Living God*, 186.

11. Rizzuto, "Psychological Foundations," 129.

12. Ibid., 134.

13. Ibid., 124.

14. Rizzuto, *Birth of the Living God*, 203.

15. The following is a brief summary of ideas that appear in Loder's book, *The Transforming Moment* (San Francisco: Harper & Row, 1981). See especially chaps. 5 and 6 for Loder's insights on the relation of existential transformation to human development.

Bibliography

Brusselmans, Christiane, convenor. *Toward Moral and Religious Maturity*. Morristown, N.J.: Silver Burdett Co., 1980.
   Papers of the First International Conference on Moral and Religious Development. Contributors include Fowler, Rizzuto, Loder, Kohlberg, and fifteen others.

Dykstra, Craig. *Vision and Character*. Ramsey, N.J.: Paulist Press, 1981.
   A critique of and alternative to Kohlberg's approach to moral development based in a Christian ethic of vision.

Fowler, James W. *Stages of Faith*. San Francisco: Harper & Row, 1981.
    Fowler's most mature statement of his theory.
Joy, Donald M., ed. *Moral Development Foundations: Judeo-Christian
    Alternatives to Piaget/Kohlberg*. Nashville: Abingdon Press, 1983.
Loder, James E. *The Transforming Moment*. San Francisco: Harper & Row,
    1981.
    Loder's interdisciplinary work on "convictional knowing," its struc-
    ture, dynamics, and context, and its relation to human development.
Rizzuto, Ana-Maria. *The Birth of the Living God*. Chicago: University of
    Chicago Press, 1979.
    Rizzuto's comprehensive study of the formation and role of representa-
    tions of God in psychological functioning.
Wilcox, Mary M. *Developmental Journey: A Guide to the Development of Logical
    and Moral Reasoning and Social Perspective*. Nashville: Abingdon Press,
    1979.

CHAPTER 6

Religious Education as a Discipline

Allen J. Moore

A definition of religious education as a body of knowledge and a field of study is still in process. Presently several currents of thought exist regarding what it means to study and practice religious education. Since it is a relatively new discipline within the history of academic knowledge, religious educators are still searching for a consensus as to its unique mission within the larger arena of scholarly learning and research.[1]

This issue of self-understanding is not uncommon to the applied disciplines of knowledge or to any discipline in which practice is central to knowing. There are those, on the one hand, who would argue that all the accumulated knowledge of humankind is already covered in the basic, or liberal arts, disciplines.[2] On the other hand, there are those who would suggest that religious teaching and learning are primarily commonsense activities and cannot become a systematic body of knowledge.

To some extent both of these positions are represented among those who teach and study religious education. Some understand the discipline as the study of how the knowledge derived from psychology, philosophy, and theology can be applied to the teaching of religious belief. Others suggest that the field requires teachers who have been successful practitioners and who can demonstrate in the classroom how religious education can be done. Although truth exists in both of these approaches, this essay will propose alternative models that allow religious education to take its place within the marketplace of academic disciplines.

Toward a Definition

A discipline may be defined as a branch of learning that has identifiable limits to its subject matter and established processes

Allen J. Moore is Professor of Religion and Personality and Education at the School of Theology at Claremont.

and procedures by which an evolving body of knowledge is formed and systematized. In a more technical sense, a discipline is a specialized, delineated slice of reality that can be explored, described, and explained. These explorations result in new theories and concepts about that particular reality.[3] Included in any discipline are predictions and control that offer a way for generalizations and theories about the specialized part of reality to be both verified and replicated. What is meant here is that a discipline serves to give order as well as dependability to knowledge. When an established operation is repeated, it can be expected to work according to the theory that is behind it. For example, the discipline of aeronautics has formulated principles of flight which provide a reasonable prediction that each time an airplane takes off according to these principles, it will fly. Similarly, within the discipline of religious education, certain formulated generalizations provide reliable indicators of how persons learn to be religious.

What is at issue in a definition of religious education as a discipline involves several questions. What is the delineated area of study, and what are the procedures suitable to it? Is the discipline education, religion, theology, or religious education? Or is it instead an interdisciplinary subject, as represented by religion *and* education or theology *and* education? We have proponents for each of these emphases. The question is whether there is a common subject matter made up of ideas, methods, concepts, and a shared community of scholarly inquiry.

There are certain agreed criteria for defining an area of study as a discipline. The criteria are generally used within the academic community as a basis for dialogue between disciplines and for holding scholarly endeavors more accountable. These criteria are: (1) a self-conscious community of inquiry, including those persons who study, practice, and teach with a critical intentionality; (2) a defined area of inquiry with identifiable boundaries, a unique subject matter that is shared by a self-conscious community; (3) common functions and goals: critically reflecting on generalized theories and concepts, supporting an emerging community of practice/research, constructing new knowledge, and teaching; (4) an evolving tradition with a body of knowledge and literature, including scholarly/professional writing; (5) common methodologies of established and agreed-upon processes and procedures for ordering the data and activities of the disciplines; (6) principles of evaluation or means by which a community of inquiry may engage in self-correction; (7) an active participation in an interdisciplinary dialogue that will lead to clarification and correction within a discipline as well as make a contribution to larger knowledge; and (8) a reflective alternation between detachment with attention to knowledge and involvement with the concern for relevance.[4]

A broad application of these criteria to religious education might provide a generic definition. Although most of the discussion of definition has been among Christian religious educators, a discipline needs a definition that would also be inclusive of other faith perspectives. Furthermore, if there is to be a self-conscious community of scholars engaged in the study of a discipline, the definition needs to allow for variations of emphasis while at the same time including common language, methods of inquiry, and shared purposes.

This leads us to suggest that religious education is an *intentional*, deliberate study of teaching-learning and the educative process as it relates to the faith and practices of a religious community. Although religious education may draw upon literature from cognate fields and the larger arena of knowledge, it should also seek in a deliberate way to incorporate the literature from its own history, as well as from the theological traditions to which it belongs. In seeking to develop a body of knowledge, religious education needs to reflect critically upon knowledge from other disciplines in an effort to reconstruct it within the frame of reference that is religious education, while at the same time it seems to construct new knowledge out of the practice of religious teaching-learning.

The task of a discipline of religious education is therefore to *construct*, *test*, *evaluate*, and *reconstruct* theory and practice of religious teaching-learning within the faith community. This needs to include both critical practice and reflective study of the religious experience of persons within the educative context, as well as experimentation in the forms of religious teaching-learning.

External Influences

In addition to formal criteria and definition, a discipline's self-understanding may be influenced by a variety of external forces and assumptions. Some of these external factors have particularly influenced the changing nature of religious education as a field of critical inquiry.

First, *political factors* within academic institutions influence the definition of disciplines. It is within these centers of learning that most disciplines function and find their own identities. The value that a discipline has and the recognition of that value are influenced by political decisions such as the distribution of budgets, the allocation of faculty positions, and the assignment of curriculum requirements. For example, the redefinition of religious education as a discipline has come about in part with the emergence of newer disciplines within theological schools (such as pastoral counseling and church administration) that share related theory and methodologies. The establishment of the newer areas has led in some situations to a reduction of faculty positions and curriculum expectations in religious education.

Second, the *profession* that has been nurtured by an academic discipline influences how that discipline is defined. This is especially critical as a profession undergoes change. Historically, religious education emerged largely as a lay profession closely related to teacher education. More recently, some denominations have directly or indirectly encouraged ordination. Thus a new professional group has emerged that might be called, for lack of a better image, pastor-educator. Many of those who are lay professionals in education today are persons who were trained in undergraduate programs for church careers or who are certified through part-time courses of study in theological schools. Few large schools of religious education remain that concentrate on training a large number of individuals for lay careers in religious education.

A third factor is the *philosophy of education* that is implicit or explicit in the way an academic institution organizes its curriculum into teaching units and programs of research and study. Beliefs regarding the nature of knowledge and the sources of truth are often at issue. Such beliefs influence the importance that is placed upon either basic (classical) knowledge or applied (functional) knowledge. The issue of what to stress has emerged again in recent times with the emphasis, on the one hand, on a return to the fundamentals of knowing and, on the other hand, on a need in our society for persons who are competent in either a trade or a profession.

This dilemma raises an epistemological issue about ways of knowing that has played a large part in shaping the modern discipline of religious education. Aristotle makes a distinction between *theoria* and *praxis* in regard to knowing. The former is more characteristic of the basic disciplines in which knowing for its own sake is central. *Theoria* involves disciplined reflection upon knowledge itself, or thinking, interpreting, and comprehending a world of ideas. *Praxis*, on the other hand, is reflection *in* action or knowing by doing. It has to be pointed out that praxis is not the same as "reflection *and* action" or the application of ideas into programs of action. Praxis also goes beyond what Aristotle called *poisis*—unreflective doing in which the accomplishment of a skillful task is the primary end. *Poisis* refers to unreflective competence or skill training.[5] Praxis, by contrast, is reflected-upon action.

The recovery of praxis as a way of knowing has been due largely to the writings of Jürgen Habermas with his emphasis on the idea that we know what we do. Knowledge therefore is embodied in human action.[6] Richard Bernstein, in developing this point of view, suggests that those disciplines that are oriented to praxis do not have as their primary end knowledge or wisdom for the sake of knowing. Rather, praxis is both a way into knowing and the way to more responsible life within the activities of life itself. The end of practical disciplines is not just knowledge (although such knowledge may have much value), but a critical knowing that emerges from participation in purposeful action. Referring again to Aristotle, Bernstein writes: "The *telos* of the practical disciplines is to change our forms of activity and to bring them into closer approximation to the full ideal of free human activity."[7]

Although all three ways of knowing—reasoning, training, and purposeful action—have significant roles within the discipline of religious education, it is praxis that tends to be central. Modern religious education, as we shall see more fully later on, has been especially influenced by experience and pragmatism. It was the teachers and researchers of religious education during the first third of this century who sought to form a discipline around John Dewey's method of learning by doing. They caught the experimental spirit of Dewey with its emphasis on the scientific method. Reflection upon the experience of religious teaching and learning became the source, as well as the methodology, of religious education theoretical structures. Experience led to hypotheses, critical testing of insights, and the reconstruction of theory and practice. George A. Coe stands out as one of those early pioneers whose empirical philosophy and psychology of religion led to a clearly defined discipline of religious education study.[8] His scholarship and research still comprise the legacy for the definition of the discipline.

In a very perceptive way, Seward Hiltner has written how religious education emerged as a discipline grounded in an empirical or active psychology of religion in which the study of persons in learning situations provided the basis for theory construction. He writes that it was religious education that made "the first move toward the study of actual people engaged in a form of religious activity and the attempts to draw basic theory of these participant observations."[9] Pushed by pressures to institutionalize religious education into denominational programs and the need to find a more orthodox theological base for its reflections, religious educators since 1940 have found themselves increasingly neglecting this kind of research and the study of the religious experience in the educative context.

The scholarly purpose of a discipline is critical reflection on action, not simply doing for action's sake. The purpose is not application itself but informing how application is to take place. Similarly, the task of an academic discipline is to nurture a profession, not to become a "stand-in" for that profession. The orientation to praxis seeks to construct the theoretical and practical foundation from which a strong profession can emerge. For example, the professor of religious education may have a great commitment to sharing the Christian faith, but in the academic context the task is not teaching per se the Christian faith per se. The scholarly task of the discipline is to discover from critical reflection on teaching-learning how the Christian faith can more effectively be communicated.

Fourth, the *context* in which the scholarly work of a discipline occurs will also influence the definition that operates within that discipline. The boundaries of religious education and its functioning as a discipline are greatly influenced by the setting in which it is taught and the kinds of relationships it has with other disciplines. The importance of the setting is illustrated by the several academic contexts in which religious education is taught and studied:

1. *The theological school or seminary.* These are usually graduate and/or professional schools with programs of studies leading to a variety of graduate and professional degrees. Religious education as a discipline may be engaged in both scholarly research and the shared task with other disciplines of training persons for the professional ministries of the church. The weight placed upon either scholarship or teaching may vary greatly according to the setting, although both are viewed as essential to a vital discipline.

2. *The university graduate school.* This context may be either a graduate department of religion (which may be an extension of a theological school) or a graduate department of education. The presence of religious education within this context has become increasingly rare, even though in former times this context was

where the discipline was most formative and influential. In this context the goals of the discipline are most clearly organized around research and the development of knowledge.

3. *Church graduate school.* This also was once a more prominent context than it is today. Here the emphasis is on a career course of study for the purpose of educating lay leadership for specialized positions in religious education in the church and similar institutions.

4. *Church undergraduate school.* This context is an undergraduate program in religion or a career-oriented curriculum designed to provide church leadership, usually in response to a regional need of religious bodies. A strong liberal arts base may be found in some programs but cannot always be assumed.

Historical Influences

As we have already indicated, the discipline of religious education is less than a century old.[10] By 1930, religious education had emerged as an established discipline with a rather clear charter to study personal religious growth and experience within the church, the school, and other character-building institutions. Although the content of the discipline was derived in part from progressive education and educational psychology, it had a rather clear self-understanding of its task as well as an awareness that it had a contribution to make to knowledge, especially theological knowledge.

Between 1945 and 1965 a growing confusion emerged regarding the discipline. The problem was largely due to the changing theological climate accompanying the rise of neo-orthodoxy, a decline of financial support, especially on the part of denominations, growing estrangement between public education and church education, reduction in faculties, a decline in students in religious education, and the rise of specialization in theological education.[11]

The growing number of empirically oriented theological disciplines is of particular importance. Although the history of this era has yet to be fully written, evidence indicates that several of the newer practical theological disciplines are actually derivatives of religious education. Religious education, with its social and psychological understanding of persons and its emphasis upon a dynamic approach to ministry, provided the cornerstone for the rise of pastoral counseling, church administration, social mission, and religious communications. In addition, psychology of religion

has become independent from religious education. This separation has led not only to competition for territory within the
theological curriculum but has resulted in a lack of sharp definition
of content and teaching methods for all of these fields.[12] The
problem is further complicated by the growing division between
the so-called systematic disciplines of theology and the so-called
practical or ministerial disciplines. Especially within the context of
the theological school, religious education now must seek its
identity and task as a discipline within the current attempt to
clarify structures of divinity.[13]

Religious education is rooted deeply in the Judeo-Christian
heritage and in the history of education. Historically, religion and
education were closely related. The religious spirit and motivation
were inherent in the very nature of education. The historian Robert
Ulich writes about this phenomenon. "In our secular age we are
inclined to underestimate the role of religion in the history of
education. All early education was religious, and all early religion
was also educational."[14]

One of the earliest forms of religious education can be found in
the rabbinic tradition. The postbiblical rabbi was generally a
layperson who was known as a "master" teacher of Mosaic law.
The training of such persons was largely informal and occurred as
younger disciples taught alongside older, more experienced
teachers. The discipline was informal, but a very explicit tradition
evolved around the rabbinic movement. The three components of
practice in early Jewish education included compulsory education
for males, the religious duty of every Jew to study the Torah, and
the study of the sacred literature in the original Hebrew language.
This rabbinic practice gave rise in both the Jewish and Christian
communities to the teaching office and the need for an academic
course that would prepare persons to assume the task of teaching.

Another historical form of religious education is the Christian
practice of catechesis. Westerhoff defines catechesis as "the
process by which persons are initiated into the Christian
community and its faith, revelation, and vocation; the process by
which persons throughout their lifetimes are continually converted and nurtured, transformed and formed, by and in its living
tradition."[15] Catechesis in the early church was associated with
oral instruction, although Westerhoff argues that to take that
meaning in an overly literal sense is to miss the richness of this
tradition. The pedagogical significance of catechesis is in its
emphasis upon discourse, interaction between learners and the

catechist, and the role of the community as a whole in forming Christian lives.[16]

Catechetics as a science of oral instruction was undoubtedly one of the earliest attempts to form a discipline of religious education. To a large extent, catechetics was a theological discipline that was formed and defined as a churchly discipline in relation to the early study of education. It was deeply informed by the work of Greek and Roman philosophers of education who were preoccupied with both the nature of knowledge and the oral processes by which persons came to knowledge. In time the discipline of catechetics became a subdiscipline of practical theology and remained there until the emergence of modern religious education in the early 1900s.

This discussion of history leads us to the awareness that the modern discipline of religious education has its roots in both the theological practice of the religious community and the ancient science of education. As we have observed earlier, the weight given to each of these elements varies greatly and is influenced by a variety of outside factors. The two sources have not always been viewed as compatible and at times are in tension and even conflict.

The first of these streams is practical (or pastoral) theology. Friedrich Schleiermacher (1768–1834) is generally credited with the formulation of this third branch of theology and with establishing it as an independent body of theological knowledge.[17] For him practical theology was a positive science concerned with the welfare of the church. It seeks to respond to the problems of church life and serves to enable the church to do better what must be done. He understood practical theology to involve those concepts and methods that would *maintain* and *perfect* the church. This belief involved the study of those acts and functions necessary to the life of the church and to the daily life of the Christian. What is significant about Schleiermacher's contribution is that practical theology was conceived not as applied theology (the application of norms), but as theological practice (reflecting theologically upon experience). Catechetics was a subdiscipline in Schleiermacher's system of practical theology, and he apparently understood it to be related to the pastor's concern and care for the welfare of the people. He did not mean by this an individualistic approach to religious instruction but saw it as a central activity of the life of the church for which the pastor had the primary responsibility.[18]

The development of practical theology as a theological discipline took place first in Europe under the influence of scholars such as Van Oosterzee of Utrecht and Vinet of Lausanne.[19] In this country it is believed that W. G. T. Shedd of Auburn and Union Theological Seminary first introduced practical theology as a discipline of study in 1867.[20] In all these instances, practical theology was conceived as a generic discipline concerned with the study of all the functions of ministry and their relationship to one another. Within practical theology, teaching ministry, known also as catechising or "doctrinal instruction," received major attention. Nowhere among these major pioneers is there evidence that Christian pedagogy, or pastoral teaching, was anything less than a central discipline of study. It was, in fact, an essential element in the scientific study of ministry and the activity of the church. It was also a theological discipline with a concern for both theological understanding and practice.

The second of the streams of influence emerged from the recovery of the religious significance of education. As we have already observed in the history of education, one cannot easily separate the religious elements from the essential nature of the educational experience. Without reviewing the whole history of this vision, it is significant to note that the benchmark for this emphasis of religion in education came in the founding of the Religious Education Association in 1903. The intent, as Westerhoff has reminded us, was "to inspire the education forces of this country with the religious ideal; to inspire the religious forces of this country with the educational ideal."[21]

What was emerging in this new coalescence between religion and education was a set of assumptions that would eventuate in the discipline of religious education. No longer were religious teaching and learning understood solely as an activity of the church concerned with the initiation of the young into religious faith. Education was being redefined as personal realization and development, and Dewey brought a new emphasis on the religious qualities inherent in the achievement of one's human capability. In addition, William James's psychology of religion contributed a way by which experience—already a concern of practical theologians—could be studied scientifically, and the findings could lead to the construction of a more systematic theory of religious education. It is little wonder that the new field expanded so rapidly.

George Albert Coe might be considered the architect of the new discipline of religious education. He was certainly steeped in the subject matter that would come to be a source for the new discipline. Coe's academic field was philosophy of religion and his specialization in philosophy was psychology of religion, which at that time was still a branch of philosophical studies. Coe's first two academic appointments were in departments of philosophy, first at the University of Southern California and later at Northwestern University. Not until 1909, when he moved to Union Theological Seminary as professor of practical theology, did he set forth a discrete field of religious education. Coe was interested not only in the psychological study of religious experience but also in how psychology of religion could inform constructive theology. He wanted to formulate a theological system that grew out of life experience rather than from abstract speculation. The unity between a psychology of religious growth and experience and a theology learned out of life experience provided Coe with the content for a system of religious education. His famous quote was "We learn by doing that which we wish to do when we have learned it."[22] Rood describes Coe's religious education as "a way of living which unites ideas and action by drawing upon the learner's own experience and projecting the resultant convictions into actual social regeneration."[23]

Those who followed Coe, such as William Clayton Bower, Ernest J. Chave, and Harrison S. Elliott, were grounded in philosophical psychology and gave attention to the nature of human growth and how religious experience could inform both the nature and meaning of faith. They were as much at home in general educational dialogue as in religious discussions and were committed to wedding the two together.

The understanding that these formative figures had of religious education as a discipline is significant to our search for a definition. They did not understand their task as simply borrowing insights and concepts from other disciplines. Although they were deeply informed by philosophy, psychology, and the other sciences of education, they saw these sciences as providing only raw data to be reconstructed into new theoretical concepts and conclusions, always in the light of the study of actual data of religious experience. In short, religious education was in its formation a discipline in which what we now call praxis was central. The accusation that is sometimes made against religious education that it is primarily games and techniques cannot be laid against these early pioneers. What they attempted was to evolve a field of study that had a unique body of content and a clear methodology. What they sometimes left behind in their enthusiasm for a new science was a clear appreciation of theological tradition.

Only much later did the psychology of religious education reestablish its relationship with systematic theology of practice.

Possibly Randolph Crump Miller should be given the credit for restoring the theological stream to religious education, although persons such as Lewis J. Sherrill and Ross Snyder earlier contributed a new practical theology of education by integrating the psychological and theological. This integration resulted in a reformed body of religious education knowledge.[24]

Contemporary Attempts at Definition

Presently the discipline of religious education is developing in two major directions.[25] Each of these directions is rooted in the history of the discipline and is represented by major theorists.

The first direction centers around the attempt to formulate a practical theology of education. The work here seeks to clarify the theological context for the study of religious education and especially to reconceptualize the teaching-learning experience by the use of theological metaphors. The image of pastoral has been enlarged to refer to more than the office of pastor and can be broadly understood as the activity of mutual guidance. From this perspective, a practical theology of education is concerned with mutual guidance in matters of faith or what Westerhoff calls catechesis and Jack Seymour describes as a "pilgrim guide on the journey of faith."[26] The pastoral image is projected here as a paradigm for education, the content of which is how persons within a religious community come to faith. The boundaries of the discipline are established by ecclesiology (the life of the faith community), not by general education and schooling.

Westerhoff seeks to formulate religious education as a pastoral discipline that is largely dependent upon theology for its content. Catechesis, therefore, "is a pastoral ministry of the Word, the energy or activity of God which continuously converts and nurtures those whom God has chosen to witness to the Gospel of Salvation. The aim of catechesis is to make God's saving activity or liberating/reconciling Word known, living, conscious, and active in the personal and corporate lives of God's baptized people."[27]

Howard Grimes believes that a practical theology is required to give unity to the specialized disciplines of ministry and to provide a critical theological context for the whole of Christian praxis. For him, the purpose of practical theology is "to bring judgment on what the church is doing" and to formulate what the church "ought to do."[28] He chooses a middle ground between a practical theology that is dependent upon systematic theology for its content and a practical theology that is either derived from the human sciences or from experience alone. In selecting the middle he avoids the pitfalls of earlier theorists who either developed an independent theology for religious education or who found it easy to slip from a critical study of experience into subjective norms for faith. His emphasis is on interaction between the systematic branches of theology and the practice of faith, the human sciences, and the concrete situation. In this way, the beginning point for a practical theology of education "may be the biblical, historical and/or systematic; at others it is the current situation or the 'secular' sciences."[29] From this orientation, the beginning question may be either theological or educational, and in the interaction the other question is influenced and formulated.

The second direction for a discipline of religious education seeks to keep education itself as a central focus. One cannot fairly say that theorists working around this model are any less theological than the practical theologians; their belief is that educational issues are of significant importance, and that this educational identity must also be maintained. For them the task is to define the meaning of religious education and to attempt to describe the nature of the religious education activity. Some of the work is an attempt to clarify what we do when we say we are engaging in religious education. For Groome, as an example, it is important to understand what the educational act is when it takes place intentionally with a religious community. The discipline is *religious education* in Groome's understanding, although it is appropriate to address the discipline from one's own faith perspective, that is, Jewish, Christian, or whatever. So Groome refers to the activity of education within the Christian community as *Christian* religious education. In this way he maintains a generic discipline that is at the same time theological in its orientation. Groome brings to his work a methodology which he calls shared praxis. He describes it as "a group of Christians sharing in dialogue their critical reflection on present action in light of the Christian Story and its Vision toward the end of lived Christian faith."[30]

Another attempt to preserve the integrity of education within the discipline of religious education is offered by Mary Elizabeth Moore. Her model shares much with the practical theologians (who seek a theological context for religious education), and with the shared praxis of Groome (who seeks to clarify what education should look like within the religious community). She describes her approach as a "traditioning model of Christian religious education."[31] By this she means "a process by which the historical tradition is remembered and transformed as the Christian community encounters God and the world in present experience and as the community is motivated toward the future."[32]

There are two dimensions to the traditioning model: the hermeneutical and the transformative. The educational act therefore involves the reenactment and the interpretation of the Christian story. It also involves the re-creation of personal and social experience, although Moore is clear that education as an act of reconstruction in her model goes beyond the reforming spirit of the progressive religious educator. It is here that she brings a theological vision of hope and the recognition that present activity is always viewed in relationship to God's call to the future and the promises of the coming kingdom. What is suggested is an educational enterprise. But the educational enterprise is always taking place at an intersection where the resources of Christian faith stand in relationship to the concrete moment in which persons are located in the world, and to the new possibilities for change that are made possible by God's pull to the future. What is provided is an image of a busy traffic stop with many roads leading in and leading out, and education is taking place where the roads cross.

Conclusions

The question remains: To what extent is religious education a true academic discipline in a formal sense? What seems increasingly clear as one reviews the history is that religious education in its many forms has had and does have presently the essential elements for the scholarly work required of a discipline. There is a community of scholars who are dedicated to the study of how teaching and learning take place within the religious community. There is also a rich body of literature extending over thousands of years.

The extent to which religious education scholars are at work in the development of new knowledge may still be debated. There is evidence that a considerable dependence remains upon other fields of knowledge, especially the social sciences, for the content of the discipline. As we have seen in the current directions within the field, a growing self-consciousness is motivating the search for methods and procedures by which this borrowed knowledge can be reconstructed into a unique subject matter that can be clearly identified as religious education. Growing attention to research has the promise of leading to more original thought and to a clearer direction for the field.

What seems to be most significant, regardless of whether the beginning point is taken to be theology or education, is a growing consensus as to the boundaries, language of discourse, body of literature, and goal and purposes. There is evidence that religious education in the future will not need to repeat the work of the past pioneers or follow the latest trends from the social sciences. The hope lies in the recovery of education's historical and empirical roots in the religious community and in a shared concern for an education that is intentional in matters of religious faith.

Notes

1. This conclusion and some others in this essay arise from a study commissioned by the United Methodist Association of Professors of Christian Education. The study was conducted by a task force which included the author as chair, Marvin Carr, D. Bruce Roberts, Nelle G. Slater, and Linda Jane Vogel. The unpublished report was submitted June 1980.
2. The basic disciplines are commonly identified with the liberal arts which were developed by the Greeks and Romans and became the curriculum for the medieval schools and early universities. The perennialist would argue that all other fields of study are derived from these disciplines that are basic to culture, human reason, and a life of virtue.
3. For a discussion of the problem of a definition for education, see Marc Belth, *Education as a Discipline* (Boston: Allyn & Bacon, 1965), 1-24.
4. The criteria are informed by Belth but not identical. See also Paul Deats, Jr., ed., *Toward a Discipline of Social Ethics* (Boston: Boston University Press, 1972).
5. Richard J. Bernstein, *Praxis and Action* (London: Gerald Duckworth, 1971, 1972), ix-xiv.
6. Jürgen Habermas, *Theory and Practice* (Boston: Beacon Press, 1973). For a discussion of critical theory, or praxis, see Thomas H. Groome, *Christian Religious Education: Sharing Our Story and Vision* (San Francisco: Harper & Row, 1980), 152-83.
7. Bernstein, *Praxis and Action*, 316.
8. George Albert Coe's best-known works are *The Social Theory of Religious Education* (New York: Charles Scribner's Sons, 1917), and *What Is Christian Education?* (New York: Charles Scribner's Sons, 1935). For Coe, Christian education was understood as making and reflecting on experiments that would lead to further experimentation.
9. Seward Hiltner, *Preface to Pastoral Theology* (Nashville: Abingdon Press, 1958), 50-51. Hiltner enlarged this point in "The Psychological Understanding of Religion," in *Readings in the Psychology of Religion*, ed. Orlo Strunk, Jr. (Nashville: Abingdon Press, 1969), 87-90.
10. See John Westerhoff, "A Discipline in Crisis," *Religious Education* 74:1 (January-February 1979), 7-8. According to Westerhoff the Hartford School of Religious Pedagogy, founded 1903, was among the earliest. Soon after, there were programs at Boston University School of Religious Education and Social Work and at Union, Chicago, and Yale. By 1912, fifty of the sixty-three Protestant seminaries had at least one course in religious education, and by 1925 departments of religious education were common.
11. Ibid., 9.
12. H. Richard Niebuhr, Daniel Day Williams, James M. Gustafson, *The Advancement of Theological Education* (New York: Harper & Brothers, 1957), 79; also, 102-11.

13. Historically, the ordering of the theological disciplines was referred to as "theological encyclopedia." This issue first emerged in 1764. Today Edward Farley has written about the problem of the structures of divinity. See "The Reform of Theological Education as a Theological Task," *Theological Education* 17:2 (Spring 1981), 93-117.

14. Robert Ulich, *A History of Religious Education* (New York: New York University Press, 1968), v. There have been few attempts to write a definitive history of religious education. The standard work has been Lewis J. Sherrill, *The Rise of Christian Education* (New York: Macmillan, 1953).

15. "The Challenge: Understanding the Problem of Faithfulness," in *A Faithful Church: Issues in the History of Catechesis*, ed. John H. Westerhoff III and O. C. Edwards, Jr. (Wilton, Conn.: Morehouse-Barlow Co., 1981), 1.

16. Ibid., 1-9.

17. Friedrich Schleiermacher, *Die Praktische Theologie nach den Grundsäzen der Evangelischen Kirche*, 1850. This systematic treatment of practical theology was published after Schleiermacher's death and apparently has never been translated into English. Although Schleiermacher is given the credit for the development of practical theology, works in this direction can be dated to at least the mid-eighteenth century, e.g., C. T. Seidel, *Pastoral-Theologie*, 1749.

18. Frederich Schleiermacher, *Brief Outline in the Study of Theology*, trans. T. M. Tice (Richmond: John Knox Press, 1970).

19. J. J. Van Oosterzee, *Practical Theology* (New York: Charles Scribner's Sons, 1878); Alexander Vinet, *Pastoral Theology* (Nashville: A. A. Redford, Agent, Methodist Episcopal Church, South, 1876).

20. W. G. T. Shedd, *Homiletics and Pastoral Theology* (New York: Charles Scribner's Sons, 1867).

21. Cited in Westerhoff, "A Discipline in Crisis," 8.

22. Cited in Wayne R. Rood, *Understanding Christian Education* (Nashville: Abingdon Press, 1970), 188.

23. Ibid.

24. Lewis J. Sherrill, *The Gift of Power* (New York: Macmillan, 1955); Randolph C. Miller, *The Clue to Christian Education* (New York: Charles Scribner's Sons, 1950); Ross Snyder, *The Ministry of Meaning* (Geneva: World Council of Churches, 1965). See Allen J. Moore, "Religious Education as Living Theology: Some Reflections on the Contributions of Ross Snyder," *Religious Education* 73:5 (September-October 1978), 541-50.

25. A third possible direction is reflected by James Michael Lee, who views religious education as a social science and not as a theological discipline or an independent field of study. *The Shape of Religious Instruction* (Mishawaka, Ind.: Religious Education Press, 1971), 94-99.

26. Cited from the "Report of the Task Force on Defining the Academic Discipline of Religious Education," United Methodist Association of Professors of Christian Education, June 1980.

27. Westerhoff and Edwards, eds., *A Faithful Church: Issues in the History of Catechesis*, 298.

28. Howard Grimes, "What Is Practical Theology?" *Perkins Journal* (Spring 1977), 29.

29. Ibid., 33-34.

30. Groome, *Christian Religious Education*, 184.

31. Mary Elizabeth Moore, *Education for Continuity and Change: A New Model for Christian Religious Education* (Nashville: Abingdon Press, 1983), 121.

32. Ibid.

Bibliography

Belth, Marc. *Education as a Discipline*. Boston: Allyn & Bacon, 1965.

Cooke, Bernard. *Ministry to Word and Sacraments*. Philadelphia: Fortress Press, 1976.

Groome, Thomas H. *Christian Religious Education: Sharing Our Story and Vision*. San Francisco: Harper & Row, 1980.

Moore, Mary Elizabeth. *Education for Continuity and Change: A New Model for Christian Religious Education*. Nashville: Abingdon Press, 1983.

Westerhoff, John H., and O. C. Edwards, eds. *A Faithful Church: Issues in the History of Catechesis*. Wilton, Conn.: Morehouse-Barlow, 1981.

CHAPTER 7

Research in Religious Education

John H. Peatling

A Search for Understanding

Research in religious education is a challenging search as well as a diverse and quite human activity. Across the years since 1950, both that diversity and that challenge have been recorded in the previous volumes of this series (see the introduction). Each of the three predecessors of this report recorded a vision of what research in religious education could or should mean. Each of those visions was different because it was a human vision of what would help religious educators understand their field. Each was the work of a person of experience and insight. Thus the diversity of visions is more a function of the sheer humanness of the searchers for understanding than it is of the search itself. Even so, as creatures in this creation, we do need to recognize that the research important for or related to the field of religious education is a remarkably diverse set. No one discipline has a true monopoly on such research.

A *Vision of Research in Religious Education from 1950*

When Philip H. Lotz edited *Orientation in Religious Education*, Ross Snyder contributed a chapter entitled "Experimentation and Research."[1] In the optimistic years immediately following the end of World War II, Dr. Snyder envisioned a real contribution from research and experimentation in the field. Thus he identified six then-present trends in "personality and group life" as of particular importance for religious education. While those trends still are adventurous challenges, it is important to remember that they were identified well over thirty years ago. We now know at least a bit more about what is involved in each challenge and so may be a bit more prepared to meet them. Snyder's trends were:

John H. Peatling is Rector of St. Stephen's Episcopal Church in Schenectady, New York.

1. An increasing concern with the study of the total personality as it functions in realistic situations.
2. A concern with the study of the process (or processes) of representative religious experience.
3. An interest in the study of the actual dynamics of religious phenomena.
4. An increasing use of participant observation, so that studies are done within ongoing processes.
5. A growing concern to use studies to test human hypotheses.
6. An increasingly cooperative, cross-disciplinary team approach to studies of religious education.[2]

Now, in the early 1980s, it is all too easy to regard these six visions as mere optimism, because each of them is still a challenge to those who seek to understand. It is obvious that Snyder envisioned more than actually took place in the intervening years. However, we must not forget that in his time those trends were real. That they still remain a challenging part of the search for understanding says a great deal more about the searchers and the ever-shifting context in which they seek understanding than it does about the search itself, or about Snyder's 1950 vision.

A Vision of Research in Religious Education from 1960

Ten years later, when Marvin J. Taylor edited *Religious Education: A Comprehensive Survey*, Walter Houston Clark contributed a chapter entitled "Research in Religious Education."[3] Clark's vision was both clearer and more obviously social scientific. Not only was Clark an active psychological researcher, he was also chairman of the research committee of the Religious Education Association of the United States and Canada at a time when it was active and remarkably influential. Thus he reminded the reader that research in religious education had a history. He specially mentioned the Rockefeller-funded Character Education Inquiry (CEI) of Hartshorne and May from the 1920s and the then still active Lilly-funded Character Research Project (CRP) of Ligon and his associates. Neither should be forgotten, for each witnesses to the sometimes-awesome cost of good research. Both the CEI and the CRP involved large amounts of time, expertise, and money. Without that triad, neither would have been possible.

In addition, Clark's vision of research in religious education included the use of a variety of devices: the questionnaire, the interview, rating scales, tests, and the statistical procedure of factor analysis. For Clark, research included experimentation and the use of control groups, a general developmental approach to both problems and data, and the use of clinical methods such as projective devices. The breadth of concern in Clark's chapter is truly remarkable. Thus, at the end of the 1950s, Clark considered research in religious education to be interested in a consideration of religious leadership as a social elite; the development of religious experience, human sexuality, conversion; and the influence of the family group. For him, research in religious education was clearly a wide-ranging, largely psychological/ sociological search for understanding. Just as clearly, Clark thought that much of real importance to the field had already been done.

A Vision of Research in Religious Education from 1966

Just over half a decade later, when Marvin J. Taylor edited *An Introduction to Christian Education*, D. Campbell Wyckoff contributed a chapter entitled "Research and Evaluation in Christian Education."[4] The years since Clark's chapter had been important ones for research in religious education in North American Christian denominations. They were years of intense activity and of a self-conscious effort by the field to understand itself and the realities it repeatedly encountered. As a result, Wyckoff could identify six types of research and, as well, six types of evaluation. He was also aware of an even more extensive history of research in religious education than Clark had been. In addition, he sought to address the foundational question of where and how research and evaluation fit into the field's continuing search for understanding.

Possibly because of his own considerable involvement in cooperative curriculum development for Christian education, Wyckoff was acutely aware of the processes of research. He was, for instance, clearly aware of both the potentials and the limitations of research. He was also just as clearly aware of the cyclic or iterative nature of evaluation as a conceptual tool for educational progress. Wyckoff's recognition of a place for basic research in religious education was unique. His identification of a four-step sequential process was classic. The task of research began, Wyckoff maintained, with problem identification, moved on to the formulation of hypotheses, which were then tested, and finally reached an interpretative stage. He also clearly recognized that for such a sequential process to work, the only stance a researcher could take was one of detached involvement. Thus he seemed to understand that research in religious education could and should be part of an iterative cycle of theory production, in which a deductive phase of theory testing was followed by an inductive phase of theory revision (or refinement). In a word,

Wyckoff described research in religious education as basically *scientific*.

A More Contemporary Vision of Research in Religious Education

The visions of Snyder, Clark, and Wyckoff form a progression. Snyder was concerned that the then new work in social psychology and personality theory be available to the field. He was an informed consumer. Clark continued the concern that the field have available the new work from psychology and sociology but, as well, was concerned that religious education understand and support research into its own problems. He was both an informed consumer and an active participant. Wyckoff, on the contrary, was more concerned with the field's relation to research and, particularly, its use of the research sequence as a tool for its own educational problems. He was a critical consumer and supporter. In the mid-1960s, when Wyckoff wrote about research and evaluation in religious education, his vision was no mere dream: national denominations had research staffs and, increasingly, Christian education seemed to accept research as a valuable conceptual tool. However, by the early 1970s, what Wyckoff knew to be became history. The decade of the 1970s saw a return to something very like what Snyder knew during the 1940s. The denominational research staffs were either dispersed or restricted, and the field once again had to depend upon work done in related albeit cognate fields.

That is the situation which Peatling found in 1978, when he wrote the section on "Research and Religious Education" for *Pioneers of Religious Education in the Twentieth Century*.[5] By the time that fifty-year retrospective was written, the situational context for research in religious education had changed from what Wyckoff knew in the mid-1960s. By the late 1970s, the field was once again in the position of an informed (it could be hoped) consumer, and research important for or related to religious education was increasingly coming from cognate disciplines. During the years since 1966, the field had become increasingly aware of work in cognitive, moral, and character development. The studies of Jean Piaget, Ronald Goldman, and Lawrence Kohlberg led the field to become more and more aware of epistemological and pedagogical problems and of the research that sought to understand those problems. In addition, perhaps as a carry-over from the 1960s, there was evidence that religious education was beginning to be sophisticated enough to appreciate the important research questions of reliability, validity, and generalizability. While not overwhelming, there were signs that research in religious education was passing from childhood into adolescence and, at last, developing toward a maturity which had been envisioned for at least thirty years.

Definitions and Types

This chapter follows in an honorable line. Like its predecessors, however, it is clearly based on a quite human vision of research in religious education. The author is very much like Snyder, Clark, and Wyckoff. He understands research as both a critical consumer and a practitioner of the research process. But he remains very much a creature of his time and place in this creation. What follows is his witness.

What IS Research in Religious Education?

When one considers the history of religious education, one sees a clear diversity of answers that have been given to such foundational problems as the scope, stance, extent, and nature of the field itself. It is still useful, however, to seek an answer to the problem of the nature of research in religious education. Unfortunately, the problems of scope, stance, and extent are often presumed to be primary, rather than secondary, and that assumption tends to only confuse everyone. Wyckoff was almost certainly right: the researcher's stance is detached involvement, as long as he or she functions as a researcher. The real confusion results from the fact that research important for the field is a human activity which focuses upon the activity of humans. That is why a stance of detached involvement is peculiarly apropos.

1. *An initial definition of research.* At a very general level, Peatling's definition of research in *Religious Education in a Psychological Key* seems quite adequate.[6] That is, research is studious, critical inquiry and examination aimed at the discovery and interpretation of new knowledge. Research, in those terms, can be considered as a way to learn through the process of inquiry and examination. Thus it is something reasonably common and clearly human. In addition, it is a process of discovery, a way of keeping human knowledge open-ended.

Research, so defined, does four valuable things. First, it includes a great deal of human activity. Second, it focuses attention upon a surprisingly general method of learning. Third, it supports critical studiousness as a standard. Fourth, it specifies interpretable new knowledge as the aim. As a result, all that is scientific is included and so is most of what disciplines trying to be scientific do. However, a good bit more is also included—for example, the literary and historical study of tests and a fair amount of what is often regarded as the result of sensitive pastoral experience.

Research is not just a vaster form of apple-counting, nor is it only the practice of the semi-esoteric forms of statistical analysis. Research is not just the massing of data from large numbers of persons. It can be these things, but it can also be much more. Research can be conducted with small groups or with a sample of one person. Research itself depends upon the presence of a human intent, or purpose, which is no less than the discovery and interpretation of new knowledge. That is why research is so diverse, for human purposes and intentions are often similar but rarely identical.

Implicit in this recognition of the importance of the intention to discover and interpret new knowledge is a boundary for research. It is a boundary that can be expressed in terms of equally human purposes of intent. Research is not possible where there is no intention to discover or interpret new knowledge. Thus research is not a part of human activity which simply affirms what is already known; it is not a part of any human sense that everything worth knowing is already known about any field. Research is a part of that foundational human trait of curiosity. Where there is no curiosity, research is not. When all the answers are known, research is useless . . . disruptive . . . even antithetical.

2. *A further definition of research.* When the *Annual Review of Research: Religious Education* series was begun in 1978, the focus was upon the collection of identifications of empirical research related to or important for the field. However, since that series was to be built upon a base of identifications from interested, concerned scholars from a variety of disciplines, the definitional question was quite important. A definition was needed that would be general enough to be understood by both religious educators and nonreligious educators, yet specific enough to identify research that could be legitimately called (1) research, and (2) empirical. The result was a broadly general yet concisely formal definition, one which could be shared with an international and interdisciplinary network of scholar-identifiers of research. During the first four years of that series, it seems to have worked reasonably well, for the network of identifiers has listed clinical studies, experiments, evaluations of classroom interventions, explorations of single and multiple variable effects, and the search for developmental

sequences. The definition itself is fairly simple: Research is any inquiry or examination which seeks to answer, in some way, the question, *What happens to A in B when C occurs, as measured by D?*

Between 1979 and 1982, more than five hundred studies were identified through use of this definition as of importance for or related to religious education. That was probably because the four-letter symbols in the basic query were defined as follows:

A—some group, class, or category that can be described in terms of size or number, and some criterion of inclusion.

B—some situation or context that can be described in terms of some specific time, place, or places, and the specific personnel involved.

C—some action, process, or procedure that can be described in terms of a rationale, a design, and a set of appropriate behaviors.

D—some form of assessment that can be described in terms of some specific instrument, procedure, or other application of a criterion.[7]

By this definition, empirical research of potential importance for or related to the field of religious education can be generally defined as those inquiries or examinations that seek an answer to the basic query, which, in an expanded form, asks:

What happens to some group/class/category	(defined by size/number/criterion)
. . . in some situation/context	(defined by time/place/personnel)
. . . when some action/process/procedure occurs,	(defined by rationale/design/behaviors)
. . . as measured by some form of assessment?	(defined by instrument/procedure/criterion)

Only a little thought should be necessary for most persons to recognize that this expanded statement is little more than a structured specification of what most humans mean by curiosity. The statement and the curious query (What happened?) are closely related. Research and curiosity are inherently related. Thus research is a human activity that does not exist where there is no human curiosity, where all answers are known (or accessible through the "correct" index system), or where simple-but-powerful taboos prohibit such human curiosity. Unless there is some open end to the range of human knowledge, there is a profound absurdity in the curious search for understanding via the discovery of new knowledge. This may explain why religious education is periodically suspicious of the research enterprise.

The Question of Types of Research

Human curiosity has a truly awesome range of interests. That is one reason why the research sequence has been put to use by so many seemingly disparate disciplines and fields. That sequence is, we have found, surprisingly general in its applicability. As a result, humans have used the generalizable sequence for a quite varied set of problems: research has proved to be a surprisingly useful conceptual tool for a number of queries a curious humankind has chosen to put to itself or to the creation in which it exists. Thus it is not at all surprising that "religious" humans (and, especially, "religious" humans who are educators!) have repeatedly found the research sequence interesting, useful, or acceptable. What is continually at issue is just how much certainty such "religious" human educators want to assert in the face of human curiosity.

The late Clive Staples Lewis once described the Christian as very much like a gambler for the highest of stakes. Lewis noted that such a gambler made the wager on the best available information and waited to learn whether the bet was won or lost. Research is like such a gambler. Research makes a "bet" on a result whenever it specifies a hypothesis, guess, or estimate of anticipated outcome. Only an after-the-fact statement of observed occurrence can determine whether any such "bet" was a winner or a loser! Thus, "bet" or wager precedes an event which, once having happened, determines correctness.

If C. S. Lewis was at all correct in his estimate of Christians, they and the researchers are remarkably similar persons. Each is a gambler on an unknown. Each anticipates quite clearly what winning might mean. The difference, if any, is that researchers try to learn from their losses and make further bets on some future. In both instances, a process or sequence of perceived potential holds out a promise of considerable and obvious worth. It is an appeal that curious persons find difficult to ignore.

As a result, curious humans intent on searching for under-standing have come to recognize at least four levels or kinds of research. Human curiosity disciplined into a search for under-standing has been and is interested in research that can legitimately be called (1) theoretical, (2) basic, (3) applied, and (4) evaluative. While the first is often exclusively cognitive and frequently foundational, the second is a kind of testing of that which cognition determines to be foundational. Thus theoretical and basic research have a kind of pragmatic, structurally hierarchic relationship with one another. Similarly, basic and applied research have such a hierarchic relationship, in which the results of basic research are assessed to determine their actual, observable effects. Evaluation is somewhat similarly related to applied research because, although it can be considered a sub-type of applied research, it seeks to determine the accuracy with which prior intent is achieved by present procedure. As a result, through the two complementary processes of differentiation and de-differentiation, it is possible to move from one to another of the levels of such a pragmatic, structurally hierarchic set of levels of research.[8] That is, it is possible to consider evaluative research related to theoretical research through the intermediate levels of applied and basic research, and to consider the exact reverse. Like Piaget's formal operations, it seems that a marked characteristic of research is a certain inherent reversibility. Level is related to level; yet it is possible to achieve understanding at one level (e.g., the evaluative) prior to achieving understanding at another level (e.g., the basic). Thus, curiosity is often-to-always necessary for research.

Some Examples of Research Important for the Field

In the essay "Medical Lessons from History," Lewis Thomas maintained that, since medicine was an applied rather than a pure science, the best "bet" on future importance involved the element of surprise.[9] R. Buckminster Fuller made a similar point in his long free-verse poem "How Little I Know," when he maintained that research was a creative, left-handed science which was truly important.[10] Using those ideas, Peatling found that when he used a stringent criterion with the some two hundred fifty studies identified for the 1981 and the 1982 editions of the *Annual Review of Research: Religious Education*, approximately 10 percent could be regarded as offering surprise or witnessing to a left-handed, creative use of the research sequence.[11]

The following listing represents a very human vision of the kind of research related to religious education that seems like a best "bet" for future importance or a nicely creative use of research to reach a surprising result. In addition, it witnesses to several present facts. First, research related to religious education is an international phenomenon. Second, such research is often now carried out as part of an academic dissertation project. Third, a good bit of research important for the field will now be found in journals of cognate fields—thus it is important for religious educators to avoid restricting their interests solely to their own field. Fourth, the field today is most often a consumer of research done by others and is not too often a stimulator or supporter of its own research.

Blazer, Doris A. "The Influence of Parental Participation in a Parent Education Program upon the Self-Concepts of Children." Ph.D. diss., University of South Carolina, 1981.

Breslin, Ann. "Tolerance and Moral Reasoning Among Adolescents in Ireland." Ph.D. diss., St. Patrick's College, Republic of Ireland, 1981.

DeGrace, Gaston. "Effects of Meditation on Personality and Values," in the *Journal of Clinical Psychology* 32, no. 4 (1976): 809-13.

Dickinson, Sister Valda. "The Relation of Principled Moral Thinking to Commonly Measured Sample Characteristics and to Family Correlates in Samples of Australian Senior High School Adolescents and Family Triads." Doctoral diss., Macquarie University, 1979.

Exum, Herbert A. "Ego Development: Using Curriculum to Facilitate Growth," in *Character Potential: A Record of Research* 9, no. 3 (November 1980).

Francis, Leslie J., et. al. "The Relationship Between Neuroticism and Religiosity Among English Fifteen and Sixteen Year Olds," in the *Journal of Social Psychology*, no. 114 (1981).

Gorman, Sister Margaret, RSCJ. "Moral and Faith Development in Seventeen Year Old Students," in *Resources in Education* 13, no. 8 (August 1978). ERIC No. ED 151-643.

Hanford, Jack T. "Moral Reasoning in a Bioethics Course," in *Faculty Research Reports at Ferris State*, 1979.

Hayes, Donald S., and Dana W. Birnbaum. "Preschoolers' Retention of Televised Events: Is a Picture Worth a Thousand Words?" in *Developmental Psychology* 16, no. 5 (1980): 410-16.

Heikkinen, Helena. "The Renewed Confirmation School and Trait-Anxiety Among Youth: A Follow-Up Study." Helsinki, Finland: University of Helsinki, Department of Practical Theology, 1981.

Larson, Reed William. "The Significance of Solitude in Adolescents' Lives." Doctoral diss., University of Chicago, 1979.

Limoges, Jacques. "Life Planning: A Conceptual Approach to Career Education Within an Interactional Model." Doctoral diss., Boston University, 1980.

Mark, Timothy J. "A Study of Cognitive and Affective Elements in the Religious Development of Adolescents." Ph.D. diss., University of Leeds, U.K., 1979.

Mellor, Steven, and J. Andre. "Religious Group Value Patterns and Motive Orientations," in the *Journal of Psychology and Theology* 8, no. 2 (1980): 129-39.

Mischey, Eugene J. "Faith Development and Its Relationship to Moral Reasoning and Identity Status." Ph.D. diss., University of Toronto, Canada, 1976.

Ninomiya, Katsumi. "A Study of Children's Moral Judgments: An Experimental Test of the Sequentiality of Gutkin's Four Stages," in the *Japanese Journal of Educational Psychology* 28, no. 1 (March 1980).

Okwor, Comfort O. "Attitude of Secondary School Students Toward the Study of Bible Knowledge." Awka, Nigeria: N.C.E. Project, College of Education, 1981.

Peatling, John H. *A Father and His Two Sons: Finnish Students' Responses to a Piagetian Moral Puzzle*. Schenectady, N. Y.: Character Research Press, 1979.

———. *Signs of Structure and Signs of Dissonance: Adult Responses to a Piagetian Puzzle*. Schenectady, N.Y.: Character Research Press, 1976.

Resnik, David. "The Development of Children's Comprehension of Proverbs." Ph.D. diss., Columbia University, 1977.

Rholes, William S., et. al. "A Developmental Study of Learned Helplessness," in *Developmental Psychology* 16, no. 6 (1980): 616-24.

Sami, Doris Renate. "Joys and Tribulations of Parenthood in the Middle Years." Doctoral diss., University of California, Berkeley, 1978.

Singer, Jerome, et. al. "A Factor Analytic Study of Preschoolers' Play Behavior," in the *Academic Psychology Bulletin* 2, no. 2 (June 1980): 143-56.

Tamminen, Kalevi. "Religious Experiences Among Children and Youth. Project on the Religious Development of Children and Youth—Report 2." Helsinki, Finland: University of Helsinki, Department of Practical Theology, 1981.

Walters, Thomas P. "A Study of the Relationship Between Religious Orientation and Cognitive Moral Maturity in Volunteer Religion Teachers from Selected Suburban Catholic Parishes in the Archdiocese of Detroit." Ph.D. diss., Wayne State University, 1980.

Wyler, Alain. *Recherche sur la communication de l'evangile* [Research on the Gospel's Communication]. Bern-Francfurt & Las Vegas: Publications Universitaires Europeenes & Peter Lang, 1980.

In this listing nine studies are exclusively focused on adolescents, while two are focused on both children and adolescents. Thus eleven (or 42 percent) are concerned with adolescents. Similarly, five studies are focused on preschoolers, while only three of the studies are concerned with children. Thus a maximum of eight (or 31 percent) are concerned with children prior to adolescence. There are four studies that focus on young adults in the listing, and five studies involve adults. Thus 15 percent of the studies focus on young adults, while 19 percent focus upon adults. It is clear that recent research important for or related to religious education tends to be dominated by a search for an understanding of adolescents and children. As yet, research on adults constitutes only about one-fifth of the listing, even though adult religious education has been acknowledged to be important for years. There is, then, a challenge to future research implicit in these simple descriptive statistics of the first twenty-six of the Sam Gamgee Awards for Surprising Service to Religious Education Through Research.[12]

Notes

1. Ross Snyder, "Experimentation and Research," in *Orientation in Religious Education*, ed. Philip Henry Lotz (Nashville: Abingdon Press, 1950), 404-15.

2. Ibid., 405-9.
3. Walter Houston Clark, "Research in Religious Education," in *Religious Education: A Comprehensive Survey*, ed. Marvin J. Taylor (Nashville: Abingdon Press, 1960), 78-86.
4. D. Campbell Wyckoff, "Research and Evaluation in Christian Education," in *An Introduction to Christian Education*, ed. Marvin J. Taylor (Nashville: Abingdon Press, 1966), 144-56.
5. John H. Peatling, "Research and Religious Education," in *Pioneers of Religious Education in the Twentieth Century*, ed. Boardman W. Kathan (New Haven: Religious Education Association, 1978), S-101–S-125.
6. John H. Peatling, *Religious Education in a Psychological Key* (Birmingham, Ala.: Religious Education Press, 1981), 271.
7. John H. Peatling, ed., *Annual Review of Research: Religious Education—Volume 2* (Schenectady, N.Y.: Character Research Press & Religious Education Association, 1981), 135.
8. Jean Piaget, *Structuralism* (London: Routledge & Kegan Paul, 1968, 1971).
9. Lewis Thomas, "Medical Lessons from History," in *The Medusa and the Snail* (New York: Bantam Books, 1980).
10. R. Buckminster Fuller, "How Little I Know," in *And It Came to Pass—Not to Stay* (New York: Macmillan, 1976), especially 48.
11. For commentary on each of the twenty-six research studies, see the following:
    a. John H. Peatling, "Annual Review of Research in Religious Education: 1981," in *Religious Education* 76, no. 4 (July-August 1981), 442-45.
    b. John H. Peatling, "Annual Review of Research in Religious Education: 1982," in *Religious Education* 77, no. 4 (July-August 1982), 448-51.
12. For a description of the Sam Gamgee Awards and their criteria, see "Annual Review of Research in Religious Education: 1981," in *Religious Education* 76, no. 4 (July-August 1981), especially 441-42.

CHAPTER 8

Changing Patterns of Religious Education Practice in Protestant Churches Since World War II

Howard Grimes

The one word that describes most accurately the life of the church in the latter half of the twentieth century is *diversity*. Historians in the future might be able to sort out the changes that have occurred and are occurring; participants in these changes find it difficult to do so because they are many and varied. Even in a restricted area such as religious education, one must be selective. A catalog of changes might be possible though difficult, but such an approach is hardly appropriate for this essay. What I will do, therefore, is consider some key issues as I see them concerning the *practice* of religious education, with theory included since the theoretical impinges on practice.

The focus is the "mainline Protestant churches," by which I mean those communions that arose directly or indirectly from church leaders such as Martin Luther, John Calvin, John Knox, John Wesley, and the Campbells. With some exceptions such churches are older than other Protestant groups. A further characteristic is that they participated to some degree in the theological and educational changes that emerged during the late nineteenth and early twentieth centuries. Many of them now contain strong evangelical movements in reaction to those changes.

Our primary concern is with the congregational "program" of religious education and with the denominational and ecumenical organizations that influenced congregations. The public school and, more recently, the Christian day school are minor themes. The family as an agency of Christian nurture is always in the background, either for its effectiveness or lack thereof.

Howard Grimes is Professor of Christian Education Emeritus at the Perkins School of Theology, Southern Methodist University and Director of Communications at First United Methodist Church in Dallas, Texas.

The Past as Prologue

What the church does now by way of organized religious education is clearly an outcome of the genuine innovation that occurred through the Sunday school movement of the late eighteenth century. It is not correct to say that there had been *no* formal schooling in the church prior to the Sunday school; it is the case that *the school as the focus* for religious education began with that institution. The Sunday school, in fact, reflected the general culture as the formal school increasingly became, during the nineteenth century, the principal agency of general education for all rather than the few. The nineteenth century may rightly be characterized as the century of the common school.

As is generally known, the Sunday school was originally a school on Sunday for poor children, organized into a movement by Robert Raikes about 1780.[1] In the United States—earlier than in Great Britain—the churches began to "adopt" the Sunday school during the first decades of the nineteenth century and to change it into the churches' principal agency for both teaching and aiding in evangelism. Partly because it was taken over by the churches rather than originated by them, it tended to remain an appendage to the congregation—or at best a parallel movement—for more than a century. Lay led and largely lay controlled, it came to be understood as an *agency* of the church, often called the "Sunday school department," usually with negligible pastoral oversight.

Beginning about 1870, other structures concerned with or at least related to teaching emerged: agencies such as women's groups, youth societies, teacher training institutes and classes, men's groups, and, in the first decade of the twentieth century, the vacation Bible school. These groups were at first independent of one another; later, especially in the 1930s, the mainline churches began to bring many of these separate agencies together in a tentative unity to form the *church* school, with the Sunday morning session as the center. The unified church school—as precarious as its unity always was—was the prevailing pattern of organized religious education in mainline churches at the end of World War II. That is, the church school consisted of a number of teaching occasions held together by an over-arching committee on education.

Somewhat earlier the mainline churches had been influenced by "liberal" theology and by the progressive educational philosophy stemming from Pestalozzi and Froebel in the nineteenth century, followed by John Dewey in general education and George Albert Coe in religious education. Although the changes affected individual congregations in varying degrees, it is important for understanding the emergence of the recent evangelical movement to recognize the influence of both forces on the structures and curriculum materials of the mainline churches. During most of the nineteenth century, for example, two (perhaps three) purposes of the Sunday school had been clear: teaching the Bible; conversion; and, to a lesser extent, nurturing persons in faith. In the twentieth century the Sunday school has tended to emphasize nurture at the expense of conversion, or more clearly "modifying experience along Christian lines."[2]

Among other significant changes that spilled over into more recent times was the development of a *profession* of religious education.[3] Throughout the nineteenth century, denominational and interdenominational meetings of Sunday school workers were primarily gatherings of laypeople. Increasingly in the twentieth century, such meetings were transformed into meetings of professionals, both lay and clergy, but all identified by special interest and expertise. The payment of teachers never became widespread; the *supervision* of lay personnel and the control of the judicatory agencies increasingly became the realm of the professional, and education on the graduate level for such persons flourished.

A Period of Growth and Change

At the end of World War II, local church education was officially a unified whole in mainline churches but did not always function in this manner. Although laypeople did most of the teaching, professionals were supervisors in larger churches as well as in judicatory and national agencies. Perhaps most important of all, a new spurt of church and church school growth began during the war and continued for more than a decade after it was over. Indeed, the period was a time of growth and vigor for the mainline Protestant churches.

It was also a time of more theological change. In 1940, Harrison Elliott published his defense of the religious education that had emerged during the previous decades, the "liberal progressive" school. A year later H. Shelton Smith, who had earlier been a part of that movement, presented a challenge to its approach in his *Faith and Nurture*.[4] Shortly thereafter the International Council of Religious Education appointed a committee to consider the changes.[5] As these influences became more common, churches, now operating separately rather than ecumenically as in the past, began again the process of developing new curriculum resources.[6]

While theological changes were evident in many curriculum materials, the experience-centered (rather than the Bible-centered) approach to teaching continued its dominance. Religious education professionals also continued their efforts to improve the quality of teaching; the degree to which improvement actually occurred is difficult to ascertain. In any case the criticism that there was not enough Bible in curriculum resources continued.

In spite of criticism, however, the church schools of mainline churches continued the growth that had begun during World War II. Furthermore, adult education entered into its greatest period of expansion since the days of the adult Sunday school movement of the 1920s. A new emphasis on the laity in the church in both Europe and the United States spawned teaching occasions for adults. Adult Sunday school classes were still flourishing in some parts of the nations, and they had become primarily couples' groups, for "caring" as well as teaching. Special young adult and other singles' groups were also emerging.

Para-church groups arose in Europe—the "lay academies" of Germany and similar agencies elsewhere, often not closely related to the organized church. In the United States the special adult groups were more often a part of the congregation—on Sunday evening, during the week, at a conference or retreat center. Perhaps the most common form was the small group for study, fellowship, prayer, or therapy.[7] Increasingly in the 1960s such groups were associated with counseling and therapy, but in the earlier period they were more often related, at least peripherally, to teaching-learning.[8] The groups were often more or less independent of the unified "church school."

On the other hand, the "school for children" at the church was reasonably successful—with its Sunday morning form, its additional sessions during the week in some churches, perhaps a Sunday evening session, and almost always the vacation church school. Children's "work" (later "ministry") was supported by a network of local church and judicatory people who tended to follow the "party line" by echoing the latest point of view coming out of Nashville, Richmond, Philadelphia, or Indianapolis.

The attempt to define youth as "young laity" and to destroy the "youth organization" was only partly successful, and in many ways disastrous. Churches were usually not willing to accept youth as fully participating laity, and young people were more interested in their own organizations than many adults believed them to be. Para-church groups such as Young Life came into being and attracted some youth. It does not seem unfair to say that youth ministry was in something of a shambles by the 1960s.

Under the influence of the professionals, however, the ideal was that of a "school of the church." The aim was to improve teaching so that persons might be educated into discipleship. Much time, money, and energy were spent in developing curriculum resources, new structures, more professional leadership, and better methods of teaching. Such efforts were understood as being the answer to whatever problems the growing church school movement might still have.

Decline and Confusion

What had begun as a time of great optimism for the mainline churches after World War II, however, became a time of decline and confusion during the 1960s. Statistics for The United Methodist Church are typical: the largest church school enrollment occurred in the early 1960s; by 1968 significant decline was evident, and the decline continued during the following years.[9]

The decline in enrollment coincided with two kinds of dissatisfaction with the church school. On the one hand, there was a growing feeling that teaching was not what it should be—an opinion heralded by Wesley Shrader's often-cited article in *Life* magazine calling the Sunday school "the most wasted hour of the week."[10] Accompanying this belief was a questioning of conventional church structures and the origin of para-church movements as an outgrowth of the academy and small-group movements of the previous decade.[11]

On the other hand, a growing evangelical movement began to question the mainline churches in regard to the theological changes that had occurred in the earlier years of the century.[12] Evangelicals raised questions especially about the curriculum resources produced by the mainline churches. Such criticism was not new, of course; the accusation that there was not enough Bible in such materials had begun more than half a century earlier. Now the criticism came from organized groups, however, and there was an increasing number of nondenominational alternatives from which congregations could choose.

The more conservative groups now spoke from strength, for they continued to grow while the mainline churches began to decline. In 1968, when *Christian Life* magazine compiled its first list of Sunday schools with an average attendance of more than two thousand, only twelve were listed. By 1975 there were thirty-three, and not a single congregation listed was from the mainline denominations.[13]

All of these changes were happening when individuals and groups were protesting against many traditional institutions of society. Even the public school did not remain unaffected, and critics such as Ivan Illich and John Holt questioned whether schooling had prevailed too extensively as the means by which society educates its children.[14] John Westerhoff had raised a similar question concerning the church's school. In his *Values for Tomorrow's Children*, he had startled the world of religious educators by suggesting that the question was no longer *how* the church could provide better schools but rather, How can a reformed church create a new model for church education?[15]

But then the turmoil of the sixties gave way to the apathy of the seventies, and society, including the church, proved more resistant to change than the enthusiasts of the previous decade had thought it to be.

Recent Developments

Jack L. Seymour concludes in his analysis of the American Sunday school movement that the basic identity of congregational Christian education was formed *not* in the progressive, liberal period of the twentieth century but rather in the earlier period when the Sunday school became an institution of the church—a period which he identifies as extending from 1860 to 1900.[16] And Richard T. Murray, while primarily concerned with the adult Sunday school class, maintains that the Sunday school is as much a caring community as it is a learning community. The strength of the Sunday school, he writes, lies in what it does for people "in experiencing the vicissitudes of life *in the presence of* the witness of the Christian faith."[17]

From a somewhat different perspective, John Westerhoff has proposed that the school can no longer be the only model of church education and that Christian education which takes the entire life of the congregation as its context might not require a school at all.[18] Westerhoff, of course, was by no means the first person to recognize and stress the importance of the entire congregation as the context for teaching; what was new was his questioning of the necessity of there being a church *school*.

These three writers, in quite different ways, have raised questions about the ideal model of the church school that developed prior to World War II and continued in the decades that followed. That model, called here the unified church school, understood its aim as educating people into the Christian faith through better teaching, better curriculum resources, and a more adequate following of good educational procedures. Without denying the importance of such developments, it appears that the church school model encouraged the cognitive (ideas, facts, data) without adequately emphasizing the affective (feelings, commitment, values). Even the critics of the Sunday school have centered their criticism on its failure to teach Bible content or on its not being a "real school."

Intergenerational settings were an attempt to recover some of the flavor of the original Sunday school. My own limited experience is that when content was emphasized in such settings, they tended to fail. On the other hand, when the affective was brought to focus—through, for example, worship—they came alive. Other innovations during the recent past have also emphasized learning content or acquiring skills. For example, I have found that the "learning center approach" is an efficient and effective way of teaching content; it provides less opportunity for encouraging commitment and faith. The same evaluation of the use of educational technology such as the computer also seems fair.

The question that must be raised about the emphasis of all such methods and approaches is their appropriateness for *faith* teaching and the function they serve in such education. We are forever looking for the key to better teaching and do not always pause to ask how a particular innovation serves our overall purposes of encouraging a faith response.

The decade of the 1970s was not only a time of innovations in teaching; it was also a time of burgeoning theory concerning the goal, nature, and approach of religious education. This was partly the result of the entry into the field in unprecedented numbers of Roman Catholic educators, with understandings ranging from the social science approach of James Michael Lee[19] to the praxis emphasis of Thomas Groome.[20] Such educators have both drawn from and influenced Protestant religious education and have provided an important resource for rethinking what the church's teaching ministry might become.

An impetus for rethinking the past came in 1980 as the churches celebrated the two hundredth anniversary of Robert Raikes's beginning of the Sunday school movement. As Frank Booth has decisively shown, Raikes did not begin the Sunday school but began the *movement* through his access to the public media.[21]

The distinction between the Sunday school and the *movement* provides a clue to a major difference between the present and the past. The movement, which persisted in mainline churches until well into the present century, included conventions, lay involvement in the overall national and international structures, and other means of helping participants see themselves as part of a larger whole. When the mainline church organized *church* schools—a new institution—much of this enthusiasm tended to be lost. Whether it is possible to recover the enthusiasm of the Sunday school movement—as the conservative churches have done—or whether it is even desirable, is something that the mainline churches need to consider.

An additional trend, more common in the evangelical churches, was the growth of Christian day schools during the 1970s. In reaction to the perceived threat of "secular humanism" in the public schools, many conservative Christians have chosen to send their children to small Christian day schools. What this means for mainline churches, most of which have continued to support public education, is not clear; that it must be considered as part of the total picture, however, seems equally certain.

A Look to the Future

And what of the future? One fact that affects the future is clear in the present: there is a great deal of diversity among lay and professional church educators concerning both theory and practice. Further, there is often little connection between theory and practice. Much of what is tried and often discarded has no clear relationship to what theorists are saying. "Faddism" is a perennial problem for Christian education: encounter groups, simulation games, intergenerational settings, learning centers, values clarification, and a host of other approaches have been tried for a time and then discarded so that the permanent values of such innovations are often lost. What is needed is a more careful planning of the life of the congregation, including its teaching ministry, so that structures and approaches are chosen with greater deliberation, and the old is not discarded for the sake of what might turn out to be nothing more than a gimmick.

In face of diversity, is Westerhoff right that churches need to seek new models for education? Probably—but will such models replace the Sunday church school? Probably not. I believe that the Sunday school will continue, though it will probably continue to be unsure of its identity unless a more inclusive kind of thinking is brought to bear on the life of the congregation.

We need a recovery of the three-part function that developed in the earlier days of the Sunday school: for instruction, for caring, and for evangelism. The mainline churches must recognize that the Sunday school is school *and* movement, that it is both *more than* and *less than* a school. Such recognition need not be in opposition to the search for better teaching. Mainline churches also need to recover something of the mass appeal of the original Sunday school.

Such a change will mean that the Sunday school cannot be considered the only occasion for teaching in the congregation. Larger churches, in fact, may recognize three kinds of teaching: the mass movement of the Sunday school, the socialization that occurs through the entire life of the congregation, and special in-depth teaching of content for a minority. The smaller churches can implement this same approach, provided the pastor recognizes and carries out his or her responsibility as the "teacher in the congregation."

It also seems clear that the churches must make a major thrust toward the family. There is always the danger that the family of a century ago will be romanticized and that those families which carry out the work of Christian nurture today will be forgotten. Without committing either error, however, the church can recognize that the forces causing the breakdown of family life today are too great to be ignored.

Whatever a congregation may do to offer a wider range of teaching, however it may improve what it is now doing, the fact remains that the relatively few hours spent at the church in learning, worship, and other forms of activity are inadequate. They simply cannot offset the influence of mass media and the pressures which such media place, both directly and indirectly, on persons of all ages. Families must recover their sense of mission for both themselves and the world.

Most attempts to work through the family as an "ally" of the church school have failed. There are no clear patterns to follow in building more stable foundations for family life. It is also clear that the family is no longer just a father and a mother and one or more children. The one-parent family is common, and adults of all ages choose the single life. Any effort to build family life foundations must take into account this wider variety of families. Thus there is no easy answer. However, because of the uncertainties, we are all the more responsible.

It is unlikely that the mainline churches will disappear in the wake of growing fundamentalism and more moderate forms of evangelicalism. There is what the church growth people call a "target audience" for the mainline churches—especially those persons in their twenties, thirties, and early forties who were part of the baby boom after World War II. Many of these people were disaffected with the church in the 1960s and are no longer actively associated with organized religion. The Sunday school, modified to appeal to this group but with some of the spirit of its earlier day, can still be an instrument for outreach and caring. I have seen it happen on a small scale; with a concentrated effort I believe it can happen on a larger one. Once such persons are engaged in church life through a caring group, they may be open to more intentional forms of education.

Can we learn from the past? I believe we can as long as we are not slaves to it. The mainline churches are not likely to fulfill their mission by imitating the past, as might be done by groups with a different target audience. Our problem is not that we do not have an audience. It is rather that we have not thus far discovered the means for reaching it or do not use the means we have. The churches must have the commitment and the courage to take risks in the effort to find the proper means required to proclaim and teach the gospel in our time.

Notes

1. For a history of the origins and the growth of the Sunday school, see Frank Booth, *Robert Raikes of Gloucester* (Nutfield, Redhill, Surrey: National Christian Education Council, 1980). For a popular account of the American Sunday school, see Robert W. Lynn and Elliott Wright, *The Big Little School*, rev. ed. (Nashville: Abingdon Press, 1980).

2. For a discussion of this change, see Harrison S. Elliott, *Can Religious Education Be Christian?* (New York: Macmillan, 1940), especially 62.

3. See Dorothy Jean Furnish, *DRE/DCE—The History of a Profession* (Nashville: Christian Educators Fellowship of The United Methodist Church, 1976), for documentation of this development.

4. Elliott, *Can Religious Education Be Christian?*; H. Shelton Smith, *Faith and Nurture* (New York: Charles Scribner's Sons, 1941).

5. Paul H. Vieth, *The Church and Christian Education* (St. Louis: The Bethany Press, 1947). The book grew out of the work of this committee.

6. For an account of this period, see Kendig Brubaker Cully, *The Search for a Christian Education—Since 1940* (Philadelphia: The Westminster Press, 1965).

7. Two sources that describe the movement are John L. Casteel, ed., *Spiritual Renewal Through Groups* (New York: Association Press, 1957) and Robert C. Leslie, *Sharing Groups in the Church* (Nashville: Abingdon Press, 1970, 1971).

8. For an appraisal of such groups, see Thomas C. Oden, *The Intensive Group Experience* (Philadelphia: The Westminster Press, 1972).

9. United Methodist statistics, given by quadrenniums, are found in Warren J. Hartman, *Membership Trends: A Study of Decline and Growth in The United*

Methodist Church 1949–1975 (Nashville: Discipleship Resources, 1976), 30. Statistics for other churches are in *Yearbook of the American* (later *and Canadian*) *Churches*, published since 1973 by Abingdon Press.

10. Wesley Shrader, "Our Troubled Sunday Schools," *Life* 42 (11 February 1957).
11. Cf. Rüdiger Reitz, *The Church in Experiment* (Nashville: Abingdon Press, 1969).
12. See Richard Quebedeaux, *The Young Evangelicals* (New York: Harper & Row, 1974), especially chaps. 2–4.
13. Elmer Towns, *The Successful Sunday School and Teachers Guidebook* (Carol Stream, Ill.: Creation House, 1976), 32-49.
14. Ivan Illich, *Deschooling Society* (New York: Harper & Row, 1971); John Holt, *Freedom and Beyond* (New York: A Delta Book, 1972).
15. John H. Westerhoff III, *Values for Tomorrow's Children* (Philadelphia: Pilgrim Press, 1970), 11.
16. Jack L. Seymour, *From Sunday School to Church School: Continuities in Protestant Church Education, 1860-1929* (Washington D.C.: University Press of America, 1982).
17. Richard T. Murray, *Strengthening the Adult Sunday School Class* (Nashville: Abingdon Press, 1981), 23 [italics added]; see also 24-29.
18. Cf. Westerhoff, *Values for Tomorrow's Children*, esp. chap. 6, and "A Socialization Model," in *A Colloquy on Christian Education*, ed. John H. Westerhoff III (Philadelphia: United Church Press, 1972), chap. 9.
19. See, for example, James Michael Lee's *Flow of Religious Instruction* (Birmingham, Ala.: Religious Education Press, 1973 and later).
20. Thomas H. Groome, *Christian Religious Education* (San Francisco: Harper & Row, 1980). While the publication date is 1980, the book is a culmination of the development of his thinking in the 1970s.
21. Booth, *Robert Raikes of Gloucester*, especially 70-78 and chap. 5. Booth makes it clear that Raikes borrowed the Sunday school from others.

Bibliography

Booth, Frank. *Robert Raikes of Gloucester*. Nutfield, Redhill, Surrey: National Christian Education Council, 1980.

Cully, Kendig Brubaker. *The Search for a Christian Education—Since 1940*. Philadelphia: The Westminster Press, 1965.

Groome, Thomas H. *Christian Religious Education: Sharing Our Story and Vision*. San Francisco: Harper & Row, 1980.

Lynn, Robert W., and Elliott Wright. *The Big Little School: Two Hundred Years of the Sunday School*. Rev. ed. Birmingham, Ala.: Religious Education Press and Nashville: Abingdon Press, 1980.

Murray, Richard T. *Strengthening the Adult Sunday School Class*. Nashville: Abingdon Press, 1981.

Seymour, Jack. *From Sunday School to Church School: Continuities in Protestant Church Education, 1860–1929*. Washington, D.C.: University Press of America, 1982.

Westerhoff, John H. III, ed. *The Quest for a Religious Education*. Birmingham, Ala.: Religious Education Press, 1978.

CHAPTER 9

The Practice of Evangelical Christian Education Since World War II

Clifford V. Anderson

Who is an evangelical? One historian remarked that "evangelicalism is a battle-torn flag that has waved over many different Protestant encampments since the reformation."[1] The term has been utilized in the official names of denominations and in titles of associations of churches and individuals.[2] Within more pluralistic denominations there are churches and individuals that are classified as evangelical. Bernard Ramm suggests that "in the most general sense, evangelical Christianity refers to that version of Christianity which places the priority of the Word and Act of God over the faith, response, or experiences of men."[3] More specifically, Christian beliefs like the sovereignty of God, divine authority of Scripture, total depravity of man, substitutionary atonement, salvation by grace, faith alone, primacy of proclamation, scriptural holiness, the church's spiritual mission, and the personal return of Christ have been identified as hallmarks of evangelicalism.[4] Throughout the history of the church there have been Christians who have held to a core of evangelical belief. The use of the term *evangelical* became prominent after the Reformation when the evangel or gospel was emphasized as a distinctive. Pietists, Nonconformists such as Methodists and Baptists in England, and the churches that were touched and planted as a result of the Great Awakening in America were in this evangelical tradition. Within the Church of England there were influential lay and clerical leaders known as evangelicals who stressed conversion, strict morals, a life of active service to others, and simplicity in worship.[5]

Evangelicalism has stressed the authentic in religion. Its life of devotion, missionary zeal, social concern, and evangelism has burst into flame from time to time in the older churches and in new communities of faith. Evangelicals believe the Bible is the authoritative revelation of God and that faith and conduct should

Clifford V. Anderson is Professor of Christian Education and Dean of the West Campus (San Diego, California) of Bethel Theological Seminary.

be shaped by the guidance it provides. We sorrowfully confess that we do not adequately live in the power of the Spirit of Christ, pray in the confidence that God hears and answers according to his will, or work as committed followers of the Way. But we rejoice in the gospel and in God's action on man's behalf and recognize that God is at work in the believer and in the world.

The Setting for Evangelical Christian Education

In the years following the Second World War, the long-standing trend of church membership growing at a faster pace than that of the United States population continued. Estimates of percentage of church membership in the population of the nation climbed from 6.9 percent in 1800 to 15.5 in 1850, 35.7 in 1900, 47.1 in 1940, and 57 percent in 1950.[6] The Gallup Poll has stated that church and synagogue attendance reached an all-time high in 1955 with 49 percent of adults eighteen years of age or more in church weekly. By 1979 this figure had declined to 40 percent.[7] Church growth is in part linked to concern for outreach and commitment. Hence, evangelical churches were well represented in new church starts. Minority-group Christianity is largely of the evangelical type, and growth among minorities due to immigration and birth rate contributed to the numbers. What had been a little-understood element in the more recent past became widely known through evangelical heads of state, media reports of mass evangelism, and effective outreach efforts and ministries of local evangelical churches and para-parochial organizations.

Following the war there was an advance in world missions and world relief efforts. Some veterans prepared themselves to return as missionary soldiers of the cross. Churches contributed to the needy overseas, and the nation through the Marshall Plan and other relief efforts greatly assisted in the recovery of war-torn peoples, especially in Europe. Seminary enrollment climbed with the G.I. bill funding students in theological education. Urban development witnessed the flight of white churches from the central cities to suburban neighborhoods and the planting of new churches where growth was promising and rapid self-support assured.

Whether or not the success of the churches in bringing larger numbers of people into their constituencies was paralleled by growth in knowledge of and commitment to the Lord is not known. We do, however, note the way in which religious faith was viewed positively, and with this view came the full flowering of civil religion. It became good business to be religious—to a point. Prayer was offered at political rallies, sporting events, and community clubs. While often watered down theologically to cause the least offense, religion—especially Christianity—became more popular. As Americans witnessed the Korean War, the Eisenhower period, the civil rights movement, and the Vietnam War, evangelicalism became more prominent. Prayer breakfasts in Washington, D.C., and in state capitals became almost common. Born-again legislators and sports heroes were publicized through the media. Finally a born-again president who regularly taught a Sunday school class came to office. It was the time of the evangelical as the nation celebrated its bicentennial. Eventually a large proportion of the populace, greater than church membership, claimed to be born again. The term was picked up by the general public and "born again" came to mean much more and far less than what Jesus spoke of as reported in John's Gospel. Evangelicals and others pointed out that if evangelicals were such a large proportion of the population, why were crime, immorality, and poverty so great? Perhaps distinguishing between authentic maturing faith and mere self-centered institutional religious affiliation provides an explanation for the lack of life-transforming power in the lives of many adherents of religion. Large numbers of North Americans have been exposed to the evangelical message but lack understanding and appropriation of the action of God in Christ reconciling the world to himself.

Education in the Churches

Evangelical churches are, of course, similar to other churches. There is no distinctive architecture or liturgy. Schedules are not greatly different except that the evangelical church may have more activities during a typical week. Giving on a regular basis will probably be higher per member in an evangelical church. Outreach efforts at home and abroad are also likely to be heightened.

A closer look does show a difference in the area of *objectives* of the Christian education ministry. Conversion and Bible knowledge are highly visible goals in the evangelical church. Many Sunday school classes and clubs, as well as church services, provide opportunities to receive Christ as personal Savior and Lord. Individuals are helped to see their need for salvation and how God in his great love has provided for our salvation through the person and work of Christ. The inquirer is counseled to pray to receive Christ and is usually given literature and guided into classes or relationships that encourage growth. Some churches have carefully developed discipleship programs that lead converts through first steps in growth and encourage them to share their Christian witness with others. Christian life and attitudinal development, church tradition and membership involvement, and Christian outreach are also important but do not find as widespread acceptance as do the new life and Bible understanding. Outreach is primarily focused upon evangelism and missions, but a growing number of evangelicals are sensitive to social concern ministries as part of outreach.

That there is no uniform pattern among evangelicals becomes abundantly clear when the socially active and prophetic evangelical is contrasted with the quietist or the personal ethic issue activist. Evangelicals differ on issues of political involvement; nuclear weapons control; role of women in ministry; sexual, racial, and economic liberation; and biomedical procedures. There are also differences in our views toward the age of the earth and the method by which God the Creator brought the universe into existence. An issue that is peripheral to some assumes great importance to others. In this sense there is diversity among evangelicals.

The Bible is prominent in the teaching program of the church. Whatever the curriculum materials used, the Bible is the textbook. It is used both as a starting point and as a resource to which students turn for guidance. Both functional and factual use of the Bible are employed with a growing awareness of the need to relate Bible teachings to the situation of the learner. Psychology and pedagogy contribute to the shaping of learning experiences. Perhaps the greatest strides have taken place in early childhood and adult education in recent years. Learning process, values education, and stages of growth find expression in curriculum and teacher development.

While the Bible is the source for virtually all Sunday school lessons, devotional input in other agencies, and preaching, there is not a carefully developed curriculum plan that embraces all the agencies of education. Overlaps and omissions in Bible coverage exist, but for the most part the major themes of the Bible are taught in a spiral pattern so individuals progressing in age and experience will review and deepen their exposure to biblical truth. Bible memorization is not promoted with the enthusiasm it was in the early part of the period under review. This is due, in part, to the variety of Bible versions that are used in evangelical churches. It is no longer true that the King James Version is *the* approved version in evangelical churches. Implicit in the evangelical educational program is the notion that the student become a lifelong Bible reader. In actuality, this ideal is only partially achieved since many laypeople appear to develop dependence upon their pastor-teachers for their understanding of Scripture.

The application of Bible truth to personal and community life is increasingly sought. Interest in the utility of biblical teaching for practical life has risen. Unfortunately, this interest sometimes is limited to a personal healing and wholeness kind of appropriation of truth. Evangelism and discipleship are viewed as critically important responses to the gospel. Social concern applications are evident in the history of evangelicalism, contemporary church ministries, and in current literature. In practice, many evangelicals, like others, have privatized and domesticated their faith. Evangelicals believe they possess the truth. They are sometimes aware that the truth does not possess them.

The evangelical church provides worship, proclamation, teaching, fellowship, service, and witness experiences for its people. The extent of these experiences in the *life curriculum* of the church varies with the strength and emphasis of the church. Sunday opportunities are certain to include proclamation and teaching. Evangelical churches meet for worship, fellowship, and instruction around the Word of God. The Sunday school is found in nearly all churches except for the very few that merge instruction with worship in an all-church family time.[8] Within the Sunday school, children and youth are grouped in age level classes, departments, and divisions. Adults may be classified by interest or some combination of age fellowship groups. Curriculum materials are probably provided through a nondenominational evangelical publisher except where denominational curriculum provides a historic reformation or evangelical orientation. The usual organization pattern of Sunday school officers is in use, except in some of the larger churches where professional age level staff guide the program. Teacher training materials are utilized, but the effectiveness of planning and training varies greatly. Some educational programs are guided by an effectively functioning staff that meets regularly in workers' conferences. Other workers have little or no training and few opportunities to interact about their common task of teaching. There has been some success in recruiting men to serve in early childhood and children's divisions of the Sunday school.

The evangelical church will likely provide worship time activities for the younger learners. This sometimes takes the form of an extended session of the Sunday school lesson but more often is an unrelated children's church time that features Bible stories with life applications and activities that interest the child. Home living and nature centers are no longer unusual in early childhood rooms of the church.

A decline in youth fellowship programs has occurred. There is less emphasis on expression and training and more on involving youth in outreach with planning and program operation assumed by paid youth ministers. Previously, planning was a joint effort by youth with lay sponsors.

Youth group ministry sometimes occurs on Sunday evenings but more frequently is scheduled during the week. Community agencies, such as scouting and the YMCA and YWCA, changed or reinterpreted their religious objectives in order to serve a broader public. Avowedly evangelical club programs, including Christian Service Brigade (1937), Awana Youth Association (1945), and Pioneer Clubs (1939), replaced them in many areas. Some denominations developed distinctive programs for children and youth in their churches. Learning opportunities for all age levels are found between Sundays. They may take the form of the traditional midweek prayer and Bible study time or some combination of children's clubs, adult Bible studies, and youth nights.

Special learning opportunities include vacation Bible schools. Lack of volunteer workers and competition from community events have had an impact on VBS; and where leadership and vision are lacking, this opportunity for additional teaching is lost. Camps and retreats are available to children, youth, and adults of most evangelical churches. Some churches offer day care for young children, pastor's instruction classes for older children, a wide range of youth activities, graded music groups, athletic competition, Bible study programs, parenting classes, men's and women's organizations, senior citizen functions, singles' groups, and formal Bible institute-type classes conducted at the church. Church libraries range from nonexistent to filled with unusually helpful collections that have heavy circulation.

Evangelicals are aware of the breakdown of the family and are responsive to books, seminars, and classes that strengthen the *Christian home*. The struggle to offset the challenge of worldliness is very real in evangelical churches. While attitudes have changed and greater freedom is permitted, there is an uneasy awareness of non-Christian influences that sometimes results in guidance—resembling legalism—out of concern for a proper environment for

Christian growth. There is a suspicion that excessive church-sponsored peer activities can weaken the family. Premarital counseling is offered by many churches. Growing divorce rates in the wider community are paralleled in the evangelical church, though to a lesser degree.

Parents are expecting more from the church and are organizing Christian day schools in efforts to compensate for perceived weaknesses in public schools and in the home. Busy schedules, with both parents working to meet expenses, contribute to the loss of cohesion and tradition in some homes and impinge upon the time available for volunteer work in the churches. Day care centers are available in many communities as a ministry to working parents of preschoolers.

Some churches are developing "church as family" life-styles to provide singles and the aged as well as nuclear families with quality Christian experiences of worship, instruction, and fellowship. A fairly wide range of experimentation is occurring in some evangelical churches with the purpose of strengthening the Christian home. Intergenerational learning groups are not uncommon.

Facilities have changed from the assembly hall with small classrooms surrounding it to larger rooms that are useful for a variety of purposes. Recent architecture represents both functional and aesthetic considerations. Homes throughout the community are being used for midweek Bible study and growth groups and for backyard Bible schools in the vacation periods. Curriculum publishers make available literature on facility usage and development. Some denominations offer assistance in planning to churches that are adding or upgrading facilities.

Methods of instruction vary from the lecture method to discussion, small-group processes, visuals, drama, role playing, tapes, and most of the other techniques used by all educators. There is a growing practice of learning through doing without a full appreciation of the philosophy or rationale behind the method. A pragmatic approach is practiced. In many churches the lecture is enhanced by the use of the overhead projector. Learning activities help guide growth in understanding, appreciation, and skills, especially among children and youth. The Sunday school opening assembly time has often been eliminated in favor of total session teaching, giving teachers more time to involve students in self-discovery of Bible truth. There is some understanding that the language of learning includes relationships and not just words.

Theology is confessional but also relational in both content and process.

Greatly improved films with an evangelical orientation have been produced for use in churches and in neighborhood theaters. Telecommunication technology is coming as seen in Baptist TelNet, in which programs presented from Nashville will be received by a television receiver dish at the church or association site and viewed live in church instruction or recorded by a videotape recorder for later use.[9]

While *Sunday school* enrollment reflects broader demographic shifts, there has been rapid growth followed by plateaus and dropoffs in many evangelical churches. The science of church growth, while increasing in its acceptance, has not yet matched the results obtained in earlier days by community canvassing, busing, guest events, and friendship evangelism that brought a procession of new prospects into the churches. Today there are some rapidly growing Sunday schools in which pastoral and lay leadership give impetus and training to member-ministers who aggressively reach out to their community. On the other hand, there are churches with improved worship, preaching, training, curriculum resources, and facilities that have declining enrollments. Qualitative improvements have not always resulted in quantitative increases.

Southern Baptists are an evangelical fellowship of churches that are not a member group in the National Association of Evangelicals. They number over 36,079 churches, varying in size from a membership of two to 22,732. They are the nation's largest evangelical denomination and have a total membership of over 13 million baptized believers with 7.5 million enrolled in Sunday school. They have developed a strong Sunday school organization which is their vehicle for church growth. They expect to have 8.5 million enrolled in Bible study by 1985, and they are ahead of schedule.[10]

An explosion of interest in Christian education occurred in the decades following the Second World War. Growth in resources, enrollment, facilities, training, and supporting evangelical agencies was dramatic. The churches now had upgraded evangelical literature, girls' and boys' clubs, camping and retreat programs, and para-parochial organizations to draw upon and to supplement their ministry in the wider community. Seminar leaders crisscrossed the country with specialty helps on youth, family, teaching, and Bible content. Sunday school associations took on new life. Evangelical education responded to needs in the churches and community.

Related Evangelical Organizations

An array of church-related organizations serving the Christian cause developed immediately before and following the Second World War. Much earlier, evangelical Christians started home and foreign missionary associations, Sunday schools (1780), the YMCA (1844), temperance societies, and benevolent organizations such as schools and colleges, hospitals, homes for the aged and the orphaned, and rescue missions for the poor and the chemically dependent. It seems that the truly converted and enlightened person reaches out to share the good news and at times is led to form voluntary associations to help meet critical needs.

As the Sunday school movement expanded, there were needs for better curriculum outlines and leadership training. Over a century ago the uniform lesson series and a program for the training of teachers were implemented. The David C. Cook Publishing Company (1875), Scripture Press Publications (1934), and Gospel Light Publications (1933) are among the well-known nondenominational *curriculum publishers* for evangelical churches. An examination of the materials shows that biblical, graded, sequenced, and balanced content are presented in an attractive format.

Supporting the *leadership training* programs of the evangelical churches are denominational services, the Sunday school associations, the Evangelical Teacher Training Association, and the International Center for Learning. The largest Sunday school associations are now located in Detroit, Los Angeles, and Chicago. There are many smaller associations that are virtually unknown except at local levels. The National Sunday School Association was founded in 1945. It concluded its work in 1975. The strength of some of its area associations made funding and focus for the mother organization difficult. The Evangelical Teacher Training Association was founded in 1930 out of a concern for upgrading and certifying teachers in the local church. It publishes courses of study and seeks to certify faculty for local church and community training efforts. Over two hundred colleges and seminaries are members of ETTA. The International Center for Learning was founded in 1970 and has trained over 100,000 teachers in age division, administration, and special interest seminars. These seminars are conducted in strategically located cities in the United States and Canada. They are staffed by trained persons involved in Sunday school work who both model teaching skills and structure an intensive learning experience for participants. These six-to-twelve-hour seminars have ministered to persons from a variety of denominational backgrounds.

Training is conducted by the larger denominations in districts or in connection with annual meetings and, in the case of Southern Baptists, at highly developed learning centers at Ridgecrest, North Carolina, and Glorieta, New Mexico. Denominational resource persons are available for church consultation.

The youth clubs also offer training for leaders in their work. These opportunities often take the form of a class conducted by a staff member of the organization in the local church that offers the program. Regional conventions for church youth workers are ecumenical in composition.

A remarkable development of *Christian schools* has occurred in recent years. This growth may be traced to further loss of confidence in the environment of the public school, ethical relativism, sense of an increasing loss of discipline in the classroom, declining scores in achievement tests, and the secular orientation of some teachers and classroom resources. Neighborhood changes in socio-economic and racial composition contributed to the formation of some schools.

One out of every nine American school children attends a private school. Eighty-four percent of these are in religiously affiliated schools (4.2 million pupils). Catholic schools enroll 3.2 million students or 63 percent of the private school total.[11] About 1 percent of all school children are in evangelical schools.[12] The Association for Christian Schools International (La Habra, California) grew from 1,051 schools with 185,687 students in 1978–79 to 1,728 schools with 320,950 students in 1981–82. Christian Schools International (Grand Rapids, Michigan) estimate their current growth at 2 to 3 percent a year. The American Association of Christian Schools (Normal, Illinois) grew from 125 schools with 25,000 students and staff in 1972–73 to 1,078 schools and 170,000 students and staff in 1982.[13]

Evangelical Christians have, despite some fear of higher learning, given serious attention to the *higher education* of youth and church leadership. Many of our oldest universities had the training of biblically sound leadership for the churches primary in their founding charters. At the present time, there are about one hundred evangelical liberal arts colleges. Sixty-eight are members of the Christian College Coalition, and thirteen are also members of the Christian College Consortium. In addition, there are about 125 Bible colleges related to the American Association of Bible Colleges. These range from smaller schools with limited resources to institutions that are large and strong in faculty, library, facility, and support resources. There are about sixty seminaries represented in the Evangelical Seminary Presidents Fellowship. About two-thirds of all Protestant theological students in the United States are enrolled in evangelical seminaries.[14]

There are several *professional groups* that serve the evangelical community. The Evangelical Theological Society, founded in 1949, is a two-thousand-member fellowship of evangelical teachers and scholars. The purpose of the group is to foster conservative biblical scholarship by providing a medium for oral exchange and written expression of research in the theological fields. The *Journal of the Evangelical Theological Society* is in its twenty-fifth year of publication and has a circulation of 2,400. *The Christian Scholars Review* is sponsored by thirty evangelical colleges. Its articles seek to relate the Christian faith to all fields of arts and sciences.

The National Association of Professors of Christian Education (1971), formerly the Research Commission of the National Sunday School Association, provides fellowship and communication among evangelical teachers in the field of Christian education. It has about one hundred teachers in its membership. The National Association of Directors of Christian Education has about four hundred members. *Infocus* is its communication vehicle. Annual meetings, often held in connection with the NAPCE or another organization, provide information and fellowship for members. The recently formed National Christian Education Association is an attempt to rebuild an organization like the earlier NSSA by the National Association of Evangelicals.[15] Christian Camping International (1963) serves the camping industry. With 750 camps and conference centers in its U.S. membership and seven other divisions worldwide, it offers regional and international conventions that provide training and communication among members. It publishes the *Journal of Christian Camping*. Its Foundations for Excellence certification program has helped member camps meet professional standards in their operation.[16]

Evangelical seminaries and colleges have established Christian education departments that have benefited from the substantial growth in evangelical schools. An increasing number of male graduates serve as ministers of Christian education or age group directors within larger churches. Women continue to minister at all age levels but are usually related to children, youth, or family ministries in the local church. Perhaps in no other area has the evangelical impulse found greater expression than in the *para-parochial* ministry organizations. The Navigators, Inter-

Varsity Christian Fellowship, Young Life, Youth for Christ, and Campus Crusade have fired the imaginations of young adults for evangelism and discipleship.

Founded in 1941, Young Life has emphasized incarnational evangelism in its weekly club meetings, contact work by staff among high schoolers, and summer camps at several locations. They emphasize teaching the person and work of Christ. They receive support from persons representing many denominations. The staff is provided with basic theological training, primarily at a summer institute in Michigan that was established in the mid-1950s in Colorado. While they are committed evangelicals, they are broadly ecumenical in their relationships.

Youth for Christ originated in Chicago in 1944 with youth gathering on Saturday nights for evangelistic rallies. The rally provided a common meeting place for youth from various church backgrounds to which they brought their friends. In time the rally was succeeded by weekly club meetings, lifeline camps, and special programs that included disadvantaged youth. *Campus Life*, its magazine for adolescent Christian education, has a circulation of 250,000.

The Navigators (1933) have had an extensive ministry with service personnel during and following the Second World War. They continue to work with young adults in both military and civilian settings. Their Scripture memorization and discipleship programs are conducted in one-to-one or small-group settings. They have developed discipleship programs to assist local churches.

Inter-Varsity Christian Fellowship of America (1941) is widely recognized for its triennial missionary conventions at the University of Illinois at Urbana. About seventeen thousand persons attend. At the local level Bible study, retreat, and interpersonal witness and nurture programs are focused upon colleges and professional schools. Inter Varsity Press provides high-quality study materials for thinking Christians and serious seekers. *His* (1941), its magazine, has a circulation of more than thirty thousand.

Campus Crusade for Christ began in 1951. It has attracted wide interest and has grown rapidly. Known for its religious surveys, four spiritual laws, and effective training, it has initiated aggressive evangelism with follow-up discipleship programs on campuses and in communities around the world. Recent developments include a graduate school of theology, plans for a university, and consultant services to churches.

Child Evangelism Fellowship provides programs and training for evangelistic work among children. Staff and volunteers work through homes and churches in reaching children in a wide variety of communities in our nation and around the world.

These para-parochial organizations have brought vigor, training, and clarity of thought for outreach to the churches.

The Wider Evangelical Influences

Radio and television have become attractive fields for evangelical initiative. Presently there are 1,400 religious radio stations, 35 religious television stations, and four religious television networks. The general consensus is that these ministries are especially significant to the elderly, infirm, and handicapped. The "electronic church" has helped some listeners toward greater involvement in a local church.[17]

Evangelicals are also served by *periodicals and books*. Leading evangelical publications include the *Journal of the Evangelical Theological Society, The Reformed Journal, Bibliotheca Sacra, Westminster Theological Journal, Christian Scholars Review,* and *Review and Expositor*. More popular magazines are *Christianity Today* (established 1956; circulation 180,000), *Eternity* (1931; 51,637), *Moody Monthly* (1900; 280,000), and *Christian Life* (1939; 95,000). Denominations provide a variety of periodicals to inform and guide their membership.

Zondervan, Eerdmans, Baker, Regal (Gospel Light), Tyndale, Fleming H. Revell, Broadman, Word, Victor (Scripture Press), and David C. Cook are among well-known evangelical publishers. Other publishers also provide evangelical resources. Many denominations publish educational resources that are evangelical.

Revenues from religious book sales totaled nearly $269 million in 1977. In 1981, the projection was to realize $350 million. Religious radio and television revenues reached $675 million, magazine revenues were $40 million, and record and tape sales were $33 million in 1977.[18] In the very recent past, revenue has reached a plateau, and, in the case of broadcasting, declined.

The Basic Youth Conflicts, Youth Specialties, Walk Through the Bible, International Center for Learning, and Focus on the Family *seminars* are among the more well-known opportunities that are presented in urban communities. Some are available on film for greater exposure to the Christian public. The Women's Bible Study Fellowship has brought an ecumenical evangelical emphasis to many communities. Christian Women's Club, Christian

Businessmen's Association, Gideons, and other evangelical organizations provide interchurch fellowship and outlets for service.

The citywide *evangelistic crusades* conducted in recent years by the Billy Graham Evangelistic Association team, together with similar efforts by the Luis Palau team and others, have provided a platform for cooperative evangelism. Evangelical Christians from different theological, social, and economic backgrounds have met together for planning, prayer, training, and service. Church members are strengthened and converts assisted into the life of the churches. Films and television broadcasts have added to the impact of these evangelistic efforts. Local church campaigns with guest evangelists or Bible teachers are declining. Friendship evangelism and lay outreach teams receive growing emphasis in the churches.

Compassion, World Vision, World Impact, NAE (National Association of Evangelicals) World Relief, and Food for the Hungry are highly visible ministries of relief to depressed and disaster areas of the world. The Seminary Consortium for Urban Pastoral Education, located in Chicago, is an evangelically oriented program, preparing seminarians to understand and minister in the cities.

Evangelical Christian education takes place in the home, church, and wider community. A richly varied and potentially effective environment for growth is available to learners of every age. The old story of Jesus and his love still commands attention and elicits response when it is presented with clarity, concern, and under the influence of the Spirit of Christ. The evangelical seeks with heart and mind to serve the Lord and the world that is so loved by God.

Evangelicals need to struggle anew with the meaning of being in but not of the world. We risk losing our distinctives of conversion and Bible application as we take on the values of our culture. We stumble as we exchange spiritual power for programs, responding to God's Word for debating our loyalty to it, and concern about lost mankind for church games. We are content to teach with words and reluctant to act as Christians. We build walls to maintain our spiritual heritage only to find the glory has departed and walls alone remain.

As we draw near to God, he will draw near to us. From that renewing encounter we dare to go to a world in need and respond with good news and good deeds.

Notes

1. Sydney E. Ahlstrom, "From Puritanism to Evangelicalism: A Critical Appraisal," in *The Evangelicals*, ed. David F. Wells and John D. Woodbridge (Nashville: Abingdon Press, 1975), 269.

2. Evangelical Lutheran, Evangelical Mission Covenant, Evangelical Alliance, and National Association of Evangelicals are examples.

3. Bernard Ramm, *The Evangelical Heritage* (Waco, Tex.: Word, 1973), 13.

4. Donald G. Bloesch, *The Evangelical Renaissance* (Grand Rapids: Wm. B. Eerdmans Publishing Co., 1973), 48-49. Other but similar lists of distinctives are found in John Gerstner's chapter "The Theological Boundaries of Evangelical Faith" in *The Evangelicals* (see n. 1); Millard Erickson, *The New Evangelical Theology* (Westwood, N.J.: Fleming H. Revell Co., 1968); and *The Orthodox Evangelicals*, ed. Robert E. Webber and Donald Bloesch (Nashville: Thomas Nelson, 1978).

5. Kenneth Scott Latourette, *A History of Christianity* (New York: Harper & Brothers, 1953), 1030.

6. Ibid., 1410-11.

7. *Yearbook of American and Canadian Churches—1981* (Nashville: Abingdon Press, 1981), 266.

8. Traditional, renewal, and aggressive approaches to evangelical Sunday schools are presented by Sherman Williams, Gene Getz, and Elmer Towns in the *Journal of Christian Education* 3: 10-36. This biannual journal is published by Scripture Press Ministries.

9. Grady C. Cothen, "Cogitating on Communicating," *Facts and Trends* 26 (June 1982): 2, The Sunday School Board of the Southern Baptist Convention.

10. James Lowry, "Average Church Portrayed," *Facts and Trends* 26 (June 1982): 1, The Sunday School Board of the Southern Baptist Convention. Also see 3, 6, and 7.

11. "Counting Noses: Who Goes to Private School in the U.S.?" *San Diego Tribune* (18 June 1982): A-29. Charles Kniker, "Changing Perceptions: Religion in the Public Schools," *Religious Education* 77 (May-June 1982): 251-68, reviews the relationship of religion to public schools and addresses the rapid development of Christian day schools.

12. George Van Alstine, "The Christian and Public Schools," *The Standard* 72 (June 1982): 38. Van Alstine's book by the same title was published by Abingdon Press in 1982. Long-standing efforts to provide financial assistance to parents who choose a private school for their child are increasing. Some evangelicals are turning away from traditional opposition to public support of private education in their search for relief from "double taxation." Others support the freedom to provide private schools, but without using public tax funds to assist these schools and/or the children enrolled in them or the parents who must bear the costs.

13. Gerald B. Carlson, "Christian School Growth Continues," *AACS Christian School Communicator* 2, no. 6: 1 and letter dated 28 May 1982.

14. Interview with Dr. Carl H. Lundquist, president of the Christian College Consortium and convenor of the Evangelical Seminary Presidents Fellowship, St. Paul, Minn., 3 September 1982.

15. Mark H. Senter, "Christian Education: Analysis and Proposal," *Infocus* 4 (Spring-Summer 1982): 11.

16. Christian Camping International, *Guide to Christian Camps* (Carol Stream, Ill.: C.C.I., 1981), 13.

17. George Gallup, "Many Say TV Religion Spurs Local Worship," *Minneapolis Tribune* (30 January 1981): B-9.

18. Interview with C. E. Ted Andrew, Executive Director, Evangelical Christian Publishers Association, 17 September 1982.

CHAPTER 10

Protestant Religious Education in Canada

Doris Jean Dyke

In a certain isolated village, there were delight and gratitude among the people when the telephone operator added to her responsibilities that of giving the time of day. Previously the only reliable source of the correct time had been the large town-hall clock, and of course the townspeople still checked their watches by it when they had occasion to be on Main Street. During the rest of the week, it was reassuring to know that the correct time was immediately and graciously provided by the telephone operator. Although there were several calls each day asking for the time, the operator was aware that one request came in daily at five o'clock.

As time went on, however, some of the townspeople who had been to other places returned and challenged the accuracy of the town-hall clock. The custodian of the clock would not listen to any such charge because, he told them, he checked the time every day at five o'clock with the telephone operator. When the same people challenged the telephone operator's time, she dismissed any possibility of inaccuracy. She could see the town-hall clock from her window, she pointed out, and it was from this reliable source that she derived and maintained the correct time.

The foregoing story symbolizes the way the relationship between the church and the school was formed in the mid-nineteenth century in regard to religious education. The Protestant churches and the schools came to depend on each other in such a manner that they reinforced each other's high defenses against any form of criticism. The interpretation that has been given to religious education as the outcome of this coalition between church and school can be seen in both institutions.

The fact that the same term, *religious education,* is used in both institutions is worthy of critical consideration. Any understanding of the relationship between religion and education may be severely

Doris Jean Dyke is Professor of Christian Education at Emmanuel College of Victoria University, Toronto.

144

limited by the fact that the expression *religious education* clearly connotes a purpose to be achieved by education for religious ends. *Religious* modifies *education* both grammatically and functionally. If we had recognized the possibility of an alternate relationship wherein the emphasis was on education for its own sake, we might have approached an understanding of religion and education that would be appropriate for the schools. Education is used to inculcate religion, surely appropriate for the church and clearly connoted in its use of the term *religious education*. The schools, on the other hand, require a theological understanding of education which would not only take account of specific religious phenomena such as the Bible, religious elements, and Sacred Scriptures of other traditions within the curricular fields of history, literature, music, and art; but also would have encouraged the student to see the appropriate religious questions which are evoked by the entire educational enterprise. Any activity that is carried on in the classroom ought to be justified on educational grounds. Although in most of its provinces during the twentieth century Canada has had some form of multiple establishment rather than disestablishment as in the United States, in the latter part of the twentieth century the symbiotic relationship between church, school, and home has broken down.

Historical Background in the United States and Canada

From the beginning of the Puritan settlement in New England, religious enthusiasm was the *raison d'être* for the schools. While the totality of the educational picture in the colonial period was but a frontier version of the situation in England, religious fervor had begun to wane long before the colonies became independent. Of the colonial period, Ellwood Cubberly wrote that it was "essentially a period of transplanting, during which little or no attempt at adaptation or change was made."[1] While historians disagree as to how clear-cut the motivation in education was for the colonist,[2] certainly the religious motif was predominant in the curriculum materials of that period. Samuel Morison argued that the Puritans were not narrowly interested in preserving orthodoxy, but were seeking to achieve "the ideal of transmitting a civilization."[3] He insisted that Harvard was "founded for the advancement of learning in the broadest sense of that word."[4] The education of ministers may have been the immediate purpose, and the fear of an illiterate clergy no doubt was the dynamic motivation in founding Harvard, but the "advancement and perpetuation of learning were the ultimate objectives of the foundation."[5] The main reason for founding the college was to advance the life of the mind so that the people would not lapse into barbarism. The clergy was a significant means of transmitting a culture; therefore, it was imperative not to leave an illiterate clergy to the churches.[6] Perhaps in the colonial period the preservation of orthodoxy was so interpenetrated with the transmission of culture that they were indistinguishable as separate motives.

When Canada became British in 1763, the population was largely Roman Catholic. In guaranteeing the French population the right to practice its own religion, the control of education was included. As the Roman Catholic archbishop of St. Boniface pointed out during the establishment of the school system in the Canadian West:

A Catholic population does not enjoy full religious freedom when impeded from having schools in accordance with their own ideas or convictions. This was well known to the Governor General of Canada when he promised respect and attention for our religious persuasions, when he assured the Catholics that their religious rights and privileges would be respected. It would have been a mockery to add that there would be no protection for Catholic schools.[7]

While some historians say that "equal rights dictated that non-Romanists should have similar advantages,"[8] it is more to the point to realize that the Church of England fully intended to establish itself as a state church and to control education.[9]

The Founding Fathers of the United States could not have imagined the dimensions of the controversy and confusion which ensued from their concise and crisp statement forbidding Congress "to make any law respecting an establishment of religion, or prohibiting the free exercise thereof."[10] The crucial role that Jefferson saw for education in a free society necessitated a complete divorce of the civil from the ecclesiastical in public affairs. "The liberty Jefferson championed was at bottom the freedom to believe and he found the most critical restrictions on that freedom to be traceable to the policies and practices of one or another church, especially as churches and states maintained alliances."[11]

In Canada, however, political leaders chose to harness religion and make it a unifying instrument for social and political ends. The War of 1812-14 was viewed with some consternation, and in 1819 the Lieutenant-Governor said, "To restore the Province to real tranquility, and to render it truly English, our principal attention must be paid to the religious education of the people."[12] The Anglican Bishop Strachan provides a clear hierarchy for the values which he determined should be inculcated in the schools. "Children should be taught to understand and admire the beneficence of their Creator in the works of His hand, to feel that they are immortal and accountable beings, that Christian virtue is the first distinction among men, and that useful knowledge is the second."[13]

Jefferson's point, on the other hand, was that human liberties were God-given attributes, and frustration of their fullest expression would be tantamount to opposing the will of God.[14] It was not inconsistent with this thinking that exclusive efficacy could be attributed to education. Jefferson's well-known statement makes this point clear. "Enlighten the people generally, and tyranny and oppression of the body and mind will vanish like evil spirits at the dawn of day."[15] The human liberty inherent in a free society was viewed as God's will and could be ensured only by education.

Horace Mann's vision of the common school as the instrument which would fashion a new America out of the many conflicting traditions included a moral consideration of the highest order. In seeking out the moral foundations of an educational system in a religiously diverse society, Mann faced the issues that still plague the public school. Since he considered morality as the ultimate purpose of the school, he sought a common core of religious doctrine which would incorporate the variety of sectarian creeds. "The fact that this new corpus of knowledge closely resembled his own optimistic, humanistic Unitarianism did not seem to trouble him."[16]

If it was not apparent to Horace Mann, it has been apparent now for some time that the Bible cannot be read in the public schools merely on the basis of private interpretation. Although private interpretation of the Bible is an inaccurate representation of the Protestant doctrine of the priesthood of all believers, belief in the efficacy of Bible reading without comment is based on a Protestant understanding of the Bible. The Protestant presuppositions regarding Mann's suggested use of the Bible have not always been clear to non–Roman Catholics.

Mann argued that morality and religion are inseparable. Cremin indicated that Mann's clue to this problem was that "morals can be taught outside of their historic context in particular religious doctrines."[17] Both Lawrence Cremin and Neil McCluskey made the point that in order to have the common school, it is necessary to compromise on the historic doctrines of religion.[18] Historically Cremin was accurate in pointing out that in the rise of the common school as fashioned by Mann, it was clear "for the first time that moral education could be given outside the context of the sectarian religious beliefs of a given denominational faith."[19] Mann did not, however, try to separate morality from religion, and in his effort to locate religion within education as only a foundation for morality, he failed to do justice to religion.

Horace Mann's Canadian counterpart, Egerton Ryerson, entered the arena in Upper Canada violently opposed to church-controlled schools as shaped by the Anglican Bishop Strachan. But not for a moment did he consider education in any way separated from Christianity. His faith was that "the inculcation of morality based on Christian teaching should occupy a central place in any system of public instruction; that in the Bible there existed a body of common doctrine sufficient to form a basis of such instruction."[20]

Ryerson apparently assumed that a system of public education that included religious instruction could be acceptable to all denominations including Roman Catholics. State-supported Roman Catholic Separate Schools were firmly established, but Ryerson thought they would die out. In a letter Ryerson said,

I have always thought the introduction of any provision for separate schools in a popular system of common education like that of Upper Canada, was to be regretted and inexpedient; but finding such a provision in existence, and that parties concerned attached great importance to it, I have advocated its continuance, leaving separate schools to die out, not by force of legislative enactment, but under the influence of increasingly enlightened and enlarged views of Christian relations, rights and duties between different classes of the community.[21]

Just how erroneous Ryerson was in this matter is indicated by the Catholic Separate School Minority Report in connection with the Royal Commission on Education in Ontario, 1950.

Despite what may have been in Ryerson's mind concerning Separate Schools, Catholics . . . considered Catholic Schools an essential concomitant of the practice of their religion. The original provision for Separate Schools in the Act of 1841 was regarded not as a special privilege, but as a right—a natural, moral, and historical right which became a legal right when incorporated into the Act.[22]

There is no evidence that the Catholic body would have accepted a "common" system of education that did not include with it a system of Catholic schools for Catholic children.[23]

Ryerson, however, believed that a minority of "foreign ecclesiastics" wished to inflict clerical control on an unwilling

Roman Catholic people. This was not freedom of education; rather, in Ryerson's words, "a despotism in the state over the state—despotism in the family over the parent—a surrender of the rights and functions of both the state and the parent to a clerical absolutism under which humanity withers and society retrogrades."[24]

In the meantime the Church of England was charging that the schools were godless institutions. Ryerson was able to point out that the Bible was being used in nearly all the schools. Clergy of various denominations were allowed to teach in the schools, subject to several restrictions and protections. The major responsibility of the teacher was to impart those general principles which have a direct moral application. Another set of critics challenged the competence of teachers to give religious instruction. Ryerson's reply points to a different issue—the one he saw as crucial.

The reading of the Bible and the giving of instruction from it are two very different things. The question is not the competency of teachers to give religious instruction, but the right of a Protestant to the reading of the Bible by his child in the school as a textbook of religious instruction. That right I hold sacred and divine.[25]

The Churches and the Public Schools Now

By the time the twentieth century got established after the First World War, Roman Catholic Separate Schools maintained by government funding were well established in most provinces across Canada. There was agreement, even if it was sometimes uneasy, that religious teaching in the public schools should be provided by the churches. The sociology of religion could well be seen in decisions regarding the weekly period of religious education. In the small town in Ontario where I was teaching school in 1950, the ministerial association organized the hierarchy for religious instruction. With the understanding that any parents could on written request have their children excused from the one-hour period of religious instruction, which by regulation must be either the first or last hour of the teaching day, the United Church of Canada minister taught eighth grade. The Anglican minister had seventh grade, the Presbyterian minister had sixth grade, the Baptist fifth grade, and so on until the Salvation Army and the Pentecostal Assembly ended up with first and second grades. After each of the world wars there was a flurry of legislation which endeavored to ensure that public morality, presumably threatened by the instability of war, would be restored by increased emphasis on the teaching of religion in the schools.

Twenty-five years ago it seemed as if much of Protestant Canada was beginning to move out of the Christian imperialism in society, so well established since its beginnings in the nineteenth century. The class bias of the school promoters was becoming clearer as post–World War II waves of immigrants became Canadian citizens. It became relentlessly clear that the Protestant church should withdraw from its relationship with the public school. The multiple establishment of the Christian churches, an apparently splendid Canadian compromise between the situations in the United Kingdom and the United States, was not working. Liberal Protestants were simply not prepared for what is happening in the eighties; biblical literalists have organized in a new way. It is not religion they want to teach in the schools, they say, but "creation science." Modestly, they ask only that it be given equal time in science classrooms with the theory of evolution. In Ontario thirteen thousand names have been collected by the Creation Science Association and sent to the Minister of Education calling her to require teachers to include creation science in the curriculum and to use textbooks that refer to it as another view of creation. Under this kind of pressure the Government Ministry of Education stated in 1981 that evolution must not be taught as a fact, and that alternate explanations of human origin must be included.

So the benign neglect of the schools on the part of liberal Protestants has in fact left the public schools vulnerable to this well-organized pressure from interest groups who seem sometimes to represent more people than they really do. And since that pressure appears to come from what we now call the right wing, elected school board members and politicians who would like to stay in office are likely to respond. The plea for equal time works like magic in a democracy. One of the leading spokespersons for the "creationists" says, "In a truly liberal public school system, it is mandatory that all alternative theories . . . should be taught." The pressure is working. A 1973 textbook, *Biology: Living Systems* (Charles Merrill), had in its index seventeen lines of page references to evolution; in the 1979 edition, references have been reduced to three lines.

So in the eighties the public schools are again requiring the attention of the liberal Protestant churches, but this time very much at the request of teachers, school boards, and a Provincial Government Ministry of Education which must in a sense reflect the will of the majority. There is not in Canada at this time a nationally organized Moral Majority as there is in the United States. Nonetheless many Canadians do respond positively to the television programs that originate in the United States, and there are in Canada similar "electronic churches" with approximately the same agenda. It is not at all clear whether the liberal Protestant churches can offset this latest assault by the "creationists." Many Protestant denominations do have at the national level— sometimes at the regional—a department that has within its mandate issues concerning the public schools. For several years now, this concern has been limited to the teaching of moral values. Since the concentrated organization of the major Protestant denominations is at the national level, the structure does not lend itself to offsetting the local initiative of the biblical literalist. Liberal Protestantism does not seem to be well organized for coping with the well-funded onslaught of the "new right."

Teaching, Preaching, and Church Schools

Most of the educational ventures within congregations are those that are related to preaching and liturgy. Sometimes the curriculum uses the same church school structure that was in place when the congregation was using centrally produced curriculum. But the most dynamic changes seem to develop where the whole congregation is involved in organic structural change rather than simply groping for changed content.

One such example comes from a United Church of Canada congregation near Toronto. What seems to be a significant departure in this plan is simply that it represents new directions in relating worship and education. One of the benefits of the intentional relationship between worship and education is the easy access that the whole congregation has to Christian education and the new access that children have to worship. Since a team effort is basic to the whole endeavor, resource people can teach for short periods and teachers can participate in worship; the church school for everyone (as it is still called) meets before the congregation gathers for worship. Christian nurture within the family is enhanced. And, since children and adults are learning together, there is the possibility for follow up and discussion later. The beginning point for both education and worship is the Bible; the whole congregation is experiencing nurture and development at the same time. For instance, the children simply see more of the ministers; the ministers are perceived to be more involved in and caring about Christian education; and the laity, including children, is seen to be more involved and participating regularly in worship.

In speaking about children participating in worship, Bruce McLeod, the United Church minister, says that if we keep the children away from the worship service, we will be bereft of the voices than we need to listen to. "Without them, we will seem more organized than we really are. The service may go more smoothly. The ushers will be in step as they bring up the offering. What a change when children look after the offering. They just go and get it, and there's a rustle and we remember who we really are, not needing the solemnity that we attempt. Worship is livelier and fuller when children are present, and maybe shorter." This reorganization has already given the congregation new vitality and energy. With the increased sense of commitment and cooperation, teachers are easier to find. When visiting this congregation, I found an appealing sense of family with its own rituals and way of doing things, songs and stories known and beloved, children fully a part of the worshiping community in the service with their gifts no less important than anyone else's. There's a friendly kind of reverence and devotion in worship. There's not a whiff of pretentiousness, but the informality is not self-conscious. A visitor feels welcome. I knew when I visited that I had been to a particular congregation, in the sense of not just another church, but one that had accepted responsibility for its life and work, its liturgy, and its education.

Christian Development and Social Action

Ethical questions always have educational dimensions when the faith itself is seen as the curriculum and worship is seen as creative and dynamic as well as traditional. For instance, there is an urgent educational need to change the language of songs and stories that are sexist, racist, imperialist, or adultist in the very community where there are still many persons who do not see the problem at all. Even more sensitive is education dealing with Scripture, where, for instance, many centuries of anti-Semitism cannot be sifted out of biblical records.

The past decade has seen a radical questioning of goals, objectives, and methods in education. There is a growing urgency in the realization that the work and worship of the congregation as a whole determines the growth and nurture of its members. Nowhere is this clearer than around the educational efforts for new hope, dignity, and equality in the relationships between women and men. Christian education, child care, and food preparation in congregational life traditionally have been undertaken by women. Where it is intended that patriarchal ideology be displaced, it is recognized that everyday structures are the context in which content is formed and are themselves more powerful than the overt curriculum.

An understanding of the congregation as a teaching, learning, and liberating community has not been the experience of most of us. Sharing, serving, forgiving and loving, and coping with the tensions created by social change or by the lack of social change are not the characteristics by which most congregations are known. If a church teaches by its life-style, it must constantly be seeking to bear witness to the life of Christ by commitment to social justice. Clearly, there is commitment to less formal styles of learning and increased emphasis on doing a variety of things together. Urban churches are rediscovering in the last decade a community style of being together for shared meals, dramatic events, and parties, as well as the usual camp weekends and outings. Within these events, the ways in which the work is shared is a powerful style of teaching. Politically alert men, ironically enough, are not always the first to see that cleaning up the coffee cups may be one of the most political things they'll ever do.

Another lively issue in the forefront of discussion in many Canadian churches has to do with the questions about human sexuality, which includes of course, homosexuality. In all the discussions *about* homosexuals, there has been rather little discussion *with* them. Evidence seems to be mounting that the test of Christian ethics and education will be whether or not the church can address itself in a positive and theologically creative manner to the question of homosexuality.

In conclusion it is sufficient simply to point out that the most dramatic and recent changes within the major concerns of the church have to do with the new emphasis on nuclear disarmanent. That the church that proclaims "peace on earth" would become part of the peace movement should hardly be the surprise that it actually is.

Notes

1. Ellwood P. Cubberly, *Public Education in the United States* (Boston: Houghton & Co., 1934), 58.
2. Samuel E. Morison, *The Intellectual Life of Colonial New England* (Ithaca: Cornell University Press, 1961), 69. For a discussion of the economic motivation, see Merle Curti, *The Social Ideas of American Educators* (Paterson, N.J.: Littlefield, Adams & Co., 1961).

3. Morison, *The Intellectual Life of Colonial New England*, 16.

4. Samuel E. Morison, *The Founding of Harvard College* (Cambridge: Harvard University Press, 1935), 248.

5. Ibid., 247.

6. Ibid., 148.

7. Canada, *Sessional Papers of Canada* 27, no. 40C (1894); 45.

8. C. E. Silcox, *Religious Education in Canadian Schools: A Study Document* (Committee on Religious Education in Schools, Department of Christian Education, Canadian Council of Churches, 1960), 6.

9. W. E. Matthews, "History of the Religious Factor in Elementary Education" (Ed.D. thesis, University of Toronto, 1950), 56.

10. U.S., *Constitution*, First Amendment, 1791.

11. Gordon C. Lee, *Crusade Against Ignorance: Thomas Jefferson on Education* (New York: Bureau of Publications, Teachers College, Columbia University, 1961), 59.

12. Matthews, "History of the Religious Factor in Elementary Education," 65, quoting *Public Archives of Canada*.

13. Bishop Strachan quoted in C. E. Phillips, *The Development of Education in Canada* (Toronto: W. Gage & Co., 1957), 105.

14. Lee, *Crusade Against Ignorance: Thomas Jefferson on Education*, 11.

15. Ibid., preface, quoting Thomas Jefferson's letter to Du Pont de Nemours, 1816.

16. Lawrence A. Cremin, *The Republic and the School* (New York: Bureau of Publications, Teachers College, Columbia University, 1960), preface.

17. Ibid., 14.

18. Lawrence A. Cremin, *The American Common School* (New York: Bureau of Publications, Teachers College, Columbia University, 1951), 70, and Neil G. McCluskey, *Public Schools and Moral Education* (New York: Columbia University Press, 1958), 61.

19. Cremin, *The American Common School*.

20. C. E. Sissons, *Church and State in Canadian Education* (Toronto: Ryerson Press, 1959), 61.

21. Ibid., 20, quoting from Dr. Ryerson's Letters, 24 April 1952.

22. "The Catholic Separate School Minority Report," *Historical Sketch of Separate Schools of Ontario*, Report of the Royal Commission on Education in Ontario (Toronto: Royal Commission on Education, 1950), 2.

23. Ibid., 13.

24. Egerton Ryerson quoted in "The Catholic Separate School Minority Report," *Historical Sketch of Separate Schools of Ontario*, 27.

25. J. G. Hodgins, *Ryerson Memorial Volume* (Toronto: Warwich & Sons, 1889), 80.

CHAPTER 11

Roman Catholic Religious Education in Canadian Churches

Martin Jeffery

The sixties ushered in an ambitious project in religious education for Catholics across Canada. The enthusiasm of the bishops recently home from the Vatican Council embraced research and programming already under way in French Canada toward a revision of the catechism. English-language bishops joined with their French confrères in a project to publish a new bilingual curriculum for religious education to be called the Canadian Catechism. This visionary decision intended that one program in both French and English Canada be theologically and methodologically parallel. Previously, the Canadian church had suffered from various programs reflecting quite diverse pastoral and doctrinal perspectives in French and English Canada.

This historic decision made at Orléans outside Ottawa in the spring of 1966 envisioned a bold initiative of French and English bilingual catechists working together, coordinated through the Office de Catéchèse du Québec and the National Office of Religious Education. These two offices would jointly combine their efforts in the planning, editing, and publication of a unique program for renewal in the two official languages of the nation. Through the rest of the sixties, enthusiasm and optimism about this initiative abounded, and a new future for Canadian Catholic religious education looked promising.

Now in the early eighties, there has been a return to diversity and isolation of effort. English- and French-language Catholics are working quite apart without consultation or concern for the research of the other. French catechists continue to revise the original program, but very narrowly within the perspective of the Quebec milieu. While the revision in English reflects a broader perspective, a multiplicity of other programs are also in use across the nation. Many schools and dioceses have once again turned to

Martin Jeffery is Professor of Education in the Faculty of Education at McGill University, Montreal.

programs developed and published by Americans for the United States. The catechetical vision of the late sixties for Canadian religious education seems to be at least "on hold"—if not shattered.

Three Contemporary Concerns

Such return to pastoral and language diversity reflects present Canadian political preoccupation with regional autonomy and separatism. Such politics have parallel counterparts in Canadian Catholicism as well. Yet, interestingly, catechetical preoccupations and questions about directions in religious education are basically the same in both language groups and across all regions of the country: textbooks that "work," what should the students "know," eucharistic and sacramental practice, prayer and moral behavior. However these concerns are articulated and emphasized, they can be summarized in three basic theoretical questions that have remained unanswered and hence problematic through these twenty years since the inception of the Canadian Catechism program.

The most articulated of these concerns is the use of "human experience" in the methodology of religious education programs. From the beginning of the renewal in the late sixties, this question of human experience in lesson design has remained a major challenge to religious education. For many catechists and educators, the introduction of human experience into programming remains only a means of "interesting" the children to learn with more interest and enthusiasm. This means continuing a traditional approach to religion but in a better way. Consequently, the student's experience introduced into methodology is frequently reduced to the level of teaching aid. That this "experience approach" directly reflects the Vatican II Dogmatic Constitution on Revelation has never been very well understood. The constitution set forth principles concerning propositional and/or personal emphases within the process of God's revealing activity. But also seemingly ignored are educational principles and theory concerning experience as the basis for the acquisition of knowledge by the child.

Religious education is based on the theological presupposition that the human person responds in faith to God's revelation: God reveals; the human person responds with living faith. God approaches women and men with the invitation to live with him in love. God communicates the gift of faith, enabling human response. The place of this divine communication and enabling gift is within the consciousness of human experience. Consequently, religious education must examine, utilize, and develop those elements in human experience that prepare men and women to receive and respond to divine revelation, whatever form it takes and whenever it comes.

Religious education which ignores human experience and focuses solely on a theological examination of the content of faith will be truncated. Understanding the human possibilities for receiving faith requires not only theological and biblical acumen and precision, but similarly an understanding of human experience and its relationship to the divine self-communication. All academic disciplines interact with each other. "Because of the unity of human consciousness all sciences depend on one another whether consciously or not."[1]

Theology does not give the entire game plan to religious education. Educational theory can and must also contribute to effective learning. Knowledge becomes integrated for an individual insofar as it relates to and unifies knowledge gained through diverse experiences. The most essential characteristic of knowledge presented is its relation to the individual's already accumulated knowledge. This relationship becomes the basis for internalization: the ability of the learner to make connections between the idea communicated and the cognitive/affective structures of knowledge already developed. For knowledge to lead to living, it must be appropriated to a person's learning structure and, thus, assimilated to one's authentic, intimate self-experience. This internalization provides the power for an individual to organize and synthesize human experience.

The new program commissioned by the bishops was designed to help Canadian priests and catechists at the diocesan and parish levels reflect on these theological and educational principles. The intent was that the program should never be implemented without serious in-service training to help clergy and educators develop their understanding of these basic principles. However, this preparation frequently was limited to "how to do it."

Not understanding these theological and pedagogical principles, hesitation and dissension arose within the English-language Catholic community. The theological accusation of creeping "liberal Protestantism" and/or the educational criticism of "Progressive Deweyism" became steadily growing attacks from which the Canadian catechetical renewal has not yet recovered. Anne Roche, in her intemperate and extremely opinionated book, *Gates of Hell*,[2] is an example of some of this argumentation. And yet her argumentation can be found variously expressed in Catholic periodicals of the seventies. One could find such attacks for example, particularly during the years 1973–75, in Catholic newspapers such as *The Canadian Register* (Toronto) and *The British Columbia Catholic* (Vancouver), as well as in the monthly Oblate review *Our Family*[3] (Saskatchewan).

This dissension resulted in the Canadian bishops setting up an official study and evaluation of their catechism, the results of which were published in the autumn of 1974. Today, almost ten years after this report appeared, the uneasiness and debate described continue to persist.

Many of the responses suggest the existence of a large number of people who feel the Church is being betrayed by many of its leaders and theologians, who appear to be deserting them and our Catholic tradition. The Canadian Catechism appears to be just one, but by no means the only, confirmation of their worst fears and hostilities.[4]

The situation, while different religiously and culturally in French Canada, was not less stormy. The 1960 Quiet Revolution had moved the Catholic church from the center of Quebec's society to a very distant periphery. Pastoral and ideological exaggerations abounded. And yet, the disputes about the new religious education program were as contentious. The Quebec bishops participated in the national evaluation of the catechism. The prestigious Jesuit monthly *Rélations* devoted a special edition to the question when the episcopal evaluation was announced and remarked, "It seems likely that what has been called 'the war of the Catechisms' will not cease with this evaluation unless the bishops take a very clear position on the matter."[5]

The debate about the role of human experience in religious education persisted—and still persists. In the autumn of 1981, the Office de Catéchèse du Québec again called into question the anthropological approach in religious education.[6] The question was not resolved after the 1974 episcopal evaluation and continues to loom strongly in current catechetical discussion. The question needs to be thoroughly researched—on the level of theology as well as the level of education. And while significant studies have been developed, they have not had much influence on pastoral decisions and directives.

The second concern that continues to surface among those questioning current religious education is the place of sacred Scripture. Most Canadian Catholics are not yet comfortable with a biblical spirituality. Vatican II focused a new emphasis upon

Scripture in the formation of faith. The Bible in the liturgy, in personal prayer, and in religious education was henceforth to have a significant place. Focus on salvation history and the biblical word as a context for religious education became characteristic of the new programs in religious education.

The emphasis seems to have been too much on the external word of Scripture, as if it were powerful enough of itself to redeem and sanctify. Biblical knowledge and culture as well as exegetical studies are important, but by themselves they do not realize the directive of the Council "to provide the nourishment of the Scriptures for the people of God, thereby enlightening their minds, strengthening their wills, and setting men's hearts on fire with the love of God."[7]

Almost twenty years later, after numerous biblical institutes as well as new and creative religious education programs, the catechetical apostolate has not learned to transmit the Word of God so that its vitality might enable the conversion and transformation of people's hearts and lives. It is not sufficient to make the Bible interesting and appealing—nor is it enough to proclaim Scripture kerygmatically. Scripture must be presented to the faithful so that it might penetrate to the very marrow of human living. In our schools and programs, we have a long way to go before we rest.

Further probing into the meaning of the kerygmatic era uncovers an obligation too easily glossed over in current concerns: the special responsibility and role of religious education in regard to modern study of Scripture. Because the discipline of religious education is formed at the juncture of specific theological and educational approaches, its professionals utilize theology and education in their task of making accessible traditions and making manifest their transformational character.[8]

Learning about the personages, events, and teachings of the Jewish and Christian Scriptures and being able to quote phrases and texts have not resulted in a general renewal of faith. There may be more literacy among today's students about biblical lore, but the question remains. What is the educational process which leads to the development of living faith?

The third concern of the Canadian Catholic community remains the ability of the graduates of the new programs of religious education to articulate their faith in the symbols and language of a traditional Catholic heritage. For example, a student must be able to speak of the relationship of Father, Son, and Spirit as Trinity and express that belief with the sign of the cross. There is a concern that the students know the traditional prayers of the church, such as the Act of Contrition and the acts of faith, hope, and charity. There is an evident concern that the "real presence" of Jesus in the Eucharist should characterize the child's faith in Jesus. A concern uppermost over the past fifteen years has been that the young understand and utilize the sacrament of reconciliation regularly.

Two Questions Addressing the Concerns

The concern regarding articulation and tradition needs to be questioned. It is certainly sincere and expresses an authentic desire of the Catholic community that religious education may lead to knowledge which does not remain theoretical but is integrated into a life-style and pastoral practice of faith. This concern also expresses, though, the expectation that the new programs will educate youth to articulate and express their faith in language, sacramental practice, and Christian living characteristic of pre–Vatican II Catholicism.

The bishops in their visionary decision to develop a Canadian Catechism in the late sixties saw religious education as an opportunity to implement the insights and growth which they had experienced in the halls of Vatican II. The program was to be an occasion to evolve, deepen, and resynthesize our Catholic faith in the context of today's society and contemporary living. In the light of this objective, we should be asking two questions. The first question concerns what goals and objectives we should have in educating youth to live a Christian life in today's society. Given the importance of the past in clarifying and arriving at a direction, what indeed should be the aims of religious education today? Are they those of presenting and introducing our children and youth to a pre–Vatican II Catholic life-style, or are they goals providing young people with insights and attitudes that will bring deeper meaning and fuller human coherence to Christian living in contemporary society? These perspectives are not mutually exclusive. They are interrelated and mutually dependent. The heritage of the past has significance in the present. The real question, though, is how? There is a pressing need for the church to examine and clarify what indeed are the true goals of Canadian religious education today.

The second question we must ask concerns us as adult believers. Are we imposing the challenges and problems of renewing contemporary adult Catholicism into young people's catechesis? In other words, Christian attitudes and pastoral practices that were traditional and normative for adult Catholics prior to Vatican II have now undergone modification. The adult must deepen and expand both his or her understanding of the gospel and how to live it authentically in today's world. Maturity and authenticity of belief and practice do not permit a superficial thinking or unknowing obedience. Witnessing to the credibility of Christ and his gospel demands clear-headed maturity and deliberate decisiveness. Adult Catholics today have no alternative but to face up to an ongoing renewal of their Christian faith and living. But the challenges to the adult to renew understanding and faith in the gospel cannot be the norm for determining objectives of religious education of the young. The young must be introduced to Christ and his gospel. Their day of challenge to authentic Christian living will come tomorrow. They will meet tomorrow's challenges as adults if we are wise today in presenting Christ to them.

The sacrament of reconciliation is one of the most pressing examples. The failure on the part of today's Catholic community (clergy and laity) to fully renew its penitential faith and practice in the light of the theology and pastoral orientations of Vatican II will result in handing on a deficient understanding of the sacrament. It is not a question of preparing youth for tomorrow, but of renewing an adult faith today. In the light of the divine call proclaimed by Vatican II, it is necessary to rethink the framework of our heritage and how to live it so that we might hand it on with integrity. The problem is not with the youth, but with the quality of living faith among adult Catholics in today's world.

Five of the ten provinces in Canada have Catholic schools, while the other five do not. This factor is important, because Canadians continue to focus their primary effort in religious education on children and youth. The major effort of diocesan offices of religious education is still directed toward children of school age. The school continues to be the privileged place for religious education. The major emphasis in teaching is still directed toward children. Even those places that do not have a Catholic school still work to prepare adult catechists to function within a church school where children will be educated. While there has been talk of adult education over the past fifteen years, there has been little significant activity that has been imaginative or effective. In addition, where there are Catholic schools, the urban situation has evolved, and schools are less related to parish and local community. The dependence of the school on the parish has become nebulous and almost nonexistent.

The role of the family in the development of faith and in the preparation and initiation of children to the sacramental life of the church is neither the norm nor the expectation among Catholic parents. The parish does not presently educate its young in the faith, and the parents do not know how. Religious education is left to the school. The increasing secularization of the school and remoteness from the parish and the family make the role of the school in religious education very tenuous and inadequate. The former complementarity of family, parish, and school is gone. The social structure has evolved. Religious education, though aware of the shift, has not been able to respond creatively and effectively.

These conditions are experienced as very painful and threatening for the Catholic community, but they will not go away. They will not be resolved by hand-wringing, dissension, or recriminations. They will not be resolved by textbooks or programs. There is no one answer. The challenge will be resolved gradually by how the Catholic community in Canada evolves its own adult faith. Programs are important and must reflect sound research in both theological studies and educational methodology. This research must be at the service of programs in religious education. But programs remain instruments of the community that uses them. Even the Bible by itself cannot "save." The quality of faith shared and lived at the local level will determine the future faith life of young people. Insightful, practical Catholics will learn how to hand on their faith heritage.

Leadership and Questions About Directions

The Catholic bishops of Canada have exercised national leadership in religious education through their Office of Religious Education (NORE) for some twenty years. Originally the office was established to develop a Confraternity of Christian Doctrine (CCD) program, imitating the model in the United States. The impetus toward renewal engendered by Vatican II, as well as the significant number of Canadians returning from studies abroad in religious education, occasioned a change from CCD to the National Office of Religious Education and hence a broader mandate. Through the sixties and into the seventies, NORE exercised significant leadership across the country. During the seventies the leadership became less effective due to the mounting concern about the new religious education programs as well as the implications of regionalization. The bishops, desiring to address themselves more effectively to local pastoral concerns, divided the country into four regions. The lines of national and regional responsibility have never become very clearly defined. Consequently, at this time the leadership of NORE—and of the Canadian bishops as a unity—remains a bit of a question mark and is quite nebulous.

The regions have been active in religious education. Among English-language Catholics, Alberta, Ontario, and Newfoundland have put forward particularly significant efforts to structure and deepen religious education more effectively. The bishops of these provinces, utilizing a strong Catholic school system, have directed personnel and financing toward catechetical development especially at the secondary school level. Secondary school curriculum is more clearly outlined, and objectives and parameters are more clearly defined. It is perhaps too early to ask about the effectiveness of this work. But certainly the voices of clergy and parents, and teachers as well, still seem to indicate uncertainty and hesitation.

Meanwhile in Quebec, the bishops have all but relinquished their leadership through their Office de Catéchèse du Québec. The leadership has passed to the government and the highly bureaucratic Ministry of Education through its unit entitled Direction de l'Enseignement Catholique. New curricula rigidly spell out cognitive and affective objectives according to social science taxonomy for every unit and lesson of each elementary and secondary school year. Curriculum guides set out in detail the content, teaching strategies, and evaluation procedures for each classroom lesson. One wonders if the expectation is that teachers will consume the voluminous material, digest it, and emerge (robotlike?) as effective catechists. It is too soon for critical assessment, but too late to raise critical questions about the planning and priorities of the project. The five-year plan is on the move!

Meanwhile at the diocesan level across Canada, diocesan offices staffed by very dedicated and prayerful catechists continue to work. They continue their pre-service and in-service sessions for the development of school and parish catechists. These leaders deserve tremendous respect and gratitude. Amidst the uncertainties and criticisms, they continue to encourage, to strengthen, and to be examples of faith and hope. They work quietly, generally without much recognition—often bearing the heat of much contemporary criticism. They work generously with their time and talent, and they share their enthusiasm with their clientele. They are the sign that religious education has a future and may even flourish in some "tomorrow."

A number of questions might be raised about the direction of the leadership being given. The first concerns emphasis. Increasingly, the emphasis has focused upon the traditional family as the basic unit of the church and of society. Religious education programs from the outset attempted to coordinate the tripartite unity of family, parish, and school. This emphasis returns to a conviction in the early programs that the basic formative value of faith comes from the family and that the parish and the school are going to be effective only by building on the foundation laid in the home. This emphasis also marks the pastoral concern of the Canadian bishops toward a revitalization of the traditional family. Consequently, the school has been downplayed in the more recent revisions of the Canadian Catechism.

But, however laudable the emphasis on the family, what is being done to prepare and enable parents to evolve their own faith in the perspective of Vatican II so as to be effective communicators of a vital faith to face the demands of contemporary society? Only a revitalized and deepened synthesis of the "faith of our fathers" will be adequate for parent and child to live in today's pluralistic, technological, comfortable society. Again the question is raised about adult religious education which, to be effective, cannot avoid consideration of the very changing sociological situation of the Canadian family itself. The nuclear family, the extended family, such as the family existed twenty-five years ago, is no longer normative. The impact of one-parent families, marital breakdown, residence mobility, lack of appreciation for traditional and cultural roots, along with the enormous impact of modern media on human consciousness—all have created immense changes in family living and influence. A catechesis focused on family transmission will necessarily falter unless it takes into account today's conditions.

A formidable challenge, then, addresses today's parish. If the present-day family has difficulty being the focal point of stability for religious education and today's school is not able to marshall sufficient resources, the responsibility falls squarely on the local parish community to exercise leadership. This is consistent, though, with the very nature of the teaching-preaching role that priests share with bishops in the church. The triple role of bishop and priest outlined by Vatican II's *Constitution on the Church* includes teaching, sacraments, and government (prophet, priest, shepherd).[9] The Council fathers point out that teaching the gospel and developing faith is anterior in principle to celebration and administration. Difficulties in preaching the gospel abound on the contemporary scene. But this situation is not new. "The bishops should present Christian doctrine in a manner adapted to the needs of the times, that is to say, in a manner corresponding to the difficulties and problems by which people are most vexatiously burdened and troubled."[10]

The priest must teach. The expression of faith learned and lived may require new and adapted forms of sacramental celebration. We have been witnessing some of these changes over the past decades. Also, the very structure and government of the local parish may (and probably seems inevitably destined to) undergo radical transformation. But the basis of any of these changes is the teaching. It is shared faith that makes the church visible. The gospel must be proclaimed, communicated, handed on, and lived. Lived faith's expression in sacramental ritual and local communal activity follows. The sowing comes before the cultivating, pruning, and harvesting. The faith community must teach—effectively. This is of the very essence of Christ's command to his apostles.

What is the Canadian church doing through seminaries, priests' senates, and in-service training of parish ministries to prepare leaders to exercise effective and creative programming in this area? Fifteen years after Vatican II, Canadian seminaries and many priests' senate programs seem conspicuously inadequate in the effectiveness of catechetical education for priests. Repercussions abound not only for religious education but for pastoral preaching as well. After fifteen years of effort and experimentation, expectations run high among Catholic laity, particularly parents and teachers, that priests and bishops offer insight and direction to this important parish ministry.

There is indeed strong vocal concern among the clergy about the doctrinal content of religious education. "What are our young people learning about the Creed, sacraments, and commandments?" Concern for Catholic orthodoxy and the pristine purity of faith transmitted is of paramount importance and to be expected of those who have given their lives to the gospel. But responsibility does not end there. Concern with the communication process (the educational transmission of the content) also rates parallel preoccupation. Orthodoxy of faith cannot be limited solely to doctrinal expression and its precision—particularly if the norm is language traditional in theology during the past five or six hundred years. Communication of faith is a living proclamation demanding precision of theological insight and articulation in the context of the age in which one lives. Success is based on the ability to communicate in the learning processes as well as to use symbols and language understandable within the life-style of the contemporary society. The preaching of Augustine, Francis of Assisi, and

John Henry Newman springs to mind. They communicated in the idiom of their day. Surely the well has not gone dry—nor is Providence withholding grace. The charisma of Christ's grace is assured with the command of his mission. This charisma often only becomes visible through the hindsight of history. Meanwhile fidelity demands generous efforts to carry out his command "to teach all nations."

Conclusion

A constructive criticism addressed to many of these concerns involves reinforcing the conclusions of the first section of this essay: the need to determine the goal of religious education. Let us offer a perspective for future reflection and pastoral research.

The primary goal of religious education should be not to train individuals to become members of the church (confessionalisation) but to help the individual evolve his or her life through contact with Christ and his gospel (education). An individual's horizon being converted from the natural to the Christian will develop membership in the Christian community and become "church" with his or her community. This overall aim guiding insight into religious education will prevent policies and decisions from being made solely on sociological, psychological, pragmatic, or political bases. Decisions will be made in the name of the gospel and of Christian education concerning the communication of that gospel. This method immediately affects pastors, teachers, and parents in all regions of the country who, though characterized by faith and high motivation, may not be adequately renewed theologically and with sufficiently professional educational methods to competently fulfill Christ's commission. This aim also will prevent all efforts at leadership from being confined to design of programs. People formed in the light of the Christian mystery, not programs, become the focal point of energy. Programs will continue to receive attention but in the perspective of an instrument the believers use to share their faith. Pre-service and ongoing theological and pastoral seminars, as well as teacher training and in-service retraining, will be the primary commitments of leaders having responsibility for religious education. Personnel and finance may be deployed very differently.

Religious educators will become more professional. The danger across North America for professionals in almost any field today is to be too pragmatic—to work exaggeratedly toward practical ends. Theoretical knowledge is almost disdained. Yet to be practical fulfills the very intent of sound theory. Good theoretical knowledge is practical for the sake of living. Professional expertise in religious education today, more than ever, demands contemporary academic insight into what philosophers, theologians, educators, and those involved in media and communications have learned. Religious education stands at the crossroads with these numerous sacred and profane disciplines. Research concerning their conclusions can enrich Canadian religious education and can become the basis of program development in religious education. Such research can become as well the basis for religious educators of a sound knowledge combined with a faith-filled spirituality at the service of "preaching the gospel." This vision mirrors the process underlying the Canadian church leadership at the close of Vatican II.

In the sixties and early seventies, the Canadian church moved valiantly and enthusiastically to implement the documents of Vatican II. Clear, effective pastoral leadership was admired within and beyond the national boundaries. This was particularly evident in religious education. The latter years of the seventies seem to indicate a pause for people to catch their breath. Often the remark was heard, "The people are not ready." But leadership that hesitates is tempted to falter. Such is the lesson of Paul to Peter in Acts about the interpretation of the law.

Today's hesitation in Canadian religious education about new methodologies, programs, and language seems to be resulting in a tendency to look back to the past and may betray a lack of trust (faith-risk) to move forward into an ever-renewed Christianity promised by Christ. The impasse will be met for religious education insofar as bishops and clergy, professional theologians and scholars, and religious educators respect each other's authenticity and engage in dialogue together concerning this important pastoral, prophetic mission of the church. The dialogue needs to be held with respect, openness, and mutual esteem for each other's competence. The differing roles of different individuals within the community of faith call forth a different expertise and imply that no one group or individual has ultimate charisma of insight. There is a pressing need for each to be at the service of the other in the community of faith and, "like pilgrims," learn from each other as the community journeys toward definitive union with its Spouse.

Notes

1. Karl Rahner, "Theology," *Sacramentum Mundi* 6; 234.
2. Anne Roche, *Gates of Hell* (Toronto: McLelland and Stewart, 1975).
3. Cf. R. Zimmer, "Catechesis and the Canadian Catechism," in *Our Family* (Battleford, Saskatchewan) 26, no. 6 (June 1974).
4. E. Keyserlingk, ed., *Final Report of the Evaluation of the Canadian Catechism* (Ottawa: Canadian Catholic Conference, 1974), 39.
5. Julien Harvey, "Nos manuels de catéchèse: experience et message," in *Rélations: La Guerre des Catechismes*, no. 385 (September 1973).
6. *Etude sur les orientations de la catéchèse au secondaire* (Office de Catéchèse du Québec, novembre 1981).
7. "Dogmatic Constitution on Divine Revelation," no. 23.
8. Mary C. Boys, *Biblical Interpretation in Religious Education* (Birmingham, Ala.: Religious Education Press, 1980), 294.
9. *Dogmatic Constitution on the Church*, no. 28.
10. "Decree on the Bishops' Pastoral Office in the Church," no. 13.

CHAPTER 12

Women, Power, and the Work of Religious Education

Gloria Durka

The issue of women's role in religious education is tied to the whole question of power. There is considerable evidence that the issue is being ignored precisely because the implications are considered to be too staggering to be realistically confronted. But to continue to ignore them is to contribute to those oppressive structures in church and society that inhibit us all. Women's "place" in religious education can no longer be taken for granted, at least from women's own point of view.

Recently I suggested that the linking of mutually exclusive dualisms with the distinction between male and female has produced ideologies and social structures that oppress women and that have been the source of stress for women who challenge these prevailing myths by their personal and/or professional lives.[1] The ramifications of the dualisms have been especially devastating for women who work in religious organizations. When women recognize this fact and struggle to express who they really are and what they hope for, they become aware that all thinking, including feminist thinking, takes place within a network of unconscious and semi-conscious presuppositions about the wider context within which all experience occurs. Ultimately this network constitutes an implicit metaphysics whose premises are embedded in our institutions, in the structure and lexicon of our language, and in the unquestioned deliverances of "common sense." These premises, although not obviously patriarchal, nevertheless shape and are shaped by patriarchal structures and modes of thought. They are also the source of inadequate models of anthropology which have prevented women from gaining access to powerful leadership positions in church and society.

Gloria Durka is Associate Professor in the Graduate School of Religion/Religious Education at Fordham University.

The Social and Religious Construction
of Women's Reality

Even the briefest inquiry into the two prevailing models of anthropology used to describe women's experience is enough to reveal their basic inadequacies. The first model is reflected in "official" arguments against the ordination of women. Simply put, it implies a two-nature or dual anthropology in which a complementary duality between the sexes is seen as inherent in nature and therefore part of the divine plan. This duality "is the ordering principle for complementary roles, functions, and activities of women and men" (Research Report, Catholic Theological Society of America, 1978). It emphasizes the unchanging structure of nature and views revelation, tradition, theology, and ethics as past-oriented: what is has been given and must not be changed. New knowledge of the human person derived from the human sciences is irrelevant to theological discussion, since its goal is to preserve the past order as natural, as the order of creation, and as revealed.

The single anthropology is radically opposite. Besides its negation of rigidly defined roles for women or men beyond the biological, this anthropology puts emphasis on history and the data of experience rather than on "nature." It affirms the importance of the human sciences for theological reflection. Greater scope is given to human freedom and responsibility since past social patterns are likely to be construed as human products rather than as God-given permanent structures. The emphasis of history, whose changing patterns are seen as the responsibility of human agency, entails views of revelation, tradition, theology, and ethics as having sources in present experience as well as in the past.

While there are no longer assertions of the inferiority of women in ecclesiastical or theological discourse, recent official documents of the Roman Catholic Church, for example, affirm a dual anthropology, the complementary or "different but equal" status of men and women as inherent in nature and therefore as part of the divine plan. This view is the basis from which the complementary roles and functions of the sexes derive. Beyond the biologically determined psychological and sociological characteristics and the limited scope of human freedom already noted, this view finds a central analogy between nature and the economy of salvation.[2]

A third vision is struggling into existence today, a "transformative," person-centered model. This view regards both the dual and single anthropologies as inadequate because they reflect society as it was and as it is, and because they place the impetus for change on individual efforts. The new transformative model is both personal and public; it seeks to transform the old gender stereotypes at the same time that it aims to transform the social and cultural structures which are their inseparable context in human life. This transformative model received its impetus from changes that have begun in society and from the Christian faith, which calls all persons to likeness to the God of Jesus in love, compassion, mercy, peace, service, care, and community. Both women and men are called to this likeness, not to the half-personhood of complementarity which often is a hidden domination.[3]

The difference in the transformative model from the other two lies in its explicit acknowledgment that anthropological models are not merely formal, individualistic concepts, but that they are embedded in particular social contexts. Thus the dual anthropology corresponds to a hierarchic-elitist model of society. It is a model present in its clearest form since the rise of the state and the development of political ruling classes, although it was broken in principle by the English, American, and French revolutions. On the other hand, the one-nature model corresponds to the "one-dimensional" society, a product of the modern period and associated with the revolutions' ideals of freedom, equality, brotherhood, and democracy. Despite the inspiring ideals of this vision, experience has proved that "under the cloak of democracy, the real ruling groups have been hidden." In the United States, for example, blacks, native Americans, newly arrived immigrants, and women must struggle to have a voice. The upper elite is really the paradigm for all people, and thus women and minorities must conform to the single (male, white, Protestant) norm.

The stereotypes under which women have lived in religious organizations are extensions of the myths held by society in general. In recent years these myths have been under fire from feminist scholars. Historical studies demonstrate the variety of leadership roles that women have assumed in the past, showing that stereotyped notions of women's nature, place, or role are not universal or unchanging. Contemporary psychology discredits many unproven assumptions about "feminine psychology," distinctive feminine characteristics, or virtues. Many of these findings corroborate the 1978 Research Report of the Catholic Theological Society of America, which studied official theological argumentation about the question of the ordination of women. The report concludes that "the assumption of a dual anthropology, derived from cultural and religious situations which assumed the inferiority and subordination of women as a class, is unsound." The report urges the need for the church's self-criticism with regard to institutional and ideological forms which legitimate unequal views of women.

It follows that the feminist critique of cultural and religious stereotypes about women as passive, emotional, intuitive, and dependent must confront theological arguments about "feminine psychology," the headship of the male, and "complementarity of the sexes," all of which can be understood as rationalization for the subordination of women. It must also confront theories of power and leadership which have held women in subordinate positions in church and society. The educational task of this confrontation is to help women (and men) to understand power, to feel comfortable using power, and to desire power.

Women and Power: Redefining Its Dimensions

As religious educators, the question of power is central to the human challenge we have before us: that of building the earth. It is one that must be explored in the spirit of truthfulness by both women and men. But for women it has special significance, because for centuries they have thought of themselves as being powerless.

Although women comprise more than 50 percent of the world population, they were largely absent from the decision-making processes that produced the present world situation. But they are now faced with critical choices that leave them as responsible as men for the future of human history. Their responses may well depend on two factors: (1) how women assess the relationship between their history and well-being and the advancement of a more humanizing world order of peace and justice, and (2) how women perceive their powers to be and do as agents of history. To be sure, the critical assessment of their situation in this regard can have its painful moments. It can even result in anger, but that is not necessarily bad. The deepest danger is that their anger will turn inward and lead them to portray themselves and other women chiefly as victims rather than as those who have struggled for the gift of life against incredible odds. The power of anger is creatively shaped by owning this great strength of women and of others who have struggled for the full gift of life against structures of oppression.[4]

Western culture teaches persons to measure personal abilities against high standards of achievement and to compete against one another in trying to meet these standards. Power in the sense of aggressive, ambitious pursuit of these high standards, highly developed personal capacities, and achieved excellence or superior status has been an accepted cultural norm. But power in the sense of someone else's (or some agency's) control over one's own life circumstance is feared in proportion to its concentration in the hands of a few, the scope of its effects, and the secretness of its exercise. In other words, power has been thought of both as a personal capacity to do something ("It is within your power to do anything you set your mind to") and as a commodity that can be gathered and possessed like gold coins ("The real power in this country is in the banks and big corporations—where the money is"). Both of these views are misleading, and taken together they create a confusing and inhibiting ambivalence for women and men.[5]

In the 1960s power was redefined by organizational theorists as the ability to prevent others from making one act against one's will.[6] Later a more phenomenological approach was taken, and power was redefined by organizational theorists to mean the ability to create and keep the balance between adapting oneself to an organization and maintaining sufficient autonomy to influence the organization. Such an approach to power allows organizational and personal goals to be met simultaneously.

Rollo May's typology of power illustrates this shift.[7] He identifies five types of power:

1. *Exploitative*—power identified with force. It uses the other for personal gain.
2. *Manipulative*—power over another person.
3. *Competitive*—power against another; one person wins, the other loses.
4. *Nutritive*—power for the other; as in the normal parental care of children.
5. *Integrative*—power with the other; a win-win relationship.

The dignity of self and the other is respected; it is nonviolent. Integrative power can also be called *synergic* power. As power with the other, it does not benefit one at the expense of the other or the community, but tends to benefit both self and others. It is a caring form of power.[8] In this view power is not property, entity, or possession but a relationship in which two or more persons tap motivational bases in one another and bring varying resources to bear in the process of interaction. The arena of power is no longer the exclusive preserve of a power elite or an establishment or persons clothed with legitimacy. Power is ubiquitous; it permeates human relationships.

Redefining power allows us to think differently about women in leadership roles. There will never be a more humanizing world order until women participate in shaping it. And there never will be a realignment of patriarchal-hierarchical power in religious bodies until more women articulate their own experience of their call to leadership (educational, sacramental, juridical) as being "empowered" by the community among whom their functions take place, on the one hand, and as "power for," on the other hand.

The shift in understanding and describing power from exploitative control to participatory enablement has been called a shift from male bias to female construction of leadership theory. James MacGregor Burns calls it a "male bias" that sees leadership as mere command or control instead of the engagement and mobilization of human aspirations that it properly is. As we become more aware of the true nature of leadership, he said, women will be more recognized as leaders, and men will change their own leadership styles.[9] To women who are working in church-related institutions, this deduction might appear more optimistic than realistic.

Women's experience does give them some edge on moving toward egalitarian forms of leadership and power. For example, women do not come from a background or membership in a group that believes it needs subordinates. Also, women do not have a history of believing that their power is necessary for the maintenance of self-image. But women do have their own kinds of problems with power. Women's inexperience in using all of their powers openly, combined with past fears of power, is now taking on new forms. Nowhere is this more evident than in women's failure to distinguish between two *levels* of power, that is, professional and personal power. *Professional power* has to do with the formal distribution of power in organizations. It is power that can readily be displayed on organizational charts through line and staff functions. It is power that is assigned. *Personal power* cannot be effectively illustrated on charts because it has to do with norms, beliefs, and values. Power at this level is perceived and attributed; it cannot be legislated.

The difference between how professional and personal power operate has been a source of dilemma for women in complex organizations (especially in the church) because they have had, and still have, limited access to where organizational power is exercised. Today women are still largely evaluated at the level of personal power even though greater numbers of them have gained academic credentials and competencies that match (and in many instances surpass) those of their male colleagues. Women are evaluated at the level of personal power no matter how much professional power they have been assigned in an organization. As women, they are still reacted to as members of a class. Although men have problems centered around working with women as their peers or with women in positions of authority over them, it is the women who carry the burden because many men still believe they "let women in." The dilemma is further compounded because in the short run women will still be expected to function more effectively at the personal level than at the professional level. Men expect that women are more understanding, more sensitive, more "human." But it should be observed that in the long run women may not be assigned a monopoly of these qualities, because these personal skills can be taught, and men can "catch up" in learning personal relationship skills. It is a well-known fact that in recent years large organizations have spent millions of dollars for in-service training geared to improving human relationship skills of middle management and executive personnel. Churches have begun to adopt this practice, although not on such a large scale.

What does this mean for women? Clearly they ought not to concentrate their efforts to gain leadership positions solely on either the professional or personal level. Effective penetration of complex organizations can only take place ecologically, that is, in a systemic way. Systems theory identifies four distinct systems of reality.[10] A simple diagram of four concentric circles can help us imagine four levels of reality.

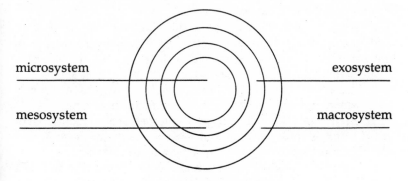

microsystem exosystem

mesosystem macrosystem

LEVELS OF REALITY

The innermost circle represents the *microsystem*, that is, personal reality, with the self in the environment, or between the self and God. The next circle represents the *mesosystem*, that is, interpersonal reality, the relationship of the self to all persons in the family, job, neighborhood, or social situations. The third circle represents the *exosystem*, that is, societal or structural reality, a level of which we are becoming newly conscious. On this level relationship is not personal, but it is nonetheless real. Until recently women have had only a vague intuition of how our lives affect the lives of all others. Understanding structural reality helps one to understand how individuals relate to all others—through the structures to which they belong, relating to the structures to which others belong. The outer circle represents the *macrosystem*, that is, the culture, value systems, and basic assumptions (paradigms) which support the other three systems.

Distinct though they are, the four levels impact one another significantly. Both interpersonal and structural realities affect the individual person. Both persons and structures affect interpersonal relationships. In addition, structures are eventually changed by persons. And all of the above interaction takes place within a cultural context of basic values and assumptions.

The Education of Women

Re-imaging the Process

For women in religious education, a systems approach to effecting transformation of religious and social bodies represents a major shift in emphasis and direction. Even now, after a century of struggling to win access to the institutions and structures that determine their history and the right to be responsible agents of their own destiny and future, women are often wrought with guilt, fear, confusion, and uncertainties about their relationship to power. Fearing to entrust themselves with power, they tend to abdicate to others (usually men) the responsibility for the way their personal lives and world history evolve. Most women, even those who have acquired professional power, tend to cling to a mode of functioning that is directed toward the personal and interpersonal dimensions of reality. This is most often true of those women who have gained significant professional power in religious organizations.

I suggest that women need to make a conscious effort to direct their energies toward the structural levels of reality. This shift from the personal-interpersonal levels to the structural level can be represented by the following chart:

A SHIFT IN EMPHASIS FROM:	PERSONAL-INTERPERSONAL	TO	STRUCTURAL
giving attention to	victim	to	cause
practicing virtues of	mercy charity compassion	to	justice peace
influencing	attitudes	to	organizations
understanding change as the result of	metanoia (conversion) influence	to	power
being motivated by	guilt/blame	to	responsibility
striving for results of	programs	to	policies
teaching for	autonomy/ relationship	to	interdependence
naming evil as	personal sin	to	social sin
the disciplines used to teach and to interpret reality	humanities psychology	to	social sciences economics sociology political science anthropology

Adapted from *Infusion: An Approach to Education for Peace and Justice*, Justice/Peace Education Council, December 1981.[11]

Reconstructing the Task

The shift represented in the preceding chart gives us a new educational agenda for women in religious organizations. Their access to leadership positions can be enhanced if all of us, both women and men, reexamine presuppositions about human nature, discover the history of women's experience and leadership that has never been told, and explicate the women-liberating insights implicit in biblical teaching about God.[12] We all need to examine the link between what seems exclusively gender related and the construction of other aspects of society, politics, and culture. But in the present and immediate future, it is women who must take the initiative and work for their own personal and professional empowerment. This process is an educational one because it involves the reconstruction of women's experience so as to shape their future experience. It entails at least two tasks.

The first task takes place at the *personal level* of reality. *Women themselves must bring more fully into consciousness and criticize their unexamined notions about the nature of things.* This self-evaluation is needed to overcome the rampant anti-intellectual bias inherent in so much of the churches' efforts to respond to women's call for empowerment. Self-criticism on the part of women cannot be overemphasized. For women not to embrace this task is simply to contribute to keeping themselves in their "place."[13] The critique of the distorted social systems in which we live is an arduous task which calls for courage, knowledge, independence, initiative, responsibility, and the ability to challenge and to struggle— qualities traditionally associated with male humanity. And in religious terms, repentance and conversion are needed not only by individuals, but also at the institutional levels of church and society since that is where the personal and public dimensions of experience are joined. But as emphasized earlier, impatience alone is not the most effective way to promote change. What is needed is systemic change.

This leads to the second educational task. At the *structural level* it no longer seems adequate or appropriate for women to seek leadership by accepting those masculine rules of the game which prize competition and domination. Rather, *women now need to focus on affirming the structures and values they bring to the question of competition versus relationships and start reconstructing organizations according to what they as women know.* Women's recent reflection on their own experience in all its variety, and their attempt to develop corresponding models of humanity, is an important development within religious organizations. It is already upsetting assumptions regarding the authority, scope, style, and nature of religious leadership. To illustrate, I offer three observations.

1. *Women are challenging traditional sources of religious authority.* Whenever women have moved into visible church leadership, the relative importance of Scripture and tradition has been reduced and the legitimacy of personal experience has been enhanced.[14] History demonstrates that it is characteristic of the leadership roles in Christianity claimed by women that they derive their authority from personal charisma rather than from office.[15]

2. *Women are already changing the styles of religious leadership.* In mainstream Christianity important leadership exercised by women is often linked to their class status. The relation of sex and class modifies the marginality of women. Although women are a subordinate "caste" within every class, they belong to all classes. So a woman who belongs to the leadership class may exercise power that derives in part from her social position. These "powers of the weak"[16] enable them to have a deep appreciation for and experience with collaborative leadership styles that are most often contrary to conventional styles of church leadership. Women in

religious organizations, excluded from institutional church leadership, have continued to represent forms of leadership that derive from a church shaped by direct religious experience, hope, and marginality within established social forms. They have represented the "lay" voice as well, united as they are with the ministry of the people.[17]

3. *Women are asking new questions about the personal and political results of greater power in religious organizations.* These questions include the following: Is it enough simply to be incorporated into paradigms of ordained ministry shaped by males for many hundreds of years in hierarchical models intended to exclude women? Or must women, by their very presence, reshape the ministry into forms that are more open, pluralistic, and dialogic? In gaining the leadership of office, will women abandon the insights gained through the authority of holiness and charisma? Also, how can women redefine the process of religious education so as to prepare persons who will transform the world rather than simply be socialized into its existing structure?

Toward the Future

Women have long been involved in religious socialization. What women can embrace more overtly is a critical stance toward this socialization process. Such a stance requires a double thrust: first, the building up of support structures, systems, and relationships which promote a more human, more just, and more peaceful world; and second, the changing of structures, systems, and relationships which dehumanize, victimize, or instrumentalize persons. And there is no better place for women religious educators to begin this transformation process than in the field of religious education itself, that is, by striving to gain access to and by assuming leadership positions in church-related institutions.

This shift in personal and structural power might well be women's most remarkable work of religious education. And, in the long run, it will be for the good of the whole community.

Notes

1. Gloria Durka, "The Religious Journey of Women: The Educational Task," *Religious Education* 77 (March-April 1982): 163-78.
2. Anne Carr, "Theological Anthropology and the Experience of Women," *Chicago Studies* 19 (1980): 113-28.
3. Mary Buckley, "The Meaning of the Human," *Catholic Theological Society of America Proceedings* (1979): 48-63.

4. Beverly Harrison, "The Power of Anger in the Work of Love: Christian Ethics for Women and Other Strangers," *Union Seminary Quarterly Review* 36 (1981): 41-57.
5. David Nyberg, "A Concept of Power for Education," *Teachers College Record* 82 (1981): 535-51.
6. See Claude Steiner, *The Other Side of Power* (New York: Grove Press, 1981).
7. Rollo May, *Power and Innocence* (New York: W. W. Norton & Co., 1972).
8. Patricia Mische, "Women, Power and Alternative Futures," *The Whole Earth Papers* (East Orange, N.J.: Global Education Associates, 1978), 1.
9. James MacGregor Burns, *Leadership* (New York: Harper & Row, 1978).
10. See especially Ludwig von Bertalanffy, *General Systems Theory: Foundations, Development, Applications* (New York: George Braziller, 1968).
11. For further information, contact J/PEC, 20 Washington Square North, New York, N.Y. 10011.
12. Joann W. Conn, "Women's Spirituality: Restriction and Reconstruction," *Cross Currents* (Fall 1980): 293-308.
13. Elizabeth Janeway, *Man's World, Woman's Place* (New York: Dell Publishing Co., 1971).
14. Barbara Zikmund, "Upsetting the Assumptions," *Christian Century* (7 February 1979): 127-28.
15. Rosemary Reuther and Eleanor McLaughlin, eds., *Women of Spirit: Female Leadership in the Jewish and Christian Traditions* (New York: Simon & Schuster, 1979).
16. Elizabeth Janeway, *Powers of the Weak* (New York: Alfred A. Knopf, 1980).
17. Bernard Cooke, *Ministry to Word and Sacraments* (Philadelphia: Fortress Press, 1976).

Bibliography

Gottemoeller, Doris, and Rita Hofbauer, eds. *Women and Ministry: Present Experience and Future Hopes.* Washington, D.C.: Leadership Conference of Women Religious of the USA, 1981.
Greenleaf, Robert. *Servant Leadership.* Ramsey, N.J.: Paulist Press, 1977.
McCall, John R. *New Leaders for Tomorrow.* Raleigh, N.C.: SPES, 1982.
Miller, Jean Baker. *Toward a New Psychology of Women.* Boston: Beacon Press, 1976.
Schaef, Anne. *Women's Reality.* Minneapolis: Winston Press, 1981.
Schillebeeckx, Edward. *Ministry.* New York: Crossroad, 1981.

CHAPTER 13

Blacks and the Religious Education Movement

Paul Nichols

Blacks in the United States have lived through an intriguing history with respect to religious education. Speciality has marked the concern for religious education among blacks for most of the time since their introduction to this land in 1620. Speciality has again become an issue, but with an important difference. The difference is that blacks are themselves demanding that religious education be made relevant to their experience. It is the aim of this essay to examine some aspects of the history of religious education among blacks, to assess the present state of the art, and to suggest some issues that are crucial to blacks with regard to Christian religious education.

Historical Overview

One of the earliest accounts of efforts to instruct blacks in the Christian faith was originally published in 1842 and reprinted in 1969.[1] The book contains historical sketches of religious instruction among blacks from the time of their introduction to the New World in 1620 to the time of the original publication in 1842.

The Society for the Propagation of the Gospel (SPG) figured prominently in the call for religious instruction among blacks. In keeping with their objective to convert the so-called heathen to the Christian faith, the SPG naturally turned its attention to the black slaves in America, who were numbered among the heathen. Strong admonition was given to slave owners who balked at providing such instruction on the grounds that it might interfere with the slave's status, and with the performance of his duty. In 1727 the bishop of London addressed an open letter to the masters and mistresses of plantations abroad on the subject, attempting to offer reassurance on both concerns:

Paul Nichols is Minister of Good Shepherd Baptist Church in Richmond, Virginia.

If it be said that no time can be spared from the daily labor and employment of Negroes, to instruct them in the Christian religion; this is in effect to say that no consideration of propagating the Gospel of God, or saving the souls of men, is to make the last abatement from the temporal profit of the masters; and that God cannot or will not make up the little they may lose in that way, by blessing and prospering their undertakings by sea and land, as a just reward of their zeal for his glory and the salvation of men's souls.[2]

On the question of Christianity's effect upon the status of the slaves, the bishop continued:

Christianity and the embracing of the Gospel does not make the least alteration in civil property, or in any of the duties which belong to civil relations; but in all these respects, it continues persons just in the same state as it found them. The freedom which Christianity gives is a freedom from the bondage of sin and satan, and from the dominion of men's lusts and passions and inordinate desires; but as to their outward condition, whatever that was before, whether bond or free, their being baptized and becoming Christians, makes no manner of change in it.[3]

In typical proof-texting style, the bishop quoted I Corinthians 7:20 to prove his point: "Let everyman abide in the same calling wherein he was called."

The above quotations illustrate the special problems posed by efforts to provide religious instruction to black slaves. They also illustrate the accommodationist approach taken by SPG, an approach so characteristic of religious instruction for blacks during the slave period.

In his historical treatment of religious education in the Episcopal Church prior to 1835, Clifton H. Brewer included a chapter on the religious education of Indians and Negroes. He indicated that what started in 1704 in New York City under the auspices of the SPG as a catechetical school and spread throughout the colonies came to include reading and writing as well as catechism.[4] Brewer suggested a motive for the attention given the religious needs of blacks during slavery: "The black man was brought to America for industrial purposes. He was somewhat patronizingly referred to as 'poor wretch,' or simply 'negro' or 'slave.' Just to make him a better man, or to improve his soul, seems to have been the aim of the efforts expended on him."[5] Brewer ultimately concluded, nevertheless, that the efforts thus expended were largely futile.

James D. Tyms agreed with Brewer's conclusion concerning the motivation for the religious instruction of blacks during slavery. He wrote: "Here it may be noted, the soul of the Negro was of primary interest to those who sought to instruct him. How to introduce God into the experience of black men so as to improve their personality seems to have been the primary motivation."[6]

At the time of the Emancipation Proclamation, various religious bodies began to investigate the condition of the newly freed slaves. With such investigations came a growing awareness of what slavery had done to blacks. One such investigation was made by the Reverend H. C. Fish of New Jersey, who had been sent to Washington by Baptists in 1863. Fish reported:

Most of their [Negroes] distinguishing traits of humanity had been effaced; their sense of self-reliance and the capacity for self-help did not show themselves; there were signs of piety among them, but it was mixed with strange elements of ignorance, superstition, and immorality; moral feeling was benumbed, conscience seemed to have been rubbed out.[7]

The response that was made to such dismal assessments about the condition of blacks under slavery led to vigorous efforts to introduce "cultural, moral, and religious standards into the life of black men."[8] Thus it can be seen that, even with the abolition of slavery, the impetus and motivation remained to expose blacks to religious education. The Home Mission Board of Northern Baptists, for example, adopted seven objectives to serve as guiding principles for the Christian education of blacks. Three of those principles are listed below:

1. That freedmen were to be educated as men, for education which fails to recognize the full, absolute, equal humanity of black men is fatally inadequate.
2. The freedmen were to be educated as American citizens. . . .
3. They were to be educated as Christians, since education is to be a matter of character and acquirement, with stress on the perfect example of manhood, Jesus Christ, kept before the black men, and on lifting up Christian influence to meet the urgent need of elevating, guiding, and inspiring optimum human nature among black men.[9]

These principles were developed and adopted by whites to guide them in their work among blacks. Blacks, however, very early after their liberation, had their own ideas about Christian education that was to be relevant for their own people.

As early as 1886, black Christians were beginning to formulate their own goals and objectives of Christian education. Tyms derived from various sources at least five such objectives. They were:

1. The enrichment of the Negro's personality under the influence of the ideals of Jesus.

2. To guide Negroes in adjusting themselves socially, morally, and spiritually, under the influence of Jesus' ideal of God in a complex social order.
3. To exalt the Word of God and proclaim its regenerative power in the hearts of men.
4. The saving of souls and the awakening and refining of the highest emotions of the human soul—the evangelistic goal.
5. As summed up in the Constitution of the Sunday School and Baptist Training Union Congress, the educational goal is to foster and stimulate all phases of religious education training in church membership, evangelism, and missions.[10]

The first two of these objectives indicate a recognition on the part of blacks that education of blacks by whites had left a great deal to be desired. The call for the enrichment of the Negro's personality betrays a suspicion that education previously received had not provided for such enrichment. In fact, indications are that blacks were being taught to admire the traditions of whites while disclaiming their own traditions. The second objective speaks to the special status which was given blacks, separate and unequal. Large adjustments had to be made by the recently freed slaves. It is one of the grand ironies of history that black Christians expected their faith to assist them in making those adjustments.

Contemporary Developments in Religious Education for Blacks

The dominant motif that may be discerned from a review of religious education among blacks in the United States is that such educational efforts required that special attention be given to their prevailing condition in any given period. Just as Christianity developed somewhat lengthy periods of catechetical training for converts during the patristic period in order to reverse the impact of their groundedness in pagan culture and religion, so the instruction of blacks during slavery was designed to overcome what was almost universally regarded to be their hopeless and depraved pagan existence prior to their arrival in America.

Blacks themselves asserted the need for Christian education that would address their special situation and respond to their special needs. So when blacks began to attempt to take control of the process of their Christian education, they asserted the principle of liberation, emphasizing self-help and self-reliance as being necessary to that process. Black-initiated efforts emphasized the importance of the social and ethical dimensions of the educational task.

One gets the impression that blackenized content for Christian education was less an issue than black control of the publication process and black contribution to the writing of curriculum materials. The hope that the accomplishment of such involvement would result in a more relevant content may have been implied. There is little evidence, however, that in the long run a distinctive content resulted from the establishment of black publishing houses and the contribution to curriculum materials by black writers. That eventuality would have to wait for another historical development, namely, the modern civil rights movement.

Before going on to that development, however, it will be useful to comment on the homogenization of curriculum materials used by both blacks and whites. The point may be illustrated by reference to public education. Edgar Friedenberg argued that public school is the place where one learns to be an American. He saw the role of the school as being the clarification of experience. He wrote: "In a school system whose historical function has been making Americans out of immigrants' children, students are likely to find that they can only win esteem by how they look and behave, not for what they are. The effect [on immigrants and minorities] is a severe form of alienation."[11] As in public education, so in Christian education, color and race consciousness were minimized in order to hasten the realization of the great melting-pot ideal.

The objectives of Christian education as set forth by the former International Council of Religious Education, as well as by the National Council of Churches of Christ, did not take racial and ethnic particularities into account. The goal was to make "Christians" out of everyone. That is why curriculum materials used by both black and white churches for most of the twentieth century were so similar, and those used by black churches reflected little, if any, relevance to the particularities of the black experience.

In 1966, at the height of the modern civil rights movement, Stokely Carmichael voiced a newly acquired sense of pride on the part of black people. His chant, Black Power, gave verbal expression to the unwillingness of blacks to live any longer under white definitions of their being. It therefore signaled a new era in black perceptions of everything from education to the process by which application is made for employment.

It should have come as no surprise to anyone that the heightened self-awareness and move toward self-determination would eventually come to be applied to Christian education. If in the late nineteenth and early twentieth centuries the issue was who would own and control the publishing companies and the racial identities of those who wrote the articles, now the concern was that the content of the curriculum be relevant to the black experience and be reflective of it wherever possible.

This concern became more pressing and persistent in the late 1960s and the early 1970s. In 1970 two important conferences were held in which these issues surfaced. One was the National Conference of Black Churchmen which met in Atlanta with a concern for the establishment of a national agenda for black churches. One of the major workshops of that conference was entitled "Black Church and Black Educational Motifs." The other conference was called Krisheim II and was held in Philadelphia under sponsorship of the Black Christian Education Administrative and Coordinating Committee, Department of Christian Education, National Council of Churches. Definitions of both Christian education and curriculum for black churches emerged from the conference reports and recommendations:

CHRISTIAN EDUCATION IN THE BLACK CHURCH . . . provides the educational undergirding for mission as seen from the black perspective—meaning the struggle for liberation and equal justice in the spirit of the teachings of Jesus Christ, in our worship, relationships with all men, our witness, and daily work. . . .

THE CURRICULUM FOR CHRISTIAN EDUCATION IN THE BLACK CHURCH is the sum of all learnings from theological reflections on the Black Experience that prepares individuals for the struggle for justice and nurtures them in the Christian faith which teaches the proclamation of liberty for the captives and the setting free of the oppressed. (Luke 4:18-19)[12]

Another statement in the same report suggests that curriculum in the black church should serve to effect change and to encourage growth, social responsibility, and commitment to goals for the community that are depicted in the biblical faith.

The National Council of Churches' office to coordinate and administer black Christian education projects has ceased to function. A spin-off from work begun by that office, however, has resulted in a new and promising development for black Christian education. That development is called Black Educational Resources Development (BERD) and was initiated in 1976 by two major denominations, the United Presbyterian Church in the U.S.A. and the United Church of Christ. BERD is a planned curriculum grounded in black liberation theology. It states as one of its underlying biblical-theological affirmations the assertion that "the history of Afro-Americans is a part of God's self-revelation and must be interpreted so that God's redemptive purpose for the people of that history can be understood."[13]

BERD is a complete curriculum resource for learners ages five through twelve and includes intergenerational mini-courses. It promises to make bold and creative use of black-oriented material which is seldom used by creators of mainstream curriculum materials. It has as an educational and pedagogical aim the correlation of biblical stories and texts with black liberation theology ideas. BERD materials are currently in use in black churches. While longitudinal evaluations must be awaited, BERD represents a courageous effort to create a quality curriculum that is relevant to black American Christians.

Some Issues in Christian Education for Blacks

A number of issues bear crucially upon Christian education that is relevant to black people. Three such issues are offered here as examples of some areas of concern.

One issue of surpassing importance in Christian education for blacks is the extent to which black persons are assisted in developing an appropriate self-image through the use of Christian education curriculum materials. It has practically become a cliché to speak of the importance of self-image to educational progress and healthy personhood these days. A plethora of psychological studies have attested to that basic fact. The need is no less dramatic in religious education than it is in secular education.

In addition to all the reasons persons suffer from a damaged self-image in society generally, black persons so suffer because blackness has been devalued in American society. Every black person growing up in America comes to realize this fact through many channels. The mass media, government, business and industry, the judiciary, textbooks used in schools, and even religious institutions are bearers of the message. Every aspect of the socio-cultural environment signals to black Americans that their blackness relegates them to an inferior status in society. Though cloaked with new subtleties, racism is as much alive today as it has ever been in the United States. This devaluation of blackness makes it difficult for black persons to develop a positive self-image. Thus the cruciality of the issue.

Some strides are beginning to be made in secular education to overcome the omissions and deficits in the treatment given blacks and their history in textbooks and the like. A corresponding effort must be made with reference to church education to which blacks are exposed and in which they are nurtured. This will mean, among other things, taking seriously recommendations such as those included in the *Manual, Black Perspectives in Church Education*, published by the Joint Educational Development project (JED). Those recommendations include promotion of attitudes of respect for self and others; identification of black models of achievement and accomplishment in American, African, and Caribbean societies; illumination and exploration of the totality of the black religious experience; and placing in proper perspective the significant role of black Americans as participants and contributors in the growth and development of the American nation.[14]

Church educators have often made the mistake of believing that by disregarding color and speaking in universalistic rhetoric the problem will be solved. That is to say, many educators contend that by treating black learners like everyone else and concentrating on the universality of the Christian faith, the greater service is rendered. With all the other signals suggesting that blackness is inferior, that approach will not do. Conscious efforts must be made to deal with the particularities of the black experience. Positive steps must be taken to negate the message of devaluation of blackness that is so persistent in society.

Another issue, not unrelated to the first, is the matter of symbolism in Christian education for blacks. Since learning is affective as well as cognitive, care must be taken by church educators not to foster a negative affective lesson while actually teaching one that is intended to be positive, cognitively speaking. The point can be illustrated by a poem written by Margaret Burroughs:

> What shall I tell my children who are black
> Of what it means to be a captive in this dark skin?
> What shall I tell my dear ones, fruit of my womb,
> Of how beautiful they are when everywhere they turn
> They are faced with abhorrence of everything that is black.
> The night is black and so is the bogeyman.
> Villains are black with black hearts.
> A black cow gives no milk. A black hen lays no eggs.
> Bad news comes bordered in black, mourning clothes are black,
> Storm clouds, black, black is evil
> And evil is black and devil's food is black.[15]

The question for black church educators is this: How can one affirm that blackness is a gift of God while using standard English in which the dominant symbol for evil is black, and the dominant symbol for all things good is white?

What is called for in response to this issue is not the substitution of so-called black English or some aberration thereof for standard English. Rather, what is called for is the creation of new symbols to express the ancient truths of the Christian faith. An alternative to the use of color symbolism can be found to express the abhorrence of sin and evil.

Sensitive educators must contemplate the question, What is being said to a young black person who is asked to join in singing a hymn with the line "Lord, make me whiter than snow"? It is of no comfort to argue that the writer of that hymn was merely drawing upon biblical imagery and had no racist intent. The issue is not the intent or innocence of the hymnwriter, but is rather the signal that is sent to the black person singing the hymn or hearing it sung.

An aggressive women's movement is seeking to correct the insensitive antifeminist language of hymns and other resources. What is being advocated here is that a similar effort be made by blacks with respect to the antiblackness so prevalent in religious resources.

Such an effort will, to be sure, meet with resistance. Artistic purists will call it tampering with art, while insensitive conservatives will ridicule the suggestion by denigrating the need for any change in symbolism. Without attempting to settle the debate, it might be noted that Roman Catholics sing Luther's hymn, "A Mighty Fortress Is Our God," but without the lines most Protestants have memorized—lines that refer to the Roman church as being crafty and powerful and full of cruel hate. It might also be remembered that many of the hymns most familiar to Christendom had, in their original forms, many more stanzas than appear in the average hymnbook. A selection process had to occur in order to choose the stanzas that would be included, and conversely, those that would be excluded. Hymnbook committees also have changed an occasional word or phrase in some hymns in order to accommodate a doctrinal or theological bias.

The point of this discussion is that it is risky business to send out signals that reinforce already present feelings of inadequacy and low self-esteem based on socio-cultural determinants. If attention is given to one of the sources of such signals, namely, Christian education curriculum materials, then a step in the right direction will have been taken.

The Christian church has failed to attract large numbers of black intellectuals, and indeed large numbers of blacks of any kind, because many blacks have been persuaded that Christianity is a white person's religion. The reference most often made in support of this perception is to the liturgies of the church which suggest that white is blissful while black is evil. The impact of this effective argument against the Christian faith on the part of many thoughtful blacks can be neutralized if the negative symbolism are dealt with in a creative way.

The third and final issue to be noted is that of theology. Thirty years ago, Randolph Crump Miller wrote that theology lies back of curriculum and that it is a tool by which learners are brought into right relationship with God.[16] Howard Grimes later suggested three functions of theology with reference to the teaching work of the church.[17] Theology functions to clarify the content of faith which is to be communicated, to inform the church's understanding of the process of teaching, and to guide the teaching church in raising methodological questions. C. Ellis Nelson asserted that "curriculum is an effort to provide meaning for the church's theology in terms that can be readily understood."[18]

The insights of the three religious educators quoted above should serve ample notice that theology and Christian education are inextricably bound to each other. Since this is true, it is of utmost importance that the theology which informs Christian education should be relevant to the experience of the learner. For black Christians this makes black liberation theology a logical choice.

As a developing theology, liberation theology might not be adequate to cover all areas of a well-rounded curriculum of Christian education. As has been shown, the most advanced European and American theologies have also failed to do this, at least where black Christians are concerned. By applying the basic assumptions and assertions of liberation theology and by adopting the action-reflection model which is so germane to it, the theological foundation of Christian education is bound to be enhanced.

As noted above, the Black Educational Resources Development curriculum offers a promising example of how curriculum based on the theological foundation of liberation theology can be developed. It must be remembered, however, that BERD is an infant endeavor and its lesson materials, so far, are directed only toward children ages five through twelve. Where materials such as BERD are not available, teachers can be taught to grapple with issues presented by use of liberation theology. Having at hand the methods and insights of this theological resource can improve the relevance of the teaching-learning process in ways that will redound to the benefit of black learners.

In summary, it can be said that speciality has characterized the involvement of blacks in the religious education movement. This was true during slavery because of their special condition of servitude. It was also true after the Emancipation Proclamation because of the special status that was reserved for blacks by the majority of the American society. Speciality has marked the new demand on the part of blacks for a curriculum of Christian education that addresses their particularity. This demand is in recognition of the fact that blacks are by reason of their history and experience in this land a special people. Special does not mean better than others or inferior to others. It means particularity, a difference born of the unique experience through which they have passed.

Christian education is expected to provide self-authentication to black Christians, just as it is expected to do for others. This will happen only when Christian education for blacks takes blacks seriously into account.

Notes

1. Charles C. Jones, *Religious Instruction of the Negroes* (New York: Universities Press/Greenwood Publishing Corp., 1969).
2. Ibid., 20.
3. Ibid., 21.
4. Clifton H. Brewer, *A History of Religious Education in the Episcopal Church to 1835* (New Haven: Yale University Press, 1924), 51.
5. Ibid., 52.
6. James D. Tyms, *The Rise of Religious Education Among Negro Baptists* (New York: Exposition Press, 1965), 89.
7. Henry L. Morehouse, *Baptist Home Missions in North America* (New York: Temple Court, 1883), 408.
8. Tyms, *The Rise of Religious Education Among Negro Baptists*, 130.
9. Ibid., 146.
10. Ibid., 178.
11. Edgar Friedenberg, *The Vanishing Adolescent* (Boston: Beacon Press, 1959), 40.
12. From "Reports and Recommendations," Krisheim II Conference, 31 August–3 September 1970, Philadelphia, Penn.
13. *Black Presbyterians in Mission*, January 1980 (Published jointly by BERD and United Presbyterian Program Agency).
14. *Manual, Black Perspectives in Church Education* (New York: Joint Educational Development, Division of Church Education, National Council of Churches).
15. Chicago, M.A.A.H. Press, 1968. Reprinted by permission of the author.
16. Randolph C. Miller, *The Clue to Christian Education* (New York: Charles Scribner's Sons, 1950), 6, 15.
17. Marvin J. Taylor, ed., *An Introduction to Christian Education* (Nashville: Abingdon Press, 1966), 32, 33.
18. Ibid., 160.

Bibliography

Harding, Vincent. *There Is a River: The Black Struggle for Freedom in America.* New York: Harcourt Brace Jovanovich, 1981.

Thomas, Latta R. *Biblical Faith and the Black American.* Valley Forge, Penn.: Judson Press, 1976.

Wilmore, Gayraud S., and James Cone, eds. *Black Theology: A Documentary History 1966-1979.* Maryknoll, N.Y.: Orbis Books, 1979.

CHAPTER 14

The Profession of Director or Minister of Christian Education in Protestant Churches

Dorothy Jean Furnish

Since the first decade of this century, Protestant churches in the United States large enough to have multiple staffs have employed specialists in education. However, there has never been unanimity about their titles and functions or their status in relation to other church professionals. In fact, the extent to which a profession of education specialists even exists has often been questioned. What is clear is that many persons have been and are employed to help people of all ages understand the heritage of the Christian tradition in such a way that they might feel themselves a part of that tradition and that they might grow in their own understanding and experience of the Christian faith. These education specialists do their work in relation to the church's total program, the developmental stages of life, the context within which people live and work, and the needs of persons and of the world in which they live.

The work of the director or minister of Christian education is done in a variety of settings and groupings. It is performed primarily within a local parish, although a limited number of education specialists are also employed by various beyond-the-local-church judicatories. In the local church, for example, they work with the Sunday school, vacation church school, camps, weekday schools, youth fellowships, informal discussion and study groups for adults, family nights, workshops, work camps, the church library, and they increasingly participate in the planning and leading of worship. For the innovative Christian educator this list may be only a beginning!

This chapter will discuss the education specialist under three major headings: (1) *The profession.* Is it a profession? Who is in it? What titles are used? What certification and standards exist? What professional organizations support the individuals in the

Dorothy Jean Furnish is Professor of Christian Education at Garrett-Evangelical Theological Seminary.

profession? (2) *The style*. What leadership style or styles characterize those in this profession? What is the place of "style" in the work of the specialist? (3) *The function*. What does a professional Christian educator do? What is the relationship between style and function? Since this is a profession in transition, the present status of these aspects—profession, style, and function—will be described with reference to the origins of the profession.

The Profession

A profession is characterized by its history, its members, their titles, membership standards, its professional organizations, and its theoretical base.

Origins and Growth

The profession known as *director of religious education* emerged during the first decade of this century. The immediate task was to permeate the church with the educational ideal, especially in relation to the Sunday school. The improving methods of teacher training for secular schools were seen as a model for education in the churches. In addition, there was a concern that the church should help turn back the moral decline among the young.

The theoretical basis for the profession was the work of John Dewey in educational philosophy and the application of the best of biblical scholarship to church education by Ernest DeWitt Burton and Shailer Matthews. The organizational stimulus for the profession came from the Religious Education Association (REA) and from its first president, William Rainey Harper. Dewey, Burton, Matthews, and Harper were faculty members at the University of Chicago when the REA was organized in 1903. The primary advocate for the profession was Henry F. Cope, general secretary of the REA from 1907 until his death in 1923. On 10 March 1910, under the auspices of the REA, the first meeting of directors of religious education was held in connection with the seventh general convention of the REA. It called for "those men and women who are employed in churches and other institutions as 'Directors of Religious Education,' or in any like capacity engaged in the supervision of such work" to meet together to discuss topics of common interest.[1]

Who Are They?

The enthusiasm for the profession and the numbers in it grew rapidly from an estimated forty-six in 1912 to an estimated eight hundred by 1926.[2] With the onset of the depression, reduced salaries caused many people to leave the profession and few new ones to enter it. Thus by 1946 the number had increased by only two hundred, to an estimated one thousand persons. Although the period between the depression and the end of World War II was a bleak one for the profession, the end of the war brought new optimism. Church programs grew, new educational buildings were constructed, church and church school attendance increased, and with it came a new wave of professional educators. Such was the growth that by the mid-1960s it was estimated that there were eleven thousand employed. In spite of the decline in church school attendance during the 1960s and 1970s and in spite of economic recession which is still rumored to be causing reductions in the ranks of professional educators, it seems certain that there are more than eleven thousand education specialists employed today. Some denominations even report a large increase in numbers since the mid-1970s.[3]

While the numbers may be remaining stable or increasing, it is not clear what percentage of these educators are lay professionals, what percentage are ordained, and what percentage might be called para-professional; that is, performing some or most of the functions usually assigned to a professional, but without meeting the educational criteria assumed to be normative. Reports from denominations indicate that the number of ordained persons serving as education specialists seems to be increasing. In fact, in some denominations persons are encouraged to seek ordination. Although there are no precise statistical data available, it appears that a larger percentage of lay professionals would now fall into the para-professional category, while an increasing number of professionals are seeking ordination.

It is a surprise to many that the profession in its earliest years consisted almost exclusively of ordained men. However, both lay men and women soon joined the ranks in large numbers so that by 1926, the profession was almost equally divided between men and women. Christian education became "woman's work" chiefly as a result of the depression, which caused married men with families to abandon the low-paying positions. By 1938 only 26 percent of the directors reported were men. This trend began to reverse during the affluent years following World War II.

Current statistics are not available to indicate accurately the percentage of men and women now in the profession. Many different factors are at work to make even an estimate difficult. At one time it would have been assumed that the growing number of ordained persons in the profession indicated a larger number of men, but with seminary enrollment of women reaching almost the 50 percent level in some seminaries, ordination is no longer a clue. Clouding the issue even more is the continued reluctance of some ordained women to work in Christian education since, not knowing the predepression history of the profession, they erroneously see it as a traditional woman's role. Suffice it to say that when national and regional meetings of educational professionals are held, a sizable number of men are in attendance.

By What Titles?

At the beginning of the profession, titles were descriptive of both function and professional status. For example, in 1910 when the first meeting of professional educators was held, the roster of the REA listed members under these varied titles: educational director, director of religious education, assistant pastor and Sunday school superintendent, minister and Sunday school superintendent, and educational superintendent of Sunday school. These were soon followed by other titles such as superintendent of the Sunday school and youth worker, and director of young people's work.

The aversion of early professional educators to limit their work to the Sunday school was reflected in the fact that *Sunday school* as a name in their titles was soon dropped. Director of religious education became the accepted nomenclature. However, two objections to this title have been voiced. First, the term *director* signals a much more autocratic and direct style of working than most directors have wanted to claim as their own. The term has persisted, however, in spite of the discomfort of many who so name themselves.

But a second objection to the title director of religious education has resulted in a change. The impulse for this change came from the new appreciation for the importance of theology's contribution to religious education theory.[4] Some see the change in title as marking a change in the development of an ongoing profession; others see it as the beginning of a new profession related to a new field of endeavor.[5] In any case, when "religious education" became "Christian education," the title was altered and the education professional became a director of Christian education.

In addition to style and theological considerations, a third factor entered into the title decision—an increasing desire among directors themselves for the establishment of standards for the profession. Since 1948 at least eight denominations have adopted a certification procedure based on denominationally determined standards.[6] In addition to other qualifications, "certification" generally indicates that the educator has some form of theological graduate work and usually holds a master's degree with a specialization in Christian education.

Since the middle of the century the title controversy seems to have subsided, and three titles have emerged among Protestant educators as normative: director of Christian education, for lay professionals; minister of Christian education, for ordained professionals; and educational assistant (or some form of this term), for persons who are employed to direct the education program but who have not met denominational standards for certification.[7]

One of the most recent changes in title has come about in response to a broadening of the educator's responsibilities from a relatively narrow specialization to supervision of the church's total program. Sometimes this results from a new appreciation for holistic approaches to church life; at other times it comes from a reorganization of church staff in order to economize. In any case, these new titles are being invented: director of program, coordinator of program, executive minister, minister of program, and program consultant. While this phenomenon has only recently appeared on the scene, it may mark a watershed in the profession which only history will be able to record.

To What Do They Belong?

Professional Christian educators often feel isolated from other educators because of geographical distance or because they feel their work is not understood. They need continuing education opportunities and moral support. Thus they are loyal and enthusiastic members of their professional organizations.

The nondenominational REA is composed of individuals of all faiths, and it was the original home for professional educators. Later the Protestant and interdenominational International Council of Religious Education and its successor, the National Council of Churches, provided a professional advisory section for directors. In urban areas, where professional educators are more likely to be employed, there may be interdenominational city or state organizations. Increasingly, however, educators have turned to their own denominational structures for support. Some denominations hold annual or semiannual regional meetings. Many Protestant educators affiliate with their national denominational organization.[8]

Summary

One way to summarize is to attempt an answer to the question, Is it a profession? In many ways it begins to meet the generally accepted criteria by which an occupation is judged to be a profession. It has recognized titles—director or minister of Christian education (although many others are used); it has a certification process based on published standards (although only some denominations certify, and standards are not necessarily the same); it suggests an academic qualification—specialization in Christian education at a graduate school of theology (although some are certified without this); its members belong to professional organizations (although membership in none of them is limited to those who meet professional standards); the profession is based on a theory of Christian education whose foundations are studies in Bible, theology, and the social sciences (although that theory is still in the process of formulation).

It may be a profession in transition, or it may be more accurate to describe it as a profession that has been conceived and is some place midway between birth and maturity.

The Style

The contemporary professional Christian educator prefers to be characterized by the words *enabler* or *facilitator* rather than words that indicate a more direct, active style of leadership. Educators understand their role as leader to be one of helping both individuals and the corporate church discover and develop their own potential. Sometimes professional educators are out ahead, urging people on. Sometimes they are helping persons realize their own abilities so that they in turn teach the professional educator. It is sometimes said that they are at their best when working themselves out of a job. A more dynamic way to see the education specialist is both as enabler of persons and as one with vision pointing to ways the church, through education, can expand its outreach to the community and world.

Consulting as Enabling

At times the enabling style of the educator requires the skills of a consultant. Problem identification, goal-setting, leader development, implementation, and evaluation are skills used not only in the education program but to facilitate the church's total program.

Resourcing as Enabling

Often the enabling style of the professional educator calls for skill as a resource person. The educator is familiar with denominational curriculum resources. Supplementary materials available from a wide range of publishers must be known so that the program can be enriched and special needs met. In the early years of the profession one of the major tasks of the education specialist was to create curriculum resources where none existed. Although the market seems flooded with such resources today, many creative educators find that from time to time their particular situations call for approaches not readily available, so they still need to invent new models and develop new resources. The educator also enables persons and programs by being familiar with "people resources" in the community who can provide long-term, short-term, or occasional services.

Another kind of resource provided is the store of knowledge about educational principles and methods, developmental theory, the traditions of the church, broader aspects of church history and Bible knowledge, denominational polity, and a general sensitivity to the varieties of life situations being experienced by members of the congregation. In a special way, the educator in his or her own personhood is a unique kind of resource. The professional educator has an opportunity to model what it means for an adult Christian to strive to continue to be a growing person within one's vocation, in relation to God, to others, and to the church set in the midst of a troubled world.

Doing as Enabling

Sometimes the enabling style of the educator calls for direct, visible leadership. This "up-front" style was more characteristic of persons in the early history of the profession when new ground was being broken. But it is still true today. When new teachers have been recruited, the director or minister of education may teach a demonstration session. When a new model of teaching is introduced (for example, learning centers), the educator may take a major role in initiating, organizing, and implementing the process. An education specialist may assume direct leadership of community and/or ecumenical endeavors in the area of education, perhaps teaching in a community leader development program. In all of these situations the intention is that the educator's doing will enable others to do or to be.

Summary

The director or minister of Christian education most often chooses to work in an enabling style. This style is sometimes misunderstood when persons not immediately involved do not see the work being done by the educator and wonder if the staff position is really necessary. In spite of this risk, educators usually resist the limelight but work with individuals and groups to help them become the church in mission to the community and the world.

The Function

The professional in Christian education performs a wide variety of functions, largely determined by the needs of the situation and the interests and gifts of the educator. These functions are described here in four categories: program development and coordination, leader development, advocacy, and modeling shared leadership in a multiple staff.

Program Development and Coordination

The programmatic aspects of a church's life are never for the sake of the program itself, but are for helping persons in their own religious pilgrimage or helping the church corporately minister to the needs of the world. It is within this understanding and in this spirit that educators join with others in the church to develop church program. Often it is the educator who has the consultation skills needed to help a church arrive at goals that express its understanding of its purpose; and it may be the educator who guides the leadership development, implementation, and evaluation phases of the programming process. It has been said that one of the tasks of Christian education is to equip persons for doing God's work in the world. One way this is accomplished is through the program efforts of the local church

The professional educator is especially responsible for coordinating the program of Christian education. In addition, however, educators from the earliest days of the profession have seen it as their responsibility to coordinate the work of education with the total program of the church. In order that persons not be fragmented, it is necessary that the work of the junior choir be consistent with the objectives of the children's church school classes; that the financial campaign of the church not exploit children; that youth projects not run counter to the church's understanding of its mission in the world; and that the one who teaches the confirmation class know what has been studied in church school. A coordinator is needed in the interest of both persons and program, and the educator is usually best able to provide this service.

Leader Development

Once program has been determined, the need is for leadership. The professional educator is at work in all phases of leader development for Christian education. Often the programmatic unit that requires the greatest number of leaders is the Sunday school. The immediate and obvious need here is for teachers. In cooperation with the church education committee, the specialist guides in setting standards for teachers, teacher selection, teacher recruitment, and finally in teaching the teachers to teach. Improvement of teaching skills may be done on a one-to-one basis, not unlike a counseling session. Or it can take place as directors and ministers of education encourage participation in beyond-the-local-church experiences such as laboratory schools, curriculum previews, and other leader-training workshops. In a similar way the educator guides the development of leadership for other aspects of the church's education program.

Advocacy

Rarely is it defined in a job description, but the professional educator is often the one in the church who assumes special responsibility as the advocate for the persons without power who seldom find themselves in leadership, decision-making positions. These may include children, youth, older adults, and persons with a variety of handicapping conditions. It is often the educator who helps the rest of the church realize that these persons are an important part of the faith community. The advocacy role may take the form of pressing for some kind of appropriate programming. It might mean helping the trustees see the need for barrier-free access to all parts of the building. It might mean an additional budget item for large-type pew Bibles; relaxation of rules on the use of the building; establishment of a drug drop-in center, recreational facilities, or a child abuse intervention service. Whatever advocacy on behalf of the powerless may mean, Christian educators are finding themselves called to be in the midst of it.

Modeling Shared Leadership

One of the functions of a director or minister of Christian education is to find a way to become a working, productive member of a church staff. The professional educator is by virtue of the profession always a member of a staff team. In the early days of the profession there were many conflicts between pastors and educators for power and loyalty of the members. Although this may occur today, educators and senior pastors are more likely now to understand the need for a team approach and will usually publicly affirm this even though it may not always feel "teamlike" in practice.

In spite of the affirmations, however, most church staffs are organized in a hierarchical fashion so that it is clear that the educator (along with other program staff) is accountable to the senior pastor with respect to day-to-day functioning. But churches vary in their understanding of the locus for ultimate accountability of the educator. In some the educator is accountable only to the senior pastor. In others, the educator is primarily responsible to the education committee, the personnel committee, or some other church-designated administrative group. Where the educator is a certified professional, theologically trained, and a full-time career specialist, there is more likelihood that he or she will be seen as a partner in ministry. If the educator is also ordained, it would seem that the last barrier to full recognition as a team member would be removed. Even then it may be necessary to overcome problems of power and status.

Summary

The functions of the director or minister of Christian education can never be limited by definition, but they emerge and evolve as the educator works within a given setting. They are much more than Sunday school related but may be seen in operation at any point in a church's program where religious growth of persons is the goal. Sometimes there is need for program formulation, and at other times there is need for leader development to implement the program. Sometimes the need may be to function alone as an advocate for the powerless, but always it is with the expectation that the educator is only one part of a total staff team that works together to enable all members and the church as a whole to perform its ministry to persons and to the world.

Conclusion

Unlike the professions of medical doctor or clergy that rest on centuries of tradition and experience, the director or minister of Christian education is a member of a young profession. It is a twentieth-century phenomenon based on confidence in educational processes for character and religious formation. In its youthfulness it is susceptible to outside influence.

One of these influences is always the prevailing theological winds that blow. They changed the field and the title from "religious" to "Christian." Another is the status of the national economy that threatens to result in diminished support even when recession does not occur. Still another influence is the evolving image of what it means to "minister," and the emerging concept of the professional educator as one who is engaged in ministry, whether that one is ordained or lay.

In spite of change and uncertainties, it is clear that the number of people engaged in a specialized form of ministry known as "the professional Christian educator" continues to grow. The titles may change, and the functions may broaden to include much more of the church's program than the Sunday school. But by whatever title, as long as the local church continues to be a setting in which Christian nurture takes place, there will be a need for persons who can guide the church's educational task.

Notes

1. "Preliminary Program, Seventh General Convention,"*Religious Education* 4 (February 1910); 13.
2. For primary sources for historical data, see Dorothy Jean Furnish, *DRE/DCE: The History of a Profession* (Nashville: Christian Educators Fellowship of the United Methodist Church, 1976).
3. Southern Baptist: 1974—1440; 1982—3049; United Methodist: 1975—1927; 1982—2739; American Baptist: 1975—400; 1982—768. (Furnish, *DRE/DCE;* correspondence from denominational staff persons.)
4. See Elliott-Smith "debate": Harrison S. Elliott, *Can Religious Education Be Christian?* (New York: Macmillan, 1940); H. Shelton Smith, *Faith and Nurture,* (New York: Charles Scribner's Sons, 1941).
5. Gabriel Moran, "The Limits of the Past," in *Interplay* (Winona, Minn.: St. Mary's Press, 1981), 24.
6. Methodist in 1948; Presbyterian, U.S. in 1959; Lutheran Church in America in 1968; Evangelical Covenant in 1975; American Lutheran Church in 1976; United Presbyterian, U.S.A. in 1981; United Church of Christ, n.d.; Unitarian-Universalist, n.d.
7. Some denominations have various levels of certification.
8. For example, American Baptist Ministers' Council, Association of Presbyterian Church Educators, United Methodist Christian Educators Fellowship, the National Association of Directors of Christian Education (related to the National Association of Evangelicals), Association of Christian (Disciples) Church Educators, and the Association of United Church Educators (United Church of Christ).

Bibliography

Beal, Will, compiler. *The Work of the Minister of Education; The Minister of Education As A Growth Agent; The Minister of Education as Educator.* Southern Baptist Sunday School Board.

Furnish, Dorothy Jean. *DRE/DCE: The History of a Profession.* Nashville: Christian Educators Fellowship of the United Methodist Church, 1976.

Harris, Maria. *The D.R.E. Book.* New York: Paulist Press, 1976.

———. *Parish Religious Education.* New York: Paulist Press, 1978.

Neiman, Joseph C. *Coordinators.* Winona, Minn.: St. Mary's Press, 1971.

CHAPTER 15

U.S. Directors of Religious Education in Roman Catholic Parishes

Maria Harris

In the mid-1960s, a new professional role, that of parish director of religious education, emerged in the United States Catholic church. Until that time, parochial education had been the province of clergy and school personnel, the latter's work carried on largely, if not exclusively, by members of religious orders. With the advent of Vatican II, declines in both school enrollment and membership in teaching orders, coupled with an increasingly aware and vigorous laity, caused a novel situation to take shape. The purpose of this essay is to describe that situation, the role which emerged from it, and the conditions and characteristics surrounding that role today.

The Emergence of DREs

U.S. Catholicism of the sixties reflected a worldwide renewal. International Study Weeks on Catechetics had begun in 1959, the culmination of at least two decades of ferment in European Catholicism.[1] These weeks were a signal of increasing interest in the teaching of religion by Catholics around the globe. Nijmegen (1959), Eichstat (1960), Katigondo (1964), Manila (1967), and Medellin (1968) attracted attention in this country, especially since their proceedings were published here[2] and were accompanied by visits from abroad by Johannes Hofinger, Alfonso Nebreda, and Marcel Van Caster, speaking the word of catechetical vitality up and down the land.[3] A rash of subscriptions went out from the States to the Belgian catechetical publication, *Lumen Vitae*, which had begun to publish an English-language edition, since no comparable journal existed here.

In 1962–65, the ferment coincided with Vatican Council II. The major contribution of the council to religious education, however,

Maria Harris is Howard Professor of Religious Education at Andover Newton Theological School.

lay not in its declaration on Christian education—to this day a little-known document—but in the *Constitution on the Church*. In that work, *Lumen Gentium*, the imagery was decisive.[4] There, the council introduced long-neglected images (people of God, family, prophetic community) which identified the church with all the people and worked against the long-standing tendency in U.S. Catholicism to equate "church" with hierarchy and/or officials.

These influences, coming from abroad, had implications for people teaching religion here, most of whom were faculty members in Catholic elementary and secondary schools, and many of whom taught Confraternity of Christian Doctrine (CCD) classes after school and on weekends. Given the heightened emphasis on teaching, these persons began to notice discrepancies between religious instruction offered in the school and outside of it, to recognize inequitable distribution of time and resources, and to examine the possibilities for the full-time designing, implementing, and offering of classes in religion for all. Coupled with a burgeoning interest in religious study on the part of Catholic adults, the realization gradually but powerfully deepened that only a small minority of Catholics of any age were receiving adequate religious instruction. Two influential books articulated the realization and moved the issue forward: Mary Perkins Ryan's *Are Parochial Schools the Answer?*[5] and the Greeley-Rossi study, *The Education of Catholic Americans.*[6]

By 1966, parishes throughout the land began to take the natural and understandable next step: the appointment and employment of someone to oversee religious education for all in the parish, with special attention to that growing segment of schoolage children not attending Catholic schools, and to the inclusion of their parents in the sacramental preparation of those children for Eucharist, penance, and confirmation. Such a role was not new. Religious orders such as the Mission Helpers of the Sacred Heart and the Victory Noll Sisters had been doing it, especially in places where parochial schools did not exist, for years. And Protestant DCEs and DREs had been performing analogous tasks since as early as 1906.[7] What was new was the emergence of the role from the grass roots, rather than from the top; and the *extent* of the role. More often than not, the impetus for employing a DRE came not from a diocesan suggestion, but from the local parish community. And where in a diocese of some one million Catholics, five DREs could be found in 1967, such a diocese might have more than one hundred by 1973.[8]

The activities of those first DREs, often referred to as parish coordinators, were many. In addition to offering religious instruction to schoolage children, they also needed to prepare persons to teach these young people and to explain to their parents and to parishioners other than parents what was happening in the Catholic subculture. These needs became apparent and often critical at the same time changes were taking place in religious orders. Life and work in teaching orders were changing, and many who had left that life-style still sought to use the skills and religious understanding developed during their years of membership. Inevitably, the first cadre of DREs included such persons: teaching sisters; women and men who were formerly members of religious orders; and often, former seminarians—all of whom were characterized by a fairly sophisticated understanding of both religion and education.

Indeed, perhaps the most obvious characteristic of this first group of coordinators and/or DREs was their competence. They were very good at what they did. They knew theology and education; they knew how to prepare classes and deal with large numbers; they understood children and how children learn. The expertise of the first DREs was therefore remarkable. More often than not they were well schooled; for those who were not, diocesan office staffs, themselves increasingly well educated, provided in-service assistance of high caliber. Typically, in the 1970s, both diocesan staffs and parochial educators knew parish life well and had engaged in serious study during year-long or summer programs at academic centers such as Manhattan College, Fordham, the University of San Francisco, Detroit's Pius XII Institute, Marquette, Loyola, Seattle, Spokane, and Houston.

A less obvious but perhaps more important quality of these first DREs was a direct result of Vatican II. This was their sense of church. For they were (and continue to be) people who believed *Lumen Gentium* and therefore thought of themselves as church, as priestly and prophetic followers of the Christ. In explaining dogma, sacramental life, or human religiousness, they were convinced—and so convinced others—that this dogma, this life, this religiousness was the responsibility of all the people in the church. It was to be applauded when it resonated as true in the lives of the people; to be examined and challenged when it did not. In other words, the DREs of the late sixties and early seventies were not afraid of educational critique, although it was a critique offered lovingly from within the church by persons who cared deeply for the church and were conscious of their own responsibility as its baptized members.

This meant, in addition, that the Catholic church in the United States had begun to have an educated corps who, in contrast to the ordained, were outside the hierarchical system. I do not mean they were people who "did their own thing"; on the contrary, they were strikingly communal Catholics, and the rugged individual did not last long in the position. But it became obvious that the DRE was someone who provided the opportunity for freedom of thought, diversity, experimentation in new forms of church life and exposure to different theologies for hundreds of thousands of church people in refreshing and thoughtful ways. Many parishioners, brought up to see the religious leader as father, confessor, and authority figure, now became involved with another kind of religious leader, often for the first time a woman, often a parent, often much like themselves. Understandably this sometimes created conflict with the clergy, a point to which I will return later. But on the whole it was a positive occurrence not only for DREs but for all with whom they worked.

Nurturance and Development

Accompanying the growth of the DRE as church role (and now I speak of the present as well as the past), significant resources came into existence and moved the role along. Although they were not always used, a circumstance true even today, these resources were available and helped many persons. In commenting on them, I restrict my remarks to those resources directed to the DRE's own self-understanding, as distinct from resources helpful in the professional design, implementation, and conducting of religious education.

No one person contributed more to the early perception and knowledge of the DRE than Joseph C. Neiman. In 1968, with the assistance and financial support of the National Conference of Diocesan Directors (NCDD), Neiman began *Project Coordinator*. From then until 1973, he wrote five major project reports as well as numerous occasional papers. These project reports provide our most significant research data on the first years of the DRE. Reporting yearly from the International Divine Word Centre of Religious Education in London, Ontario, which he codirected, he offered data on professional development, opinion surveys on national associations, studies of diocesan services, explorations of the many concepts of role, and reviews of professional preparation. Much of the data is in his 1971 book, *Coordinators*,[9] which continues to serve as a DRE handbook. The other place where Neiman's work can be found is in the 1971 and 1972 volumes of *P.A.C.E.*[10] In the 1971 volume he contributed a monthly article; in 1972, he contributed several essays. In all that he wrote, he demonstrated an awareness of the role, gleaned from those actually performing it.

P.A.C.E., begun under the editorship of Sheila Moriarty O'Fahey, has remained a leading resource for DREs. Now edited by Mary Perkins Ryan, it continues to publish articles directed to the DRE's professional understanding. The observations of DRE work by Mary Margaret Funk, until 1982 diocesan director in Indianapolis, often appear in its pages, and three major series for DREs have appeared in recent years: by John Bosio in 1976, by Daryl Olsewski in 1978, and by Gabriel Moran in 1978. In 1980, St. Mary's Press published *The D.R.E. Reader*, a collection of essays concerning the DRE culled from ten years of *P.A.C.E.* which I edited.[11]

The Living Light has also been committed to the DRE, demonstrated most recently by a special section in the fall of 1980, but dating to the beginning of the 1970s.[12] A number of pieces from *Living Light* have become standard reading for and about DREs. Stephen Nevin's "Parish Coordinator: Evaluating Task and Roles," Daniel Dolesch's "Towards a Survival Kit for the Professional Religious Educator," Paul Cook's "Contact to Contract," Joseph Moore's "The Many Hats of the Parish Coordinator," Berard Marthaler's "What is the Ministry of a DRE?"[13] and Maria Harris's "DREs in the U.S.: The First Twenty Years"[14] are perhaps the most important.

Other journals, notably *Catechist*,[15] *Religion Teacher's Journal*,[16] *Modern Ministries*, and *Today's Parish* (the latter two now incorporated as one) have demonstrated commitment to DREs over the years, often publishing a monthly column for them. Two books published in 1976 provide insight and the ring of truth. The first is Dorothy Jean Furnish's *DRE/DCE: History of the Profession*,[17] describing the role in Protestantism. The second is my own *D.R.E. Book*,[18] which continues to function as a DRE handbook and is probably a major reason the title DRE is used today by the great percentage of persons in this position.[19] Perhaps the most provocative publication of the seventies was a short-lived magazine edited, written, and produced by the Detroit Community of Religious Education Directors (CORED) entitled *Three Rings*.[20] Available only from 1972 to 1974, it discontinued publication, but not before demonstrating the possibility of a magazine specifically responsive to the role of DRE. One could surmise that the time is now right for a similar attempt, while acknowledging the superb contribution of that short-lived journal.

Two national organizations, the NCDD and the NCEA (National Catholic Educational Association), have given enormous support to DREs for well over a decade. From different vantage points, each has supplied continuing nurturance to DREs in the field. The NCDD has, from the beginning, found parish coordinators/DREs a natural constituency and provided help in many forms at local and national levels. Locally, diocesan directors and their staffs often catalyze DRE associations, supply ideas and materials, and provide job placement. Nationally, in addition to policy direction, the NCDD publishes the *Resource Guidebook for Diocesan Directors of Religious Education Concerning Parish Directors of Religious Education*, a document which in my judgment ought to be in the hands of every DRE.[21] At three dollars a copy it is a bargain, and for DREs contemplating independent organizations, it provides a plethora of suggestions on every topic from contracts to summer vacations. In April of 1980, at its national meeting, the NCDD issued a strong, supportive policy statement concerning the DRE, advocating and urging "parish and diocesan leaders to strive to provide the needed resources, policies, and public recognition and affirmation to prepare, support, and increase the number of persons who carry out this ministry in the church."[22] Most recently, in cooperation with the United States Catholic Conference, the NCDD has funded the first national profile of professional religious education coordinators, under the scholarly direction of Dr. Thomas Walters. The report, soon to be published, provides statistical data for the first time describing in detail those in the role who are salaried, full-time persons with M.A. or equivalent who have held the position for three or more years.[23]

The NCEA, first under the direction of Alfred McBride and now led by Francis Kelly, has also played a strong advocacy role. In 1973 it began a national organization of parish directors (the NCPDRE), which publishes a monthly newsletter and thus far has also produced two books: *A Day in the Life of a DRE*, edited by Thomas Smith,[24] and *The Vocation and Spirituality of the DRE*, edited by Francis Kelly.[25] In 1982 the NCEA organized, sponsored, and hosted workshops in the southwest and the northeast for DREs, bringing together national religious education experts, publishers, and DREs from many states and many dioceses.[26]

Still, aside from this professional support and the personal assistance of loving human beings and the graceful presence of God in their lives, the greatest source of nurturance and development for DREs comes from people in the same position—other DREs. Because the job demands are often exhausting, the hours peculiar, and the surprises continual, DREs have come to depend most on one another for the kind of understanding that can be given only by someone in similar circumstances. Mutual support is growing and tending to spill over parish, diocesan, state, and even ecumenical boundaries. Where the sixties saw *one* DRE per parish, the eighties witness teams of DREs—often as many as four, five, or six—who work in concert with each other. Many in smaller parishes share time and resources and exchange skills across parish lines, since the work remains the same: the design, implementation, and offering of quality religious education. In the *Project Coordinator* report of 1971,[27] Neiman found only 19 percent of dioceses had coordinator associations; the 1982 Walters report indicates 60 percent of DREs now belong to diocesan associations. The probable next step is one already taken in Wisconsin and New Jersey, that of statewide, interdiocesan federations. [28] As this occurs, however, the conflicts, tensions, and possibilities of past and present will need to be faced, or better, named as agenda for such organizations. In the final part of this essay, I turn to the conflicts and tensions, in the midst of which dwell the possibilities for the future.

Conflicts and Tensions

I begin by distinguishing between the concepts of conflict and tension, both of which, arguably, are needed for maturity. *Conflict* is a prolonged battle; a struggle or clash; a controversy; disagreement. Conflict is outright opposition. *Tension,* in contrast, is stretching, or the condition of being stretched. A tension is a device for regulating tautness and is characterized by pulls in opposing directions, both having a claim on one's energy. Tension is a positive condition created when important forces pull against each other, and in this view it is an artistic category, marking the presence of intelligence. Without the internal resistance tensions call forth, there is too "fluid a rush to a straightaway mark," in Dewey's phrase, without the chastening activities of development and fulfillment.

Conflicts

In the early days, the number one conflict for DREs was with the pastor. Given the human propensity to resist the new, the unfamiliar, and the unknown, that is not surprising. Pastors often did not know what they were getting, and DREs, although competent, were often feeling their way. In addition, the DRE appeared to threaten the pastor's position and actually often did. From the standpoint of training, DREs, in many cases, knew more about liturgy, Scripture, doctrine, and education than their pastors did; understandably, this did not create immediate camaraderie. The conflict was compounded in many cases when the DRE was a woman. Similar struggle often characterized the relationship between DRE and Catholic school personnel, and allocation of resources to school versus nonschool programs led to royal battles.

To declare such conflict over would be naïve; to declare it lessened is accurate. The absence of novelty, and knowing now what to expect, have led to the resolution of much conflict as has the move toward equitable salaries, contracts, job descriptions, mutual appreciation of each other's gifts, weekly staff meetings, and weekly prayer. On their part, advocates of Catholic schooling have recognized the legitimate grievances of nonschool religious education personnel; on their part, DREs, especially in inner cities, have seen and been part of enormous contributions by the Catholic school.

More troubling, and as yet unresolved possibly because it is sometimes under the surface, is the conflict between trained and untrained DREs; between those who strive for professional recompense and benefits and those who contribute services; between those who consider themselves professionals and those who are volunteers. At one time the conflict was symbolized by the difference between those who were in religious orders and those who were not; but more recently, both dioceses and individuals, especially sisters, are refusing the parish that wants "cheap labor" and learning to discern the parish of genuine need. The conflict more typically surfaces today in the description of who actually *is* a DRE. The 1982 NCDD Walters report, as I have already noted, uses a description that includes salary, schooling, credentials in the form of a graduate degree or equivalent, specialization, and experience. However, in many parishes in the country, the *title* DRE is held, and the *offices* of DRE (planning, designing, initiating, and offering religion programs) are carried out by persons without the above characteristics. The results are sometimes remarkably similar, yet clarity of role definition remains lacking. Indeed, no consensus is yet clear that distinctions should be maintained. Thus the issue remains unresolved. But the conflict is also apparent (where salaries *are* offered to DREs) in the pay discrepancy between those, usually married men, who are primary bread-winners and those married women whose DRE reimbursement is considered a "second salary." As of this writing, this issue too is unresolved. DREs experiencing these conflicts would be well advised to study the history of modern professions. Such conflicts are not peculiar to church people, but exist in any group moving toward professional status.[29]

One other conflict persists. Ironically, it is between the two organizations that have done most to benefit DREs, the NCEA and the NCDD. This conflict appears to me to reflect parish and diocesan conflicts on the national level. Open discussion of disagreements and the recent sharing of resources indicate the wish of both groups to come eventually to some agreement, if not to a single voice, but rapprochement has not yet been attained. Such rapprochement can only benefit the individual DRE. However, it will not be possible unless the legitimate claims of both organizations are aired, recognized, and respected, a task which both have begun to address seriously, assisted by excellent leadership.

Tensions

In turning to tensions, my thesis is that three necessary tensions characterize the work of today's DRE and that if that work is to bear fruit, the DRE must dwell within these tensions for the foreseeable future. The first is between inner conviction and outside expectation; the second is between church ministry and church education; the third is between the priestly and the prophetic.[30]

1. *Inner conviction and outside expectation.* Many reasons exist for DREs, as individuals, to decide to take on the full-time duties of directing, organizing, and planning religious education within a parish. Like any complex set of human motivations, the choices leading to this particular profession are not completely susceptible to analysis. Nevertheless, success in applying for a position; engaging in interviews; and eventually being hired by a pastor, committee, or parish board is based on certain qualities. Chief among these, ordinarily, is an awareness on the employer's part that the person applying possesses personal worth and compe-tence, a genuine concern and care for the church as a people, and some vision of a future better than the existent present.

Although it can and does happen, an individual or parish rarely dissimulates upon first meeting. Misunderstandings are certainly possible, but most times a parish and a DRE begin a relationship with a fair degree of mutuality and an honest desire to be of service to one another. Just as often, however, a tension develops between the DRE and the parish or pastor or board or all of the above. At best it is healthy, provocative, and generative of new life; at worst it is destructive and debilitating. But it is never absent. What I refer to is the inevitable tension between an individual and an institution, what in sociological terms is known as "institutional lag."

Such tension is to be expected. The DRE, as a professional person, is engaged in a continuing education, being instructed by the position itself and by the necessary study and preparation the job entails. Such study and preparation lead, by their very nature, to a deeper understanding of the underlying relationships in church life, such as those between catechesis, liturgy, and community. Firsthand contact with complex situations in the lives of parishioners can lead to questioning official sacramental or ecclesiastical positions (e.g., regarding marriage or the position of women in the church), which may heretofore have been felt only at a distance. Work with people in different communities (other parishes, ecumenical groups) can suggest to DREs a diversity of available approaches. These are only a few of the occurrences that can lead DREs to an inner conviction of the way things *ought* to be, of the necessity to order and sometimes reorder priorities, and of the desirability of institutional or parochial forms other than those accepted within their own parishes.

At the same time, the institution that has done the hiring and employing is *not* attending to parish life with the same intensity and dailiness as the DRE. For the outside community, things continue to look pretty much the same. The expectations stated when the DRE first arrived have not changed. Thus when an individual DRE, out of strong inner conviction, begins to change procedures or take on activities formerly assigned to others or (in an outside view) "lets things slide," tension is the result.

In such circumstances, several courses of action are available. Constant and open communication is necessary; a strong, supportive, and articulate diocesan office an essential partner; and continuing clergy awareness of the DRE role an ecclesial priority. Nevertheless, the tension is inevitable, and the DRE is, in my view, called to dwell within it. On the one hand, to give up one's inner convictions is intolerable. On the other, to contract for and then to negate commitments to a parish community is unjust. The solution appears for the time being to live in the tension itself, accepting as fact that compromise is part of the human condition, even though "legislation is helpless, in the end, against the wild prayer of longing" (Auden) in the heart of a convinced human being.

2. *Church education and church ministry.* In the early seventies, and even more today, DREs have spoken of their work as ministry as often as they have spoken of it as education. Sometimes the terms are used synonymously and interchangeably: "My work is educational ministry," say many; "My ministry is religious education," say others. This uncritical blurring of what are, have been, and shall continue to be *two different professions* is, in my view, unfortunate, and serves to keep hidden the genuine and productive tension that needs to be brought to the surface.

What are the distinctions? In practice the most obvious one is that ministers are officials or semi-officials of an institution, in this case the church. Therefore belonging, commitment, and a common set of assumptions or presuppositions are expected and sought from the minister as the spokesperson for the community. Essentially, the minister is *a part of* the ecclesial community. Ministerial work tends to go beyond such activities as catechesis and didache (works of schooling) to the spiritual and corporal works of mercy classically designated as *koinonia, diakonia,* and *leiturgia.* The educator, in contrast, generally works for an institution but is not one of its officers. The educator embodies, to some degree, an *apartness from* the ecclesial community. The distance following on such apartness enables the educator to carry out her or his critical responsibility to design environments where knowledge, values, traditions, and attitudes can be examined, explored, and challenged; to raise questions such as "How do we know that?" "On whose authority?" "On what grounds is this said or done?" and "Who's going to benefit?"; to share resources not only from Catholic tradition, but from the religious traditions of all people; and to keep alive the realization that with reference to God and the universe, all the data are not yet in.

In my judgment, it is important to keep both professions alive, either within the person of the DRE, or if not that, within the community where she or he works. Because of the necessary tension between them, the temptation to collapse the two into one is great, and usually goes in the direction of ministry. Being apart from the community can leave one out in the cold; being a part of the community is much more comfortable. One must acknowledge, of course, the genuinely communal and religious motives that have led many to move from education to pastoral ministry as their major work in the church. Nevertheless, one must also point out that this movement has a dark shadow side, and is sometimes the result of exhaustion, co-optation, or the desire to avoid conflict.

Despite this, I would hope for a continuance of the ministry-education tension. To me it is essential to champion the responsibilities, tribulations, sweat, and search for understanding that are proper to critical education, at the same time that ministry by all members of the church is encouraged. For in actuality, ministry is essential not to the *DRE* vocation, but to the *human* vocation. The paradox of dwelling in this second tension is that as DREs encourage ongoing education for all church members, taking seriously their own role as educators, they challenge those they educate to understand their baptismal vocations to ministry in the world. For the sake of such a church, struggling to be its own best self, both professions are needed.[31]

3. *The priestly and the prophetic.* Historically, in a religious culture, two essential elements are present: the priestly and the prophetic. In the parish context, I understand the word *priestly* to capture two notions dear to most DREs: (1) the priesthood of all believers, and (2) the Pauline injunction that we be "servants of the Christ and stewards of the mysteries of God" (I Cor. 4:1). Priesthood and priestly activity is responsibility to the *past*, expressed in the present by (a) preserving tradition, (b) remembering through ritual, and (c) gathering community. In tension with the priestly, *prophetic* activity is a focus on present activity directed to building the *future*. It is the work of the institution, in this case the church, in pushing back boundaries, in speaking the word nobody wants to hear, and in challenging society by actions in the world guaranteed to be disquieting.[32] The prophetic is that aspect of religious vocation by which a community emphasizes its responsibility beyond itself, by which it dares to call both itself and others to judgment before God, and by which it insists that personal and structured evil must be confronted and condemned. This is true even if that evil is found within the church.

I assume the tension between these two is apparent. The *priestly* or priesthood is a stabilizing force, centered on tradition, ritual, and community. The *prophetic* resists stabilizing in order to keep open questions of meaning and keep alive the process of history.[33] Prophecy is more immediately problematic, whether in art or religion: a van Gogh on the wall and a copy of Berrigan poems in the library are not threatening, but a van Gogh or a Berrigan actually present in living room or library calls much of life into question. But priesthood has a dark side too. The emergence of a priestly group or class in any work of human beings—whether law or medicine or religion—always creates the danger of a new elite.

DREs would do well to examine whether as a group they are becoming such an elite and strive to avoid it, for a new elite means some are ineluctably excluded.

Today's DRE is engaged in both priestly and prophetic work. The roles of priesthood are being claimed everywhere, indeed are acted upon throughout the country and world, although usually the name and the term *priestly* are not used. But prophecy is also alive and well and especially evident in the lives of those directors of religious education engaged in political and social activity both inside and beyond the church's boundaries. My argument, again, is that both are needed. Without the priestly, the ground, basis, and tradition upon which Catholics, especially, stand as a people are lost, and the communion of saints, especially the saints now dead, a hollow doctrine. But without the prophetic, vision is limited, hearing is selective, and tongues are too often silent. Here, church educators might note that Isaiah describes the inner life of prophecy as having "the tongue of a learner" and an ear awake "to hear as a learner" (50:4). "An ear open continually toward God to hear what God has to say to weary, broken, stumbling humanity, and a tongue ready and disciplined to speak the cauterizing and healing words—that is the true portrait of the prophet."[34]

As with the previous tensions, today's DRE dwells in this one too. Engaging in both priestly and prophetic activity, especially if the engagement bears fruit, may draw the reaction similar to that received so often by Jesus. People say to the DRE, as they did to him, "I'm not sure what you mean by that, but I'm certain I don't like it." Nonetheless, idealistic DREs continue to believe it is important to try with conviction, with lightness of touch, and with hope to stay within this tension, just as they stay with conviction and contract, with education and ministry. The pressures to avoid tension are great and are to be taken with utmost seriousness. But the stakes are enormous, too, and the DREs who choose to dwell in the shadowy light of tension may well prove to be symbols for thousands of adult U.S. Catholics who, seeing them, choose to walk in similar paths. Ultimately, such choices may be seen as an imitation of the Christ and a deeper transforming of persons into the divine image. For dwelling in tension is another way of embracing the path of paradox, a path already walked by one who taught that life and death, divine and human, crucifixion and resurrection never can be separated.

Notes

1. See Gabriel Moran, *Catechesis of Revelation* (New York: Herder & Herder, 1966), especially chap. 2, for a detailed description of this situation.

2. Among the more influential of these were those described in *Teaching All Nations*, ed. J. Hofinger (New York: Herder & Herder, 1961); see also J. Hofinger and T. Sheridan, eds., *The Medellin Papers* (Manila: East Asian Pastoral Institute, 1969).

3. See, in addition to Hofinger's edited work, his *Art of Teaching Christian Doctrine* (Notre Dame, Ind.: University of Notre Dame Press, 1961); see also A. Nebreda, *Kerygma in Crisis?* (Chicago: Loyola University Press, 1965) and M. Van Caster, *Structure of Catechetics* (New York: Herder & Herder, 1965). Of the United States, see G. S. Sloyan, ed., *Modern Catechetics* (New York: Macmillan, 1963) and Moran, *Catechesis of Revelation*.

4. Bernard Cooke, "The Church: Catholic and Ecumenical," in *Theology Today* 36 (October 1979): 358-59.

5. Mary Perkins Ryan, *Are Parochial Schools the Answer?* (New York: Holt, Rinehart & Winston, 1964).

6. Andrew M. Greeley and Peter H. Rossi, *The Education of Catholic Americans* (Chicago: Aldine Publishing, 1966).

7. See Dorothy Jean Furnish, *DRE/DCE: The History of a Profession* (Nashville: Christian Educators Fellowship of the United Methodist Church, 1976).

8. This is a personal observation on my part. I served for six years in the diocese of Rockville Centre, Long Island, New York, as a liaison for DREs with the diocese; these were the statistics in that diocese during those years. Remarkably, three of the five from 1967 are still working as DREs.

9. Joseph C. Neiman, *Coordinators* (Winona, Minn.: St. Mary's Press, 1971).

10. 1970 was the first year of publication for this journal, whose acronym stands for Professional Approaches for Christian Educators.

11. The table of contents gives a quick overview of the person and role of the DRE: five different views of who DREs are; the works of religious education and ministry; the multiple role demands such as theologian, executive, administrator, and spiritual director. See Maria Harris, ed., *The D.R.E. Reader* (Winona, Minn.: St. Mary's Press, 1980).

12. Of interest is the historical note that Mary Perkins Ryan was the first editor of *The Living Light*, succeeded by its present editor, Berard Marthaler. She seems to have been a major force in the movement, albeit a quiet and often unrecognized one.

13. See *Living Light* 9, no. 1 (Spring 1972): 48-56 for the Nevin piece; 11, no. 2 (Summer 1974): 294-301 for Dolesch; 10, no. 4 (Winter 1973): 558-65 for Cook; 12, no. 1 (Spring 1975): 57-62 for Moore; 14, no. 4 (Winter 1977): 511-18 for Marthaler.

14. *Living Light* 17, no. 3 (Fall 1980): 250-59. Since the editor of this book posed the same basic question as the *Living Light* article sought to answer, some necessary repetition of material in that piece is unavoidable here.

15. See, for example, Timothy Ragan and Norman Lambert's "DRE Newsletters" in *Catechist* 9, a monthly column from September through May; and my "DREs and the Future," *Catechist* 12, no. 3 (November-December 1978): 12-35. Gene Scapanski wrote a monthly DRE column for *Modern Ministries*.

16. "Catechetics on the Move," a resource service in the *RTJ* for years, began publication as a separate newsletter directed especially to DREs in 1980, but has subsequently, in 1982, been reincorporated into the magazine.

17. Furnish, *DRE/DCE*. Before joining the faculty of Garrett-Evangelical Theological Seminary, Furnish served as a DCE in Lincoln, Nebraska, for thirteen years.

18. Maria Harris, *The D.R.E. Book* (New York: Paulist Press, 1976).

19. The recently completed Walters' NCDD study cites the figure as 68 percent. See below.

20. Subtitled *A D.R.E. Journal*, it was published from Hazel Park, Mich. 48030. CORED also offered a placement service directed by Richard Meneau, which was subsequently taken over by the Religious Education Association. The Ad Random pages of the *National Catholic Reporter* now appear to serve this latter function.

21. *Resource Guidebook for Diocesan Directors of Religious Education Concerning Parish Directors of Religious Education* (Washington: NCDD, 1980 edition). First published, 1975. Available from the NCDD office at 1312 Massachusetts Avenue, NW, Washington, D.C. 20005.

22. For the entire text of the statement, see *The Living Light* 17, no. 3 (Fall 1980): 247-49.

23. In 1978, the USCC published "A National Inventory of Parish Catechetical Programs," researched under the direction of Eugene Hemrick, which has valuable statistical data, but is wider in its understanding of DRE than the Walters study, the NCDD statement, or this article. One further publication I would note is a report on a Model Internship Program for Religious Education Directors/Coordinators prepared for the USCC by D. Costello and F. Murphy in June 1972, describing a cooperative venture with the University of San Francisco.

24. Available from NCEA in Washington, D.C.

25. Also available from NCEA, Washington, D.C.

26. In San Antonio, Texas, in conjunction with the department of graduate theology, St. Mary's University; and in Cleveland, Ohio, in conjunction with John Carroll University.

27. Joseph C. Neiman, Research Report no. 2: "Diocesan Services to Parish Religious Education Coordinators" (London, Ont.: Divine Word Centre, 1971), unpublished ms., 8. Neiman distinguished here between regular meetings, which many dioceses did hold even then, and actual organizations.

28. See Jean Peters Pilch, "Wisconsin DRE's United in a State Federation," in *P.A.C.E.* 11, Community I (Winona, Minn.: St. Mary's Press, 1981): 1-3; and Jean Peters Pilch, "Wisconsin DRE Federation Update," in *P.A.C.E.* 12, Community H (Winona, Minn.: St. Mary's Press, 1982): 1-3. See also Marie Martens Hill, "Albany DRE's Make Haste Slowly," in *P.A.C.E.* 12, Community C (Winona, Minn.: St. Mary's Press, 1982).

29. See Gabriel Moran, "The Professions of Church Education," and "Parish Models of Education," in *The D.R.E. Reader*, ed. Harris, 81-92. See also Harold L. Wilensky, "The Professionalization of Everyone?" in *American Journal of Sociology* 70, no. 2 (1964): 137 ff.

30. See Maria Harris, "DREs Today: Dwelling in the Tensions," in *Vocation and Spirituality of the DRE*, ed. Kelly, 6-8.

31. Ibid.

32. For detailed analysis of the distinctions, educationally, between priestly and prophetic, see Maria Harris, *Portrait of Youth Ministry* (New York: Paulist Press, 1981), especially chap. 2.

33. See David Hollenbach, "A Prophetic Church and the Catholic Sacramental Imagination," in *The Faith That Does Justice*, ed. John C. Haughey (New York: Paulist Press, 1977), 242.

34. See James D. Smart, *The Rebirth of Ministry* (Philadelphia: The Westminster Press, 1968), 55.

CHAPTER 16

Changing Patterns of Protestant Curriculum

Iris V. Cully

Curriculum may be as broadly defined as to include all learning experiences—the curriculum of life. It could be limited to the planned experiences in a learning environment. It could be confined to the materials and experiences derived from a course of study. To the users of Sunday school and Confraternity of Christian Doctrine (CCD) materials, curriculum usually means a course of study. Curriculum is invariably a focus of concern for all the people involved. Those who design materials see an opportunity to improve the quality of parish religious education (in accordance with their definition of *quality*). Those who teach regard materials as the ultimate tool leading to success or failure. Parishes are in a constant process of changing curricular materials in the hope that something different will be easier to teach, more attractive to learners, or more expressive of their biblical-theological viewpoints. Everyone pins high hopes on a course of study and its attendant resources. Moreover, despite evidence to the effect that most people are visually oriented for learning—the influence of television—and although some courses of study include in resource packets filmstrips, records, and tapes, there is still heavy dependence on written directions for the teacher and workbooks with reading for the pupil.

Some Historical Reflections

The traditional content for curriculum included the creed, the commandments, and the Lord's Prayer, whether couched in lecture or question-and-answer form. These were the catechisms. Emphasis on the Bible is a nineteenth-century Protestant phenomenon growing out of the Sunday school, in contrast with school and confirmation instruction. The first widely accepted

Iris V. Cully is Alexander Campbell Hopkins Professor of Religious Education at Lexington Theological Seminary.

all-Bible curriculum was the Uniform Lesson Series, devised in 1881 by the Reverend John H. Vincent (later a Methodist bishop) and B. F. Jacobs, a Baptist layman. The goal was to present basic biblical content in a seven-year cycle, with lessons adapted on each age level. This brought some unity into what had been a fragmented curricular situation. By the early twentieth century, newly acquired child development emphases brought about the publication of a group-graded series, to be followed later by a closely graded curriculum. Denominational curricula were developed in the wake of expanding departments of Christian education. Sometimes these denominations worked cooperatively, either through outlines or in the editorial and writing process. Differences in theological viewpoint led to a desire to incorporate distinctive denominational interpretations, as in the Christian Faith and Life materials of the United Presbyterian Church in the U.S.A., a response to biblical theology. The National Council of Churches launched an ambitious curriculum development project in the 1960s which resulted in two books designed to guide denominations in their planning. At the end of that decade, several once-new curricula were reaching the end of three cycles and new planning loomed ahead. In response to economic realities as well as ecumenical considerations, twelve denominations formed Joint Educational Development and constructed the *Christian Education: Shared Approaches* curriculum with its four approaches: *Knowing the Word, Interpreting the Word, Living the Word,* and *Doing the Word.* Their emphasis on systemic planning has become a useful contribution to the process of curricular development.

Ways of Structuring Curriculum

There are several options for curricular development, each of which gives a degree of freedom or restraint to the teacher. One option is to follow a particular published course of study at each grade level throughout a school. There are advantages. There is a theological and educational consistency that assures the development of a viewpoint toward the Bible and a familiarity with teaching methods. This progression is helpful to teachers, even if they move from one grade level to another. It makes a comfortable design for learners who know what to expect from year to year. Protestant parishes that are theologically conservative have given their support to several independent publishers through the use of such materials. Roman Catholic parishes are equally loyal to several publishers. (There is no official Catholic curriculum: all materials are independently produced.) The disadvantages are that all teachers are locked into methods that may be designed for simplicity of use rather than for creativity. And there may be, in Protestant congregations, a divergence between the biblical approach to be found in the teaching materials and that which forms the basis for preaching and short-term study groups.

Some parishes choose themes for the year, gather materials from several sources, and design age level curricula. The advantages are that with one theme being used, it is possible to assemble everyone for a special film or resource person, and to hold teacher training sessions with a common focus. Initiative and creativity are encouraged. The approach demands skilled people who can plan goals, select criteria, and develop teaching outlines. They need to be willing to devote time to the process and to engage in periodic evaluation and modification of the plan. They are building a library of teaching resources year by year.

A third approach is to design a curriculum for the local situation. This is a difficult option, because the people of a parish are electing to attempt what skilled full-time staff people do in order to produce the materials that people buy. While this will be made-to-order, it will lack the professional approach to writing that helps untrained teachers, and it will lack the colorful pupil materials that are professionally designed. This option is chosen most frequently by creative people who want a freedom lacking in published materials, or by people (frequently clergy) who desire to inculcate a biblical-theological approach that they find nowhere consistently available in courses of study on the market.

In addition, there is a fourth option being quietly used in many churches with little notice. This approach is for teachers to ignore the materials ordered by someone else in favor of choosing their own. The reason may be that they find the ordered materials difficult to teach or that there is not enough biblical material or that the learners do not seem interested. Sometimes people responsible for the educational program are unaware that teachers are selecting materials independently; sometimes it seems wisest to ignore the fact in the interest of keeping a teacher. It is generally supposed that volunteers are difficult to find and should be cultivated at all costs. Although this is an argument in favor of free choice, the disadvantages are that pupils may find materials repeated from year to year with no consistent pattern, approaches to the Bible will vary, and methods of involving the learner will differ. It fosters the illusion that there is a perfect course of study that will make teaching simple and learning guaranteed.

Issues in Curriculum Development

Behind these four options lie a number of issues that may divide the producers and users of curriculum materials. Denominational designers, professionally trained, feel a mission to improve the quality of religious education in the parish. They know that the only direct influence they have is through written materials. People at the parish level want specific content, teaching outlines that are easy to follow, simple methods, and self-contained resources. Independent publishers design materials primarily with the teacher—that is, the buyer—in view.

One issue is the relationship of biblical material to experience-oriented material. There is a deep longing to "know the Bible," which usually means to know the content and have some kind of simple interpretation. This sometimes leads to a corollary that the application of the Bible to life must be made in concrete ways immediately derived from the content. Some curriculum designers would prefer that people probe life experiences and look for biblical materials that address life concerns. They also believe that the Bible addresses broad issues of social justice that are ignored when the only question asked is, What does the Bible say to me?

Another issue is that of the kind of teacher support written materials should give. Because a published course of study reaches people in churches of all sizes in many sociological contexts, it is impossible to design it for specific situations. Any material needs to be adapted. This fact runs counter to a teacher's desire for a session plan that is immediately transferable to any specific situation. Curriculum designers, to overcome the original problem, include options in the hope that teachers will read the material and make choices with a specific class in mind. Some teachers are confused by options. They seek instead a publisher whose materials are so simple and so concrete that anyone could use them. Creative teachers, frustrated by such simplicity, develop skills for making choices. In practical terms, the easy-to-use material wins more buyers, although the quality of teaching and learning might be improved if teachers were willing to expand their skills.

Designers of curricular materials for specific denominations, including the *Christian Education: Shared Approaches* materials (CE:SA), which are produced cooperatively among a number of denominations, make an appeal for the use of their material on the basis of denominational loyalty. They point out that while buying from independent publishers makes profits for a company, buying from the denomination encourages it to continue efforts to improve the quality of teaching. It is pointed out that there is a denominational "ethos" transmitted through curriculum materials. To be sure, the independent Protestant curricula transmit an evangelical ethos, and the companies whose materials are used predominantly by Roman Catholic parishes have a distinctively Catholic ethos. It is also suggested that some curricula are more open to inquiring attitudes toward biblical and theological interpretation than are others. If the basic stance of a denomination is toward openness, then the materials used for religious education should foster such an attitude.

The question may be raised whether the theological diversity to be found within any denomination makes it impossible to maintain an "official" curriculum. The wide variety of materials in use among Roman Catholic parishes is instructive here, for they run the gamut from conservative to liberal in the approach to theological interpretation and teaching methods. More important may be correlation between the biblical-theological approach and methods of teaching. When biblical interpretation and application are to some extent predetermined, then teaching methods should encourage memorization, limited forms of discussion, and concrete application. When interpretation and application are more open, methods of teaching will need to encourage thinking, exploring, choosing, and changing. Although the CE:SA material has been considered a breakthrough in interchurch cooperation, involving as it does twelve denominations, it does not offer the kind of variety that might be supposed. The biblical viewpoint is not conservative, even in the approach that centers on the use of biblical content. The teacher manuals presuppose some use of options in session planning. The basic differences among the approaches occur in the degree of content orientation toward Bible or life experience, simplicity or complexity of material, and concrete or flexible options for methods.

Materials designed for fifty-two sessions a year leave no freedom for pursuing a unit in depth or for including emphases that might be lacking in the course of study. It has been said that teachers prefer the security of dated materials, but this rigidity limits the educational options. Some questions still remain as to the adequacy of available independent and interdenominational curricula.

Specifically, the need for understanding a particular family of faith is ignored. A study of worship is important, and learners need to know the different forms of liturgy in use among Christian groups. They also need to understand the specific forms within their own communion. Children need an introduction to denominational understanding of the rites of baptism and the Lord's Supper. Learners need to be introduced to the mission of the church, not only in general terms but through the specific work their own denomination is doing. Church history is a neglected area because of the primacy given to biblical study and a general discomfort teachers have in dealing with historical materials. Their own historical knowledge is sketchy, and they do not know how to make it a lively study for pupils. The story of the development of specific Christian groups suffers from this general neglect. So the great story of the outreach and diversity of the Christian community is ignored, and its representative people are not as real as are biblical figures. To most Protestants, the history of the people of God disappears at the end of the Acts of the Apostles.

People and the Curriculum

People who use curriculum material frequently are unaware of the chain by which it reaches the shelves in a church. The process begins with a planning group. Protestants often have two departments with educational concerns: the department of religious education, whose staff is program oriented (children, youth, adult, family, minorities), and a department of publication, whose staff is materials oriented. When a new curriculum is projected, the orientation of each group is important. Position papers outlining the theological, biblical, and educational bases for a curriculum are written and discussed. Age groupings for each course are determined. Content themes for each age level are developed. Age level editors from the publications department formulate the specific outlines for each course. They choose writers and hold conferences, either individually or with a group of writers, where curriculum developments are shared and specifics for content and method are outlined. Later the writer's first draft will be submitted, edited, and necessary rewriting done.

The next people involved in curriculum are the interpreters. Field people are liaisons between the publishers and the users of materials. They are troubleshooters who show people in parishes how to make the best use of the materials. They explain and defend the basic design and show teachers how to adapt it for local use.

Whether they come into parishes or hold regional workshops, they are important links in the curriculum enterprise.

The final evaluation of materials comes at the local level. Here are the people who choose and use a curriculum. They know what they want, and they have to be convinced that a particular curriculum program fits their needs. Because a curriculum is normally used throughout a parish, some representative group should be making decisions about the choice. A religious education committee usually includes members from the governing board of the parish, teachers, parents, and clergy. Consensus is needed as to which materials best meet their educational needs. However, the committee will not be the users of materials. Teachers have the weekly task of mediating the course of study to pupils. Their felt needs may not always be consonant with those of the board, even though they are represented there. Any written material becomes, in an actual teaching situation, whatever a particular teacher wants it to become. This is why it has been said that a good teacher can teach well from any course of study. Conversely, a teacher interprets material in personal terms. An editor or a writer might sit in a class and not recognize his or her own material. Teachers alter a viewpoint, not with intent to distort, but because they see the material through their own focus. They will ignore suggested methods or materials and substitute others. Sometimes this represents adaptation to a teaching situation; sometimes it is adaptation to a teacher's needs. There seems no way to close the gap between the designer's vision and the teacher's performance. Clear teaching directions help. Field workers help. In the end, the design, writing, and use of curriculum materials involve many people, each of whom adapts according to needs.

Parish Designs for Curriculum

The Joint Educational Development group, designers of the CE:SA materials, made a forward-looking contribution in formulating a systems approach. They affirmed that curriculum planning, like any other activity, is a system with interrelated parts. If any part of the system is weak, the whole design becomes less effective. They identified five elements in the system: theological/educational presuppositions, goal setting/evaluating, educational experiences, resources, and leader development.

The first step is to gather information about the parish and the community. The grade levels chosen will be different if there are many children or few. The options run from closely graded to broadly graded, which might include grades one through six. The availability of skilled teachers will vary from one community to another, based on the educational and experiential level of members. This will influence the decision as to what makes a "teachable" course of study. The resources of the community will affect the amount of enrichment possible, whether in the area of sports, music, art, theater, or film. (The use of television as a resource, although available in almost every home, has been virtually ignored.) What is the awareness level on global issues that affect Christians: peace, poverty, environment, and other areas of concern?

The next step is to set goals for the curriculum. Some people mistakenly equate goals for religious education with goals for the curriculum. The latter are more limited yet are often designed to bear much of the burden. Goals determining what curricular materials can do to further the religious education of children, youth, and adults are limited goals that are related to but not the same as educational goals. Each parish will need to decide the place of written materials in the totality of its educational enterprise. Moreover, they might think only of materials for Sunday school or CCD classes—a further limitation. Goals can never be viewed apart from evaluation, because the two form a continuous process. Evaluation tells planners to what extent goals have been met in order that they may either redefine the goals or modify the teaching processes in relation to teacher, learner, and resources.

Specifically, knowledge of the Bible has been a goal to be fulfilled through a curriculum. This is not a simple goal. For some, biblical knowledge is paramount, and teaching methods are designed to this end. Learners memorize Scripture verses and play Bible games. To others, biblical interpretation is the goal. This may mean "What does the Bible tell me to do?"; "How does the Bible help me interpret life experiences?"; "How do biblical situations apply to my situation?"; or "What was the biblical message when spoken to the people for whom it was first written?" Still another aspect is the relation of the biblical message to a particular society.

Growth in Christian living is another goal—although the extent to which it can be conveyed through written materials is questionable. Nevertheless it is attempted, through admonitions with examples of people who made "right" decisions, that is, decisions consonant with biblical teaching, through open-ended stories and in other ways. Each method illustrates a different understanding of both the meaning of Christian living and the use of methods and materials to convey meaning.

An understanding of Christian belief has been another goal. Today, orthodoxy, right doctrine, is difficult to define. The classical creeds state that we believe *in* rather than that we believe *about*. Catechisms have attempted to define belief, but the trend is toward using catechisms descriptively rather than definitively. Exploring belief and affirming beliefs require a different approach from that used to learn definitions.

Commitment to Christ has been the ultimate goal for Christian education, including continued growth in commitment. Those responsible for choosing curriculum should read the promises that people make at their baptism or confirmation. Some clergy conduct membership classes as if this specific preparation would compensate for previous deficiencies in religious education. All religious education experiences contribute to commitment, and probably the people in a person's life are the most effective contributors. The contribution of the written curriculum to this goal is at best indirect. It helps more through the kind of teacher attracted to its use than it does through the specific content.

Biblical and Educational Assumptions

Fundamental issues need to be considered when examining the biblical approach of a curriculum. One is the understanding of biblical authority. For some the Bible is inerrant—wholly without error—because it was conveyed to its writers through the inspiration of the Holy Spirit. For others, the authority of the Bible lies in its witness to God's actions through the history of Israel and supremely through Jesus Christ. Is the Bible authoritative for answering every aspect of life, or is it authoritative where it speaks to the relationship between God and the created world? A similar issue is that of the meaning of revelation. For some, revelation is direct and immediate. The revealed word of God tells people how to order their lives to obey God's commands. To others, revelation is the self-disclosure of God, in the root meaning of the word, "to remove the veil." The revelation, in this sense, is the disclosure of the nature and activity of God by which people are drawn to love and serve the God who created and redeemed them. These distinctions are observable in any curriculum.

Another issue is the approach to biblical study. Where the Bible is viewed primarily as the source of God's laws governing human life, with Bible people as examples of what happens to those who do or do not obey, a knowledge of the content of the Bible is essential. Such knowledge is built up through years of graduated study from earliest childhood. Another approach is to view the Bible in its historical setting, viewing people's actions as response to their understanding of God's will at that time. This allows for interpretation in a sociological context. A popular method of Bible study is to put oneself in the place of a biblical person or situation. This enables a person to see how complicated our identifications are. Persons participating in the reading of the Passion story on Good Friday suddenly become aware that they, Christians though they be, dare not identify only with Jesus. They are as likely to identify with Peter or one of the other disciples, Pilate, Caiaphas, the judges, or the crowd shouting for death.

Curricular materials should give some indication that writers are aware of the many critical approaches that have illumined the text for centuries. People who study the Bible need to know the sources used by those whose interpretations they are reading. This will help learners to become more discerning in the development of exegetical skills. Literary and textual studies, form and redaction criticism, the attention being paid to the canon of Scripture, and structural studies should be evident in curricular materials.

A discerning approach to curricular materials also requires that people have a basic knowledge of the theological understandings held by the church. There is a common consensus but also broad differences in interpretation among Christian groups. One need only cite the doctrine of the atonement. A strong use of the substitutionary interpretation is basic to some curriculum designs. Others stress the moral influence of the atonement. The stress of the liberation theologies on the freedom of the whole person appears in other materials. A concern for developing an understanding of the trinitarian nature of God is important in some materials; the separation of the identities of God characterizes others. Some curricula deal with eschatology; others avoid the subject. Sensing the degree of correspondence between the theological stance of a denomination and of a curriculum is important for those using materials for the education of a congregation.

The educational presuppositions of material interact with biblical and theological viewpoints. A classical educational theory that views a thorough knowledge and understanding of the subject (here, the Bible) as essential will employ methods that help learners remember content. Such methods might be visual or aural, include teacher presentation and pupil response, but the goal is that the story of the Bible be easily recalled.

An inquiry approach stresses discovery of meaning by the learner. The teacher challenges with questions such as "What do you think?"; "Why do you think this happened?"; "What other outcomes might there have been?" Certainty is momentarily removed with the objective that self-appropriated knowledge and meaning will lead to greater certainty. The hope is that the learner can counter challenges to faith in many life situations and continue to believe in new ways.

The experiential approach begins with the learner who is asked to identify with biblical people. This may mean putting oneself into a biblical situation. It will also involve some "modernization" of the Bible by asking that one envisage a parallel situation today. This approach more frequently starts with the life experience of the learner and looks for biblical parallels. The experiences of biblical people are considered instructive, even inspirational, but the intent is that the biblical message have meaning for today. All approaches to the Bible are selective, but this one may be more selective than others because only the most basic outlines of the biblical story are deemed essential, and material used is most likely to come from the New Testament.

Any educational approach must take into account the age level capabilities of learners. In practice, anyone who examines curricula notices that the estimate of these abilities is influenced by the theological and biblical stance of the designers. A cursory examination of stories for five-year-olds used in a half dozen courses will indicate this in the material selected, the details used or omitted, and the interpretation given by the retelling of the story. Goals always need to be describable in terms of how they can be realized at each age level.

Settings for Curriculum

By putting too much emphasis on a Sunday school or CCD setting for the use of learning materials, parish planners are ignoring the many other settings in which religious education is taking place. A simple chart listing age levels, learning opportunities, and times for meeting will indicate the variety. Children may be attending a vacation Bible school. Youth have a Sunday evening meeting. Adults can belong to a men's, women's, or other special-interest group. All-parish activities include people of every age. This fact suggests that the basic curriculum should be part of the total learning opportunities. Such opportunities are especially broad at the adult level, while camps and conferences enlarge the experiences for adolescents. This awareness should be evident to pastors and others who design church membership materials at every age level, where the emphasis needs to be placed on the meaning of Christian commitment.

More attention to flexibility in age groupings is indicated. Schools have been developing ways of moving pupils into classes according to the need to develop special skills and are less bound to chronological age groupings. Churches with small memberships too often try to fit children into molds designed for larger congregations instead of designing groups that combine age levels, abilities, and experiences of learners. Adult classes seem frequently to have developed out of immediate needs for support groups based on congeniality. One would expect this approach to generate wide options in curricular materials. But in fact, few publishers make available much variety for short-term courses in the areas of Bible, theology, church, personal concern, or social concerns.

Because the key person in the use of materials is the teacher, effort has been expended in designing curriculum with the teacher's needs in view. More attention could be paid to team teaching, particularly in order to encourage flexible grading and variety in the use of methods. The trend toward encouraging the use of interest centers signals a move in this direction. The interest center gives flexibility, variety, and attention to the individual learner. Its use also requires careful planning, broad resources, and the enlistment of teachers willing to try new forms of teaching.

Questions of space, equipment, and other resources enter into the selection of materials. Usable courses of study have been rejected by teachers because a filmstrip projector was suggested. Other teachers cannot envision using specific materials when a large room has to be shared with other classes. Some materials sell because all needed resources are contained in a prepared packet of materials.

If, as was stated earlier, educational experiences and resources are essential elements in an effective educational program, then teacher support is imperative. Teachers need to learn how to use resources. They need to practice different ways of teaching. They need foundational knowledge of Bible, history, and belief. Whether such help is offered from the national level, the judicatory, the community, or the parish, only so can full use be made of curriculum material.

Teachers themselves decide what makes a teachable curriculum. Their frame of reference may not be complete, but their needs have validity. They want materials that are visually attractive and teaching outlines that let them know at a glance the order for the session. They want specific directions, particularly for completing activities. They may want some choice in activities, but not too much. Many are unwilling to commit much time to preparation, and this is a major factor in their acceptance or rejection of a curriculum. Planners may believe that the best teachers are those with sufficient commitment to spend time in preparation. At the local level, clergy frequently find it advisable to settle for willing workers. Practically speaking, until or unless more creative people are recruited, some degree of self-sufficiency needs to be built into materials. How to do this without ending up with a mechanical session outline is the problem publishers try to solve. Teachers also want an attractive pupil book, with emphasis on activities. Children may reject workbooks as being too close to a school model, but that is another problem. Some governing boards want inexpensive materials. Helping them learn the difference between price and value may be one of the tasks of those who use the material.

Conclusion

The major trend in curriculum development today lies in the increasing initiative being taken at the parish level. While individual teachers have always felt free to set aside one piece of material for another, the conscious decision for planning is recent. It could result in more thoughtful attention to local needs and can cause the development of knowledgeable educators in a parish.

This trend is encouraged by the systems approach that alerts planners to the interaction among factors in the educational program. Sensitive to the fact, planners are more likely to realize that an understanding of their presuppositions, development of goals, increasing use of resources, and teacher development are essential factors in the effective use of any curriculum.

On the production level, there is an increasing trend toward the involvement of larger units in curriculum publishing. Some independent publishers and some denominations have a large enough market to maintain their present output. Smaller units are finding it advisable to combine in order to develop materials cooperatively.

Although the suggested use of learning centers has been built into some recent curricula, there is not much evidence that a number of parishes are following that option, even when such a learning approach may be found in the public schools.

Increasing options in curriculum materials augmented by lessened loyalty to denominational or other brand names could make for imbalance in educational and biblical-theological approaches, but it could also lead to a more thoughtful involvement of parish leaders in the educational ministry of the church.

Bibliography

Colson, Howard, and Raymond M. Rigdon. *Understanding Your Church's Curriculum*. Rev. ed. Nashville: Broadman Press, 1980.

Cooperative Curriculum Project. *The Church's Educational Ministry: A Curriculum Plan*. St. Louis: The Bethany Press, 1965.

Cully, Iris V. *Planning and Selecting Curriculum for Christian Education*. Valley Forge, Penn.: Judson Press, 1983.

"Curriculum of Religious Education," *Religious Education* 75, no. 5 (September-October 1980).

Flannery, Austin P., ed. *Documents of Vatican II* 55: "Declaration on Christian Education." Grand Rapids: Wm. B. Eerdmans Publishing Co., 1975.

National Conference of Catholic Bishops, ed. *To Teach as Jesus Taught*. U.S. Catholic Conference, 1972.

National Council of Churches. *Tools of Curriculum Development for the Church's Educational Ministry*. Anderson, Ind.: Warner Press, 1976.

Sharing the Light of Faith. National Catechetical Directory. NCCC.

Wyckoff, D. Campbell. *Theory and Design of Christian Education Curriculum*. Philadelphia: The Westminster Press, 1961.

Joint Educational Development Materials

Manuals for Christian Education: Shared Approaches

Hussel, Oscar J., and Shirley Heckman. *Leader Manual*. General Assembly Mission Board, Presbyterian Church, U.S., 1977.

Michel, Bernard E. *Knowing the Word*. The Geneva Press, 1977.

Purdy, John C. *Interpreting the Word*. The Geneva Press, 1977.

Tuckett, Gwin Ream. *Living the Word*. Christian Board of Publication, 1977.

Wilcoxson, Georgeann. *Doing the Word*. United Church Press, 1977.

Curriculum Planning Guides

Developing the Congregation's Educational Program. Geneva Press, 1976.

Heckman, Shirley J., and Iris L. Ferren. *Creating the Congregation's Educational Ministry*. The Brethren Press, 1977.

Planning for Education in the Congregation. A multi-media kit. Christian Board of Publication, 1976.

CHAPTER 17

The Childhood Years and Religious Nurture

Lucie W. Barber

If one were to read Ronald Goldman's *Readiness for Religion*[1] (1965) without knowing anything about the author, it would be possible to believe that it was written by a contemporary religious educator. However, the book was written almost two decades ago. At that time many religious educators were not ready for Goldman's conclusions. Today most of them are prepared for that message and much more too. Developmental education has now been a familiar theme for some years. And increasingly, religious educators are doing something about the attempt to teach to developmental stages or levels.

Thus this chapter will start with Ronald Goldman's work primarily because of its fundamental importance in understanding current concepts regarding the religious nurture of children. Previous volumes in this series (see the introduction) have largely ignored Goldman. That oversight particularly needs correction in a chapter about the religious education (or nurture) of little children. Much of the work of religious education in the 1980s is based, in part, on Goldman's writings. However, it is also based on the work of other psychologists and persons working with developmental theory. The next section describes briefly some of the progress that has been made since the 1960s.

The Work of Ronald Goldman

At the present time (the early 1980s) Ronald Goldman is living and teaching in Australia as a psychologist, not as a religious educator. He did his doctoral work in England in the field of religious education, coming to that task from a background based on the research and theories of Jean Piaget, the Swiss psychologist. Some religious educators consider Goldman to be something of a

---

Lucie W. Barber is an author and is also engaged in research focused primarily on the religious nurture of children.

maverick. Others find in his work the marks of a genius for the field of religious education. Filled with frustration over the responses to his work, Goldman finally left the field of religious education and moved to Australia. I suspect that his decision to quit came because so many people in the institutional church considered him to be a revolutionary, a dangerous researcher, or even a mere upstart.

Yet in 1965 Goldman proclaimed these positions:

1. *Children before formal education are "prereligious."* Today James Fowler (following a Piagetian model) agrees that they are *intuitive-projective.*[2] Mary Wilcox (following a Lawrence Kohlberg model) uses the term *preconventional.*[3]

2. *Children from approximately seven to twelve years of age are "subreligious."* Both Fowler and Wilcox use the term *concrete operational.*

3. *Formal religious education begins when, in a developmental sequence, abstract reasoning is attained.* Wilcox and Fowler both propose changes upon the attainment of abstract reasoning.

4. *Religious education before the attainment of abstract reasoning is possible, but it is different.*

These four statements are paraphrases of Goldman's research findings after he and his colleagues conducted structured interviews with two hundred children and adolescents between six and seventeen years of age.

The original research findings are available in his University of Birmingham (United Kingdom) dissertation, and they have also been published in his book *Religious Thinking from Childhood to Adolescence.*[4] The volume includes numerous quotations from his subjects, and these make fascinating reading, adding a certain quality to any report of research findings. However, this is a "soft" approach to doing research. Interviewing and qualitative results are a methodology which must be refined quantitatively with large numbers and/or numerous samples to verify qualitative hunches or guesses. Goldman as a researcher did not choose to carry his efforts this far.

Goldman rather decided to follow his hunches, writing *Readiness for Religion* in 1965, one year after his first book, *Religious Thinking from Childhood to Adolescence.* He proposed a child-centered religious education which paid attention to the "needs" of the child. He proclaimed that the Bible is an adult book—not a book for children. He warned about "teaching Bible too much, too soon." He also warned that Bible stories for young children, often repeated year after year, are almost bound to be misinterpreted by children who do not have the experience to understand the underlying concepts. Goldman maintained that the repetition compounded the revolt against religion in the teenage years, when ingrained misunderstandings result in the perception that religion is both old-fashioned and childish. Although it is not possible here to give more attention to Goldman, readers interested in the religious nurture of children, especially the youngest, are strongly urged to study his two books. Goldman's point about children's "needs" is well taken. Religious education *is* concerned with individual children, not just with what adult religious educators think a child should know.

Actually, children do not know anything unless they have experienced a happening that pertains to their lives. When such experiences happen, children must integrate those new experiences before they can include them in their available structures and thus grow. Before leaving Goldman it must be said that, despite the crude research methodology which led to his curriculum advice, many of his hunches are acceptable to religious educators today as being at the present cutting edge of the discipline in its thinking about the religious nurture of children. Thus Goldman's influence can be seen in numerous curriculum series, particularly those offered by Episcopalians and Roman Catholics.[5]

On Beyond Goldman

Goldman's suggestions for curriculum materials experienced little acceptance in England. The late 1960s were a time of turmoil during which the British encountered pluralism. England was deluged by Indians and East African immigrants. Muslims, Hindus, and Sikhs appeared in substantial numbers in the school systems. And adaptations by the older Christian communities were demanded.[6]

Events in the United States during this period also worked against Goldman's ideas regarding curriculum. The Episcopal Church, which originally espoused Goldman's thought and financed John Peatling's refinement of the Goldman interview methodology,[7] experienced financial difficulties nationally. In their decision to reorganize in early 1971, thus reducing their budget, the Episcopalians eliminated research entirely. Peatling moved to the Union College Character Research Project in Schenectady, New York. And while the Character Research Project had an honorable heritage in religious education research, it is not well known. Thus continued research into and related to Goldman's insights was to a great extent lost. A glimpse at this recent history is revealing. It was Goldman who introduced many persons in North America to the religious education implications of the work of Jean Piaget. However, in order to understand the religious education or nurture of children today, one must go beyond Goldman for additional influences.

The rather modest influence of Goldman is illustrated by an examination of the predecessor volume in this series of symposia. In 1975 he was mentioned only three times in the book. One reference is found in a chapter on religious education in Western Europe. A second came in James Loder's treatment of developmental theories,[8] followed by Robert Browning's chapter on the future of religious education.[9] All three authors mention Goldman only in passing. Even so, the source standing behind Goldman (Jean Piaget) reached religious education in America only primarily through the writings of Ronald Goldman. In much of religious education in the United States, the influence of Piaget was hardly felt until the 1970s. Even then, it was far too often encountered through a variety of misunderstandings.

Two other prominent contributors to the development of religious education theory in the 1970s were Lawrence Kohlberg[10] and James Fowler.[11] Kohlberg was also initially misunderstood by many religious educators. And Fowler will almost certainly suffer similar misunderstanding for many of the same reasons. Unfortunately all too often religious educators are looking for simple answers. Piaget, Kohlberg, and Fowler have no simple answers. Their theories are extremely complex, particularly when an evaluator is dealing with an individual child and has the obligation to assign that person to one of the developmental stages or levels identified by these research insights.

Generally Christian educators are learning to live with Piagetian theory. James Loder,[12] David Elkind,[13] and John Peatling[14] have translated Piaget, as have others. Peatling's paper-and-pencil test, *Thinking About the Bible* (1973), provides educators with a sophisticated method for measuring religious thinking according to Piaget's theory. Although *Thinking About the Bible* cannot be used below the fourth grade, Iris Cully,[15] Mary Wilcox,[16] and Lucie Barber[17] have described development from birth through the early years in the system of Jean Piaget. *Sensori-motor, preoperational, concrete,* and *abstract thinking*—the terms which are used in this developmental model—have become increasingly familiar. Educators are also becoming accustomed to the concept of "adaptation," with its components of "assimilation" and "accommodation." No concerned religious educator should be—or need be—

uninformed about the work and influence of Piaget in today's world. There is an abundance of written material about Piaget and his contributions to religious education theory on the nurture of children. Piaget's developmental person-environment interaction is the theoretical basis for most current child-centered practice in contemporary religious education.

Another child-centered, person-environment approach is Lawrence Kohlberg's theory regarding the development of moral judgment. Many religious educators were attracted to Kohlberg during the 1970s. There was a strong belief that moral judgment is a responsibility of religious education, as well it is. However, the question of *whose* moral judgment was left unanswered until recently. The attention of the reader is called to the work of Craig Dykstra published in 1981.[18] It is an example of these questions being raised. Kohlberg's model has emphasized invariant, universal, and sequential as the stages which lead to "justice." However, Dykstra has suggested that "discipleship" is a more appropriate aim for Christians. His recent book challenges Kohlberg on other issues, as have other religious educators and some psychologists as well. While Kohlberg's identified stages of development from 0 to 4 do appear to be grounded in empirical evidence, stages 5 and 6 in contrast appear to be theoretically derived. Carol Gilligan, for example, has research evidence which suggests that mature moral judgment for females differs from Kohlberg's descriptions of either stage 5 or stage 6.[19]

These controversies about the adequacy and usefulness of Kohlberg's contributions to theory continue. Despite the questions, his analysis of stages 0 through 4 do appear to have value for religious educators. Both Cully and Wilcox have found that an understanding of stages 0 through 4 in the growth and development of the child are helpful to religious educators in getting to know the whole child. However, Cully has also turned to others, such as Erik Erikson, David Elkind, Jean Piaget, Jerome Bruner, and Ronald Goldman for parallel contributions to the educator's understanding. Wilcox uses Piaget as well as her own research experience and the data derived therefrom. At the present time Barber is working with a total of nine different psychological theories regarding child development in the effort to gain added insight into the problem. Today it is apparent that child-centered religious educators are concerned about understanding *the whole child*, using whatever theoretical resources and bases may prove useful in this task. The work of Lawrence Kohlberg has obviously made a significant contribution to this search.

James Fowler's theory of faith development is another example of the research-based help which is available to religious educators in understanding the whole child. As with Kohlberg's theories, Fowler's most mature stage of development (stage 6, designated "universalizing") is not specifically Christian. However, Fowler's first two stages of child development may be of assistance to religious educators. He has called stage 1 "intuitive-projective" and stage 2 "mythic-literal." Stage 1 approximates Piaget's "preoperational level," while stage 2 parallels Piaget's "concrete operational level." However, there are complexities that appear in Fowler's theory. His structural-developmental approach as illustreated in the chart of faith development[20] lists the names of his six stages in a left-hand column. In parallel vertical columns he describes what he calls "aspects of the structural whole at a given stage." These aspects include "Form of Logic," which builds on Piaget; and "Form of Moral Judgment," which represents a modification of Kohlberg. The other aspects include: "Form of World Coherence," "Roletaking," "Locus of Authority," "Bounds of Social Awareness," and "the Role of Symbols." The actual terms used reflect the complexity of the theory, adding to the difficulty in using it.

Nonetheless, religious educators should be paying attention to the research work of James Fowler. However, religious educators *of children* will be well advised to use caution in this regard. Fowler's stages 1 and 2 may be of help to teachers in their understanding of the individual children who are their learners. Teachers of children should study those first two stages as proposed by Fowler. We need to determine whether they contribute to our knowledge of the children with whom we are working. It is not yet clear whether Fowler's theoretical work will ultimately contribute to *Christian* education. However, James Fowler is at work in both research and analysis clearly related to child development, and religious educators cannot afford to ignore this work.

From Theory to Practice

A young person asked an older person, "What is the most important thing I can teach my children?" The older person replied, "Teach them to be free." That reply produced a great deal of anxiety in the younger person. And she said again, "Yes, but *what* do I teach them? What do they *need* to know?" The older person's sure response finally came. "They need to know *how* to be free. They do not need to know so much what you think they should know. They need to know what is appropriate for each of them in the world in which we live."

This dialogue dramatizes the meaning of child-centered religious education today. If it indicates a seemingly new trend in Christian religious education, I would respond that the trend already exists and extends quite dramatically across Roman Catholic, Protestant, and Evangelical denominations. We do not want to dominate children. Similarly, we do not want the children to dominate us. We all want to be open. We want to learn and discover God's grace together. That is, we want to be free, as God intends us to be free.

A Summary of Child-Centered Religious Education

There are four principles which summarize child-centered religious education.

1. *The needs of individual child learners are the focus of the educator.* This first principle means that any teacher must be acquainted with child development. It also means that a teacher must have some method for assessing each individual learner's developmental level.

2. *Each child is unique.* The teacher must not only know child development, but must also know the children individually.

3. *Assessment-based, individualized instruction is a social science translation of the term* nurture. This principle reminds us that we are beginning to understand more and more about the meaning of Christian nurture. Whereas nurture has sometimes been loosely viewed as "socialization" or "acculturation" through the social sciences, we can now appreciate that nurture is really attitude or value education that involves the whole child.

4. *The aim of religious education is the total embracing, on the part of the learner, of Christian values.* This principle indicates that children must be educated in a way that leads to their freedom to accept God's freely given grace or to reject it with understanding. Child-centered religious education is neither indoctrination nor inculcation; it is education for freedom and for responsible decisions.

It will be noted that there is no clear role for the Bible in this overall summation. Naturally, I do not discount the Christian Scriptures. But in keeping with Goldman's findings, their careful use as a supplement to the foundational religious education of little children is all that is advised.[21] Many religious education practitioners become uncomfortable with what seems to be excessive academic discussion. Others appear to long for nothing more than a thoroughly academic analysis of the approach. Perhaps some illustrations of what a child-centered religious education might mean may prove useful.

Iris Cully, in her *Christian Child Development*, describes some of the characteristics of a good teacher in a child-centered approach to the discipline. She writes:

It requires a flexible teacher who enjoys stimulating learning in others and does not depend on easy answers as a way of getting through a session. The child's curiosity is a motivating force in learning. The teacher's task is to stimulate that curiosity.

Understanding the learner as a person is essential. This means taking the time to "feel into" the situation of the child.

A good teacher bases a session on exploration. The teacher is a guide who points directions, encourages searching, shares knowledge, and gives pupils freedom to follow where their curiosity leads.[22]

A second illustration focuses on child-centered foundational religious education in action. This cannot be done with a "lesson plan" for twenty children in their best Sunday clothing sitting docilely in a Sunday school classroom. If anyone thinks that twenty children in a classroom will learn what the teacher plans, it would be well to go to such a class and observe it in action. Each young learner learns only what he or she sets out to learn! The trite phrase "it all depends" is altogether appropriate. Children *are* unique.

Imagine a father pondering about how to teach his four-year-old son to feel good about himself (a prerequisite, at the preschool developmental level, for eventually teaching love of others and love of God). The illustration is, of course, highly personalized, as all child-centered religious education must be. However, such a father might well say to himself:

Mike is pleased with himself when he completes a task. He and his Mother are refinishing the toy chest in the basement. I will tell Mike the story of Grandfather Followthrough, and I will make a poster of Grandfather Followthrough with squares to check off as Mike completes each part of the task. Mike will be proud of the completed toy chest, and he will be delighted as all the squares on the poster are checked off.[23]

The story and the poster are "the lesson." They match Mike's developmental level and Mike's uniqueness. Preschool children do need to develop a positive self-regard as a foundation for later understanding God's love. Thus the approach of Mike's father to foundational religious education is personalized and deals with those experiences which are the day-by-day happenings in the life of Mike.

Finally, there is a different illustration of child-centered religious education. In this instance think of a classroom setting. However, the illustration is only a beginning. Who could know the outcome of this class?

Imagine that you are teaching a church school class of first and second graders who hold the social perspectives of Stages 1 and 2. You have just read them the story of Matthew 12:9-14 concluding with the statement: "And surely a man is of much more value than a sheep."

At Stage 1 children may respond from the standpoint of which is older or bigger.

At Stage 2 children may respond from the standpoint of which is more useful, has the most ability, or on the replacement possibilities.[24]

The class goal inherent in this situation is that some stage 1 children will be moved toward stage 2, and that some stage 2 children will consolidate stage 2 experiences as they prepare for a transition to stage 3. The ultimate goal may be a postconventional level of social perspective. But these as yet immature learners are not burdened with anything more than what is appropriate for their developmental level.

Conclusion

What Ronald Goldman began in the 1960s has now been extended considerably. Religious educators are beginning to be more sophisticated in dealing with diverse and complex theories. Child-centered religious education has, it seems, won its place. However, that declaration does not mean that any clear consensus exists regarding the transition from theory to practice. Such a consensus will not be appropriate until religious educators have gained greater knowledge of the whole child, the actual learner. Progress has been made, and it will continue to be made. The future is filled with promise of exciting progress beyond what can be seen today.

Notes

1. Ronald Goldman, *Readiness for Religion* (London: Routledge & Kegan Paul, 1965).
2. James W. Fowler, *Stages of Faith* (San Francisco: Harper & Row, 1981).
3. Mary M. Wilcox, *Developmental Journey* (Nashville: Abingdon Press, 1979).

4. Ronald Goldman, *Religious Thinking from Childhood to Adolescence* (London: Routledge & Kegan Paul, 1964).
5. The publisher for the Episcopal Church that has most completely published Ronald Goldman's work and series built upon his work is Morehouse-Barlow. Wm. Brown publishes *The Light of Faith* for Roman Catholics. These materials are based on Goldman.
6. Krister A. Ottosson, "Religious Education in Western Europe," in *Foundations for Christian Education in an Era of Change*, ed. Marvin J. Taylor (Nashville: Abingdon Press, 1976).
7. John H. Peatling, "Cognitive Development in Pupils in Grades Four Through Twelve: The Incidence of Concrete and Abstract Religious Thinking in American Children," *Character Potential: A Record of Research 7*, no. 1 (October 1977).
8. James E. Loder, "Developmental Foundations for Christian Education," in *Foundations for Christian Education in an Era of Change*, ed. Taylor.
9. Robert L. Browning, "The Structure and Quality of Church Education in the Future," in *Foundations for Christian Education in an Era of Change*, ed. Taylor.
10. Lawrence Kohlberg, "Stages of Moral Development as a Basis for Moral Education," in *Moral Development, Moral Education and Kohlberg*, ed. Brenda Munsey (Birmingham, Ala.: Religious Education Press, 1980).
11. Fowler, *Stages of Faith.*
12. Loder, "Developmental Foundations for Christian Education."
13. David Elkind, *The Child's Reality* (Hillsdale, N.J.: Lawrence Erlbaum Assoc., 1978).
14. John H. Peatling, *Religious Education in a Psychological Key* (Birmingham, Ala.: Religious Education Press, 1981).
15. Iris V. Cully, *Christian Child Development* (San Francisco: Harper & Row, 1979).
16. Wilcox, *Developmental Journey.*
17. Lucie W. Barber, *Religious Education of Preschool Children* (Birmingham, Ala.: Religious Education Press, 1981); and, by the same author and publisher, *Celebrating the Second Year of Life*, 1978.
18. Craig Dykstra, *Vision and Character: A Christian Educator's Alternative to Kohlberg* (New York: Paulist Press, 1981).
19. Carol Gilligan, "In a Different Voice: Women's Conception of the Self and Morality,"*Harvard Educational Review* 47, no. 4 (1978).
20. James Fowler and Sam Keen, *Life Maps* (Waco, Tex.: Word, 1978), 96-99.
21. See Lucie W. Barber, *When a Story Would Help* (St. Meinrad, Ind.: Abbey Press, 1981), chap. 10 and *Religious Education of Preschool Children*, chap. 9.
22. Cully, *Christian Child Development*, 151, 155, and 156.
23. Barber, *Religious Education of Preschool Children*, 75.
24. Wilcox, *Developmental Journey*, 76.

CHAPTER 18

Youth and Religious Nurture

Michael Warren

No look at the matter of youth and religious nurture in the United States would be fully adequate without an examination of the various ways this issue had been viewed in the past. The effort called for in scrutinizing this history, even in a cursory manner, may be rewarded with a sense of perspective valuable in assessing more contemporary efforts at nurture. However, the reader must be warned that the history of religious groups in the United States is complex in that generalizations could lead to disastrous misunderstandings.[1] For instance, much of the following report reflects the experience of the better-documented denominational histories, even excluding such well documented but not fully mainstream histories as the Roman Catholic and the Southern Baptist.

Early Attitudes Toward Nurture

In the beginning, prior to the period of gradual religious decline in the colonies starting around 1700, New England Congregationalism stressed the importance of a Christian upbringing in childhood. Parents believed there was a covenant relationship between them and God that affected all members of a particular household.[2] These ideas changed, however, as a result of the Great Awakening of 1740–42, when religious fervor was stirred back to life by the preaching of revivalists such as Jonathan Edwards and George Whitefield.[3] Although the awakening fluctuated in fervor over the years through various social factors, its impact can be traced right up to the outbreak of the Civil War. During these years, emphasis was on the dramatic and radical conversion which brought a person suddenly and decisively to salvation through Jesus. Though such a "turning" could occur anywhere between

Michael Warren is Professor in the Department of Theology of St. John's University.

childhood and adulthood, it was generally expected after puberty as one advanced closer to adulthood.[4]

This revivalist stress on conversion affected the way children were perceived, if not in every denomination, then at least in general. Christian parentage notwithstanding, the child was seen to be a "child of wrath," under the domination of Satan. There was little expectation that the child could engage in the intense struggle necessary before one could move from Satan's ways to Christian discipleship. Children were allowed to remain like fallow fields building up receptivity for the eventual planting. As Luther Weigle describes the situation,

[children] were held to be lost in sin, depraved by nature, and in need of a wholly new heart. They were children of wrath until the Holy Spirit should transmute them into children of God. It mattered nothing what their parentage, or what the quality of the home in which they were brought up. . . . Older folk can do nothing for them, then, save to seek to deepen in them a sense of their need, and to pray on their behalf for the gift of conversion.[5]

As unwise as such attitudes may be, judged by later generations, they show not so much an antichild bias as they do a conviction that the church was not meant to be a gathering of any and all naming themselves Christians, but rather of a fervent elite.[6] Jonathan Edwards and the others were offering a corrective, and a religiously elevated one, to church life that had become halfhearted and half-committed.[7] Ironically, the revival of Jonathan Edwards, native of the Hartford area and graduate of Yale, was to be nuanced and, as far as its treatment of children was concerned, corrected by a Yale graduate who spent his entire life as a pastor in Hartford: Horace Bushnell.[8]

In 1847, Bushnell, after struggling intellectually with the prevailing practice of almost ignoring the religious development of children, published *Christian Nurture*, a work that set forth the theory and practice of the Christian formation of children and young people. In what is often quoted as the kernel of his position, Bushnell explained his conviction that proper nurture would make it possible for

the child to grow up a Christian, and never know himself as being otherwise. In other words, the aim, effort, and expectation should be, not, as is commonly assumed, that the child is to grow up in sin, to be converted after he comes to a mature age; but that he is to open on the world as one that is spiritually renewed, not remembering the time when he went through a technical experience, but seeming rather to have loved what is good from his earliest years.[9]

Throughout this book, Bushnell shows a keen sense of the importance of socialization in the development of children. Not only the family, but the local church community has a decisive impact, for better or worse, on the spirits of the young.

But suppose there is really no trace or seed of holy principle in your children; has there been no fault of piety and constancy in your church? No want of Christian sensibility and love to God? No carnal spirit visible to them and to all, and imparting its noxious and poisonous quality to the Christian atmosphere in which they have had their nurture? For it is not for you alone to realize all that is included in the idea of Christian education. It belongs to the church of God, according to the degree of its social power over you and in you and around your children, to bear a part of the responsibility with you.[10]

These somewhat utopian convictions of Bushnell appear to have been decisive for the eventual and increasing preoccupation of the Protestant churches with careful intervention in the lives of children and youth. What Bushnell offered as a thesis in 1847 came to be the dominant, taken-for-granted agenda for young people in the majority of Protestant churches. Even the Sunday schools, which erupted almost spontaneously along the Atlantic seaboard after the War of 1812 as a way of instructing the children of the poor in reading and writing, came eventually to be instruments devoted to Christian nurture, indeed, the key instruments.[11]

As one might suspect, not all this growing concern of the churches with the nurture of the young turned out to be fully beneficial to young people themselves. In the unplanned but effective way disparate events sometimes have of coalescing, concern for Christian nurture combined with other developments after the Civil War in a way that served to restrict the activities and even the spirits of young people. These developments reversed the experience of young people in the early republic (1790–1840), when most children moved quickly from a brief period of dependency to an early situation of semidependence, which one historian describes as a jarring mixture of complete freedom and total subordination.[12]

In the early republic, many children at an early age ceased being subject to complete parental control, even if only during a summer of labor on a neighboring farm.[13]

"Full" incorporation [into the work force], moreover, probably occurred around the time of puberty—that is, at 15 or 16, when a boy was judged physically able to carry a man's work load. Prior to the middle of the 19th century, contemporaries associated puberty with rising power and energy rather than with the onset of an awkward and vulnerable stage of life which would later become known as adolescence. . . . Since children entered the work force in stages, it is not surprising that contemporaries customarily distinguished infancy, boyhood, and young manhood. A second measure of passage out of infancy [was] the commencement of departure from home.[14]

A social system of apprenticeships, an acceptance of serious work for a child starting around age seven, and frequent orphanings due to the early deaths of parents all combined to set up myriad forms of semidependency for children and prepubertal young people.

As one might expect, the quasi dependence of so many young people at an early age affected the kinds of associations they had among themselves. Especially in the large towns and cities of the early nineteenth century, young people gathered in their own voluntary associations, organized and run by themselves. These included academies, a variety of young men's societies, and political clubs.[15] Even when all members of these groups were under the legal age of adulthood, and needed, for legal purposes only, adult sponsors, the groups themselves tended toward independence rather than toward adult domination. In fact, prior to the Civil War, few institutions at all marked the passage from one stage of life to another. The criteria for the attainment of adulthood were the following: entering marriage, leaving home for the last time, or, in some cases, the age at which one joined a church.

Evolution of Nurture as Control

However, after 1840, a number of social forces combined with the theory of Christian nurture to restrict, gradually but ineluctably, the independence of young people. One of these was the rise of the public school, begun earlier in Britain as a reform movement seeking to instill moral virtue via carefully managed schooling.[16] Another was the application of new principles of efficiency to environments carefully planned and engineered to produce the internalization of moral restraints and the formation of character. In addition, the conscious spacing of children led to a declining birth rate and to more attention to the task of child rearing.[17] Buttressed by economic forces, these philosophical and social factors combined to ensure that in the second half of the nineteenth century, more and more of the period of childhood and youth was spent in institutional settings seeking the careful nurture, if not control, of young people.

These developments eventually took their toll of young people's freedom by diminishing the opportunities they had for directing their own activities. As Kett points out,

the difference between the early and late 19th century lay not merely in the extension of ecclesiastical control over the spare-time activities of youth but in the increasing erosion of the principle of voluntary association by youth. The young men's societies of the 17th through early 19th centuries had been organized by young men themselves; the young people's movement of the 1880s and 1890s, in contrast, consisted entirely of adult-sponsored youth organizations.[18]

Within these social forces, Christian nurture was moving at its own energetic pace, ever better organized, better staffed, more carefully theorized, and with ever more evident results, which, from our present standpoint at least, are also more open to question and critique. During the period 1880–1900, particular progress was made in church youth organizations through "muscular Christianity," an import from Britain that stressed planning, structure, and discipline in youth work. The "young people's movement" spawned by muscular Christianity affected millions of Protestant youth at the end of the nineteenth century, "far more young people than did public high schools."[19]

Unfortunately, many of these efforts, operating under a rhetoric of nurture, had built into them unexamined goals of carefully protecting young people from "moral dangers" or of shielding them from reality and in some ways from adult questions and tasks. Sincerity was judged as more significant than competence, predictability more important than probing inquiry. "Even when spokesmen for the young people's movement outlined specific goals, they were so general as to be meaningless . . . or so trivial as to be ludicrous. . . ."[20] In sum,

for all the talk about activity . . . the motive force behind church youth societies in the 1880s and 1890s was defensive, a desire to shield young people from contamination by the alien culture of big cities and immigrants. . . . A common thread which ran through college "life," the high school extra-curriculum, and Christian youth organizations was hostility to precocity, to adult behavior in youth. As it acquired institutional forms, the long-standing fear of precocity changed its shape. The avoidance of precocity no longer entailed merely the removal of intellectual pressures and social stimulants from youth, but the creation of a self-contained world in which prolonged immaturity could sustain itself.[21]

The irony in these programs was that the questions and activities of youth all tended to be set by adults who at the same time seemed to be shielding youth from adult questions and adult activities. In these settings religious nurture tended toward passivity and insularity.[22]

The move in church youth work toward adult domination of youth activities continued into the twentieth century, and even increased as part of a wider societal program of exercising more and more control over the lives of young people. In part, the progress of these programs was itself tied to a growing move toward professionalization in the United States. Standards were set for training and performance, and professionals were expected to have greater technical control over the tasks they performed. Adult domination and professionalization both coalesced in the first quarter of the twentieth century in the transformation of the Sunday school from a nurture-centered to an education-centered activity.

The shift was engineered by a cadre of thinkers influenced by the progressive educational theories of John Dewey and by the relatively short-lived social gospel theology of Walter Rauschenbusch.[23] The desire of these professionals was to shift the emphasis of the church school from informal procedures and educationally haphazard materials to a professional combination of the best thinking about education and about religion. In a new century ready to move away from the unenlightened practices of the past, the religious education professionals judged that the Sunday school should become a respectable educational institution. The efforts of these reformers were greatly assisted by the formation in 1903 of the Religious Education Association. Founded by William Rainey Harper as an organization free of any sort of ecclesiastical control, the association was to be an umbrella organization for all those concerned with promoting religious and moral education.[24] At its 1905 convention, the REA set forth its ideal of fostering a proper conjunction of education and religion: "To inspire the educational forces of our country with the religious ideal; to inspire the religious forces of our country with the educational ideal; and to keep before the public mind the ideal of religious education and the sense of its need and value."[25]

One of the chief theorists of the new religion-and-education thrust was George Albert Coe, professor at Union Theological Seminary, a radical and progressive on every front: political, educational, and theological.[26] Coe was imbued with an intense faith in the human potential as it seemed to be emerging in the early years of the century. Such was his faith in the future that "few of his students [were] encouraged to study history; instead their attention [was] focused upon the present and the ongoing struggle of freeing men from the burden of a dead past."[27]

Coe and other leaders of the religious education movement succeeded for almost thirty years in professionalizing the education structures that had evolved in the churches. Lynn and Wright summarize the agenda of these reformers as follows:

[They] looked upon this hustle and bustle [of the average Sunday school] as empty efforts of well-intentioned workers, amateurs who had too long dominated the Sunday school. Amateurism was, in fact, the nub of their quarrel with the traditional movement. *Professional* leadership must take over. And why not? Experts were evident in public schools, social work and municipal life. Should Protestant education be different? Volunteer leaders, in the reformers' scheme, should be aided by a fulltime "director of religious education" if a congregation could afford one. If not, the minister was expected to assume the mantle of the professional. . . . The formula was straightforward: no professional, no reform; no reform, no school worthy of respect.[28]

Although it would distort history to suggest that all leading the religious education movement walked lock-step with each other, [29] in general it seems accurate to say that for thirty years the effort to professionalize the educational side of religious education went unquestioned, as did the effort to make the religious side more open to intellectual inquiry. The success of these reformers, however, was more complete at the theoretical level than at the level of local church practice.

The local church's educational structures rested on the foundation of the efforts of many volunteer laypersons, some of whom at least cherished their memories of the good old days of the nonprofessionalized Sunday school. In rural areas the optimistic and rationalistic faith of the new professionals was coolly received. In both urban and rural settings, some volunteers found that "the methods of progressive education—the experience-centered approach with stress on problem-solving and attention to student needs—required a sophistication and commitment of time" not feasible for them.[30] And then, of course, in many places the life of the local Sunday school had gone on as if there never had been a religious education movement.

Eventually, the social optimism of what was called liberal theology was dealt a lethal blow by World War I before collapsing entirely in the pessimism accompanying the economic collapse of 1929.[31] More and more through the 1930s, voices were raised to question the assumptions of religious education, precisely regarding its adequacy as a structure for religious nurture. Finally, in 1941, H. Shelton Smith wrote his *Faith and Nurture*, a book decisive for moving the question away from the fixities of the early religious education movement and back to a quest for the appropriate context for the development of religious faith.[32] In the forty years since Smith's attempt to critique the religious education movement, especially the Coe-Childs wing of it, the literature of religious education-Christian education has hovered between the poles of education or nurture.

Nurture in Current Thought

A substantial amount of writing has attempted to shed light on various aspects of the question in the decades since 1941, and it would be impossible here to treat even a small fraction of this literature. What is significant is that the question itself remains unresolved, so much so that some would contend that the field of religious education is in disarray. Others find in the ongoing dialectic an enriching vitality that refuses to offer or accept simplistic answers to complex questions. Indeed, there have been many attempts at synthesis and the avoidance of what is seen as a false choice between education and nurture. Because of its special relevance for youth ministry theory, the writer wishes to turn to one stream of this literature, the one that pays special attention to socialization theory.

Since about 1965, when C. Ellis Nelson gave the Sprunt lectures at Union Theological Seminary in Richmond, Virginia, later published as *Where Faith Begins*, some writers have sought to combine education and nurture through an examination of the possibilities of a nurturing community.[33] These thinkers ask whether it is possible for the community's own life to be centered in an ongoing hermeneutic that scrutinizes contemporary culture in the light of religious meaning. Such thinking moves not so much to instructional strategies as the dominant instrument for communicating religious traditions, nor to child-centered procedures organized and dominated by adults. Without rejecting the value of such procedures, these thinkers prefer to examine interaction among community members and the many informal means of communication they use to influence each other. Thus the main contention of *Where Faith Begins* is "that religion at its deepest levels is located within a person's sentiments and is the result of the way he was socialized by the adults who cared for him as a child."[34] Put in another way, Nelson's thesis "is that faith is communicated by a community of believers and that the meaning of faith is developed by its members out of their history, by their interaction with each other, and in relation to the events that take place in their lives."[35] The community's buildings and budget, its worship, its way of dealing or not dealing with conflict, its forms of leadership are all ways of communicating its core meanings. However, everything needs to be put under the scrutiny of Scripture and a quest for discipleship appropriate to the current age.

This attention to religious socialization among Protestants has created new possibilities of dialogue and mutual enrichment with Roman Catholics, whose own catechetical renewal has an emphasis on socialization. John Westerhoff's *Will Our Children Have Faith?*[36] finds a wide audience among Roman Catholics, while Westerhoff acknowledges his own debt to catechetical theory.[37] Catechetical theory holds that "catechesis in the final analysis is community education. The community of faith with all its formal and informal structures is the chief catechist."[38] However, for catechesis to be effective, the community itself needs to undergo continuous conversion, broadening its horizons, reforming and renewing itself, through an ongoing process of interpreting and reinterpreting the shape of its response to the gospel.

In Roman Catholic understanding, catechesis falls within the category of ministry rather than within that of education.[39] Without in any way ignoring education or educational theory, catechesis finds the more appropriate frame of reference for its activities within ministry. Significant to the purpose of this essay, the task of working out an ecology of church-related activities within ministry rather than within education has effected a renewed understanding of youth ministry and thus of youth nurture.

To be effective, ministry with youth must attend to the multiple needs of youth seeking to achieve a balance among many ministries: ministry of the Word, of worship, of guidance and counsel (including education). A brief overview of these ministries reveals how they revolve around the community's own life. The ministry of the Word encompasses all those activities by which the church maintains and proclaims the meanings that bind it together. The ministry of worship is the activity by which a community embodies its understandings and its group life in ritual worship. The ministry of guidance and counsel, including education, embodies those activities by which a community comforts the troubled and shares its wisdom about the human condition. This is a ministry of liberating the human spirit. The ministry of healing involves those activities by which a community follows Jesus' mandate to free the captives, feed the hungry, bind up the wounded, and be a force for justice.

Seen from this angle, youth ministry operates out of the community's life. As a nurturing activity, youth ministry is not content with summoning young people to an intense and warm peer-group fellow-feeling. Important as such intense experiences seem to be for young people, a properly nuanced ministry with youth goes beyond them to pay attention to the distance between much in current culture and the norms of human life set forth in the gospel. When seeking to critique culture, youth ministry is more about challenge than about comfort.[40]

The best youth ministry thinking of recent years has been stressing the need for a strong intellectual and educational component, worked out through innovative, deschooled strategies. Considering the manipulation of the consciousness of youth in an electronic culture and the difficulty of doing conscientization among young people, the educational stress of a renewed youth ministry will have to receive increasing attention in the future.[41] Similarly, as works such as Kett's become more widely known, those working for youth nurture through youth ministry will be more and more on their guard against offering young people domesticating strategies and trivial ideas. For the future, youth ministry seems headed for a period of creative dissatisfaction with its own achievements and of critical suspicion of its own agenda. Out of these directions one might hope that the churches will find their way to be ever more faithful to their young people.

Notes

1. Robert W. Lynn offers several such warnings in a fine article that has been of special help in preparing this survey. See Robert W. Lynn, "The Uses of History: An Inquiry into the History of American Religious Education," *Religious Education* 67, no. 2 (March-April 1972): 83-97.
2. Williston Walker, "Horace Bushnell," in Horace Bushnell, *Christian Nurture* (New Haven: Yale University Press, 1967), xxviii. Actually the situation seems to have been somewhat more complex than Walker's description of it. Even children from thoroughly Christian homes were expected eventually to undergo a conversion in adulthood. See Sydney E. Ahlstrom, ed., "Introduction," in *Theology in America* (New York: Bobbs-Merrill, 1967), 26-36, especially 34, n. 12.
3. Luther Weigle, "Introduction," in Bushnell, *Christian Nurture*, xxxii-xxxiii.
4. Although conversion was to come close to adulthood, it is important to realize it was prepared for in early years. Joseph Kett notes "the fact that in religious households piety was to begin early. Conversion in youth was often the outcome of a process that commenced at 7 or 8, with the symptoms going into

remission in ensuing years." Joseph F. Kett, *Rites of Passage: Adolescence in America, 1790 to the Present* (New York: Basic Books, 1977), 68. The Shaker communities welcomed children to live among them and gave them a careful formation until maturity (age 14 for girls, 16 for boys), when they had to make a decision—either to leave and grow toward conversion in the "world" or to remain through the making of a formal commitment. See Edward Deming Andrews, *The People Called Shakers* (New York: Dover Publications, 1963), 186-94.

5. Weigle, in *Christian Nurture*, xxxiii.
6. Ahlstrom, in *Theology in America*, 33-34.
7. See Walker, in *Christian Nurture*, xxix, and Ahlstrom, in *Theology in America*, 34-35.
8. For a vivid account of the thought about conversion prior to Bushnell, see Kett, *Rites of Passage*, 63-68. It is important for readers to note that Kett's book focuses on the history of *males*, because of the scant documentation about women.
9. Bushnell, *Christian Nurture*, 4.
10. Ibid., 5-6.
11. Kett, *Rites of Passage*, 120.
12. Ibid., 29.
13. Ibid., 15-30 for a detailed treatment of childhood during this period, 1790-1840.
14. Ibid., 17.
15. Ibid., 30-31 and 38-41.
16. See ibid., 111-15. See also 186-89 for a treatment of more technical bureaucratic controls in schools at a later point in history.
17. Ibid., 112-15.
18. Ibid., 194.
19. Ibid., 190.
20. Ibid., 194.
21. Ibid., 210.
22. A suggestion of the insularity of the Sunday school can be found in Mark Twain's depiction of Tom Sawyer's Sunday school superintendent, who "was very earnest of mien, and very sincere and honest of heart; and he held sacred things and places in such reverence, and so separated them from worldly matters, that unconsciously to himself his Sunday-school voice had acquired a peculiar intonation which was wholly absent on weekdays." Cited in Robert W. Lynn and Elliott Wright, *The Big Little School* (New York: Harper & Row, 1971), 75.
23. Ibid., 80. See also 75-85.
24. In the beginning the REA was not intended to be a professional organization but to bring together professionals and laypersons to foster communication. See Boardman W. Kathan, "Report," *Reach* 11, no. 1 (Spring 1981): 2.
25. "The Aims of Religious Education," in *Proceedings* of the Third Annual Convention of the Religious Education Association (Chicago: Religious Education Association, 1905), 474. For a good description of William Rainey Harper's desire to professionalize church education, see Boardman W. Kathan, "William Rainey Harper: Founder of the Religious Education Association," *Religious Education* 73, no. 5S (September-October 1978): S7-S16.
26. See Helen A. Archibald, "George A. Coe: The Years from 1920–1951," *Religious Education* 73, no. 5S (September-October 1978): S25-S35.
27. Lynn, "The Uses of History," 87.
28. Lynn and Wright, *The Big Little School*, 83.
29. See Lynn, "The Uses of History," 86-87.
30. Lynn and Wright, *The Big Little School*, 85.
31. A detailed account of this inflated social optimism and the gloom that followed in its wake can be found in Russell B. Nye, *This Almost Chosen People* (Ann Arbor: Michigan State University Press, 1966), 1-41. George A. Coe's social

optimism can be revisited in his work, *A Social Theory of Religious Education* (New York: Charles Scribner's Sons, 1917).

32. A valuable account of this period can be found in Kieran Scott, "Religious Education and Professional Religious Education: A Conflict of Interest?" in *Religious Education* 78, no. 5. (January-February 1983).

33. C. Ellis Nelson, *Where Faith Begins* (Richmond, Va.: John Knox Press, 1967).

34. Ibid., 9.

35. Ibid., 10.

36. John Westerhoff, *Will Our Children Have Faith?* (New York: The Seabury Press, 1976).

37. John H. Westerhoff III, "A Call to Catechesis," *The Living Light* 14, no. 3 (1977): 354-58. See also "Catechesis: An Anglican Perspective," in *Sourcebook for Modern Catechetics*, ed. Michael Warren (Winona, Minn.: St. Mary's Press, 1983).

38. Berard Marthaler, "Socialization as a Model for Catechetics," in *Foundations of Religious Education*, ed. Padraic O'Hare (New York: Paulist Press, 1978), 64-92, especially 89.

39. See "Youth Ministry in Transition" and "Youth Catechesis in the 80s," in Michael Warren, *Youth and the Future of the Church* (New York: The Seabury Press, 1982), 8-25 and 74-88.

40. See "Youth Ministry: Toward Politicization," ibid., 89-102. Also Michael Warren, "Some Reflections on Religious Media," *Catholic Library World* 53, no. 10 (May-June 1982): 424-27.

41. For background on a specific approach, see Michael Warren, "Youth Politicization: A Proposal for Education Within Ministry," *Religious Education* 77, no. 2 (March-April 1982): 179-96.

Bibliography

Harris, Maria. *Portrait of Youth Ministry*. New York: Paulist Press, 1981.

Kett, Joseph F. *Rites of Passage: Adolescence in America, 1790 to the Present.* New York: Basic Books, 1977.

Konopka, Gisela. *Young Girls: A Portrait of Adolescence.* Englewood Cliffs, N.J.: Prentice-Hall, 1976.

Lipsitz, Joan. *Growing Up Forgotten: A Review of Research and Programs Concerning Early Adolescence.* Lexington, Mass.: D. C. Heath, 1977.

Little, Sara. *Youth, World and Church.* Richmond, Va.: John Knox Press, 1968.

Warren, Michael. *Youth and the Future of the Church.* New York: The Seabury Press, 1982.

Wyckoff, D. Campbell, and Don Richter, eds. *Religious Education Ministry with Youth.* Birmingham, Ala.: Religious Education Press, 1982.

CHAPTER 19

Adult Religious Life and Nurture

Norma H. Thompson

Through most of human history, the religious life of adults has been taken for granted. It is assumed that children will grow up and take on the religious beliefs and practices of their elders and that if any concentration is necessary with respect to the nurturing of religious life, that concentration is upon the young. Throughout the world this "natural" way of nurturing still exists. It is only as the world has developed a consciousness of education as a special nurturing activity that the processes by which this education takes place have been examined with the end in view to improve the nurturing process. Even yet the tendency in the Western world, and wherever this education approach has been developed in other countries, is to be concerned for children and youth. In Buddhist countries there are now courses on Buddhism in the schools, but there is little or no consciousness of nurturing the religious life of adults except as they become monks or nuns. In India, and wherever Hinduism has moved in the rest of the world, the same is true. But in Christianity, and perhaps to a lesser extent in Judaism, there has developed as a part of the so-called religious education movement a sense that the religious life of the adult can be deepened and strengthened if conscious nurturing efforts are made both by the adults themselves and by the faith communities of which they are a part.

It is true that adults will grow up with some religious sentiments, some answers to the basic questions of life, and some rituals and myths which become their guides and their ways of dealing with both everyday aspects of existence and the crises of life. Joachim Wach divided those ultimate questions into three categories: theology, cosmology, and anthropology. In particular, he saw the basic and eternal questions as dealing with: (1) "Is Ultimate Reality pluralistic, dualistic or monistic? Is it personal or impersonal? Is it

Norma H. Thompson is Professor Emeritus, Program in Religious Education, School of Education, New York University.

characterized by distance or nearness?"; (2) "What is the origin of the universe? What kind of order pervades it? What is its destiny?"; (3) "What is the nature of human beings? How do they relate to the universe? What are the highest possibilities of earthly life? What are the hindrances to achieving these possibilities and how may they be overcome? What is the final goal of human life?"[1]

Even the most unlearned person develops some answers to these questions, and to a large extent actions are consistent with those answers. The question for religious education, then, is to what extent and in what ways is it helpful to persons to work consciously at those answers, to share with others in an intentional search for the meaning of existence, and to be a part of a community whose very being is geared to nurturing in the religious realm? The religious education movement has assumed that people are helped in this process, that faith does begin in the "community of believers."[2] The profession of religious educator is posited on the notion that within that community of faith things happen to people, and it is possible for people to make differences in their own lives, and in the lives of others.

Adults as Central to Religious Nurture

C. Ellis Nelson concluded, after studying the way by which children develop faith as they are socialized into a society in much the same way that they take over the customs and attitudes of the community, that the foundations of faith are laid in the experience of the person within the community of believers.[3] Berard Marthaler[4] and John Westerhoff[5] have developed theories of religious education based upon this same notion. Sociologists, from the study of contemporary societies, and anthropologists, from studying both past and present societies, have shaped a pattern of development within which the members of a group socialize, or enculturate, their offspring.

As persons grow within a community, some of the learning experiences (most of them, in fact) are not intentionally planned as educational and nurturing experiences. They are simply the way this particular group lives together, expressing the values and customs which they have built up, and handling the aberrations and conflicts in a manner which attempts to keep the society intact. Within the group, however, there are certain activities that are planned as educational, such as the passing on of the culture from one generation to the next and helping the young know the beliefs, attitudes, and values which it is assumed they will take on for themselves as they move from the state of childhood to adulthood. Many of these activities occur at the point where the society sees the young as making that transition—at puberty or in late adolescence.[6]

In reviewing the history of the human race, it appears that most cultures have operated under the assumption that what is necessary for persons to function as adults in the society can be transmitted in this way, and the rest will be picked up experientially. This approach depends upon the family's teaching the boys and girls what they need to know about sexuality, trades, roles as adults, housemaking and housekeeping, handling of finances and possessions, and many other matters essential for carrying on the daily functions of life. It depends upon adults sharing what they know about work, about human relations, and about the good and the bad. But it says little about the learning which adults themselves must do in order to function as adults in the society.

What it does show is the central role of adults in the educational process, both in intentional and nonintentional education. Some scholars make a distinction between intentional and nonintentional education, using different terms to express the two forms. Westerhoff appears to include both in his enculturation theory of religious education, noting the two forms but seeing them both as included in enculturation.[7] Marthaler notes that "the socialization process has been operative in the Christian community since two or three first gathered together in Jesus' name"; and insofar as it was "an intentional process, socialization was traditionally called *catechesis*."[8] Gabriel Moran distinguishes between education and schooling, noting that schooling is one form of education, "the specific kind of learning that is most appropriate to the institution of school,"[9] but there is a nonschooling part of education which consists of forms of learning found in institutions of various kinds, including the school. Others have called the intentional learning experiences *education* and the nonintentional learning experiences *nurture*. Regardless of terminology, the process can take place only as the adults of the society carry the socializing roles and provide nurturing and educational experiences for the young and for one another.

Although this socialization process does not focus on the learning which adults must do as they move through life, taking on new functions and making necessary changes, every society gives evidence of such learning. The process of passing on the culture continues daily. Ralph Linton defined culture as "the configuration of learned behavior and results of behavior whose component elements are shared and transmitted by the members of a particular society."[10] Thus the process by which the patterns of action are transmitted to individuals in many situations of life includes both everyday activities and special occasions ranging from birth to death. It includes as well the religious in life as individuals learn the values, attitudes, knowledge, and beliefs of the society.

Adults today are seeking all sorts of formal educational experiences, as well as learning from relatives, friends, and neighbors. The great activity among adults to learn arts and crafts, the use of home computers, home repairs, and more and more intricate subject material in business and in science—all of these learning experiences attest to the lifelong nature of learning. The study of gerontology has further strengthened the idea that even in advanced age adults are learning new ways as they are forced by circumstances to sell their homes and move into smaller quarters, to adjust to nursing homes, to move to completely new housing in another state, to relate to new people—often a community made up of older persons.

John Elias sums up the continuity of learning thus:

> Though some differences between the learning of children and adults must be recognized, adult learning must always be viewed within the perspective of lifelong learning. For too long researchers have looked either at child learning and development or adult learning and development. What this approach misses is the continuity that exists from the beginning of life to its end and the similarities between people at the beginning and end of the life span.[11]

He goes on to say that, though continuity is primary, this does not preclude particular emphases and phases. Even the title of Moran's book, *Education Toward Adulthood: Religion and Lifelong Learning*, emphasizes that a theory of adult learning must take into account the continuity, variety, and complexity of human life at all stages from childhood through adulthood.[12]

In this connection Elias argues that Malcolm Knowles's distinction between pedagogy (the art and science of helping *children* learn) and andragogy (the art and science of helping *adults* learn) is not adequate. Lifelong learning "goes beyond andragogy."[13] He notes that "going beyond andragogy does not mean going back to pedagogy,"[14] and cites Paulo Freire's *Pedagogy of the Oppressed*[15] as an example of an educator who did not hesitate to use the term *pedagogy* for an education clearly oriented toward adults. Finally, Elias says, "Going beyond andragogy entails recovering a sense of the unity of learning and education in human life."[16]

When one juxtaposes the idea that adults play the central role in nurture (both intentional and nonintentional education) with the concept that learning is lifelong, the importance of the life of the parish or the congregation emerges. It is in that context that the religious life of the worshiping community is shared; it is the congregation that proclaims to the rest of the community the meaning, values, practices, and attitudes which are of importance to itself. It is within that group that persons of all kinds—families (traditional and nontraditional), single adults, and the like—share their meanings and experience the meanings of others. There may be conflict within the group which has to be resolved; there may be divisions that simmer below the surface; there may be a real sense of community and togetherness in values and ideas. Whatever the nature of the congregation, each individual is learning as he or she participates in the life of that group.

Gradually a way of looking at things develops, an attitude toward the rest of the world and toward social issues. Some answers to the ultimate questions of life are evident within the group, and these become evident to the outside community. Members of the wider community "see" that congregation as active in social concerns, Bible-believing, or exhibiting a close, warm human relationship with themselves and others. They have developed a life-style into which the members are caught up and which the children inherit along with the liturgical practices and the history and traditions of the church. This way of seeing and acting may be called a congregational life-style, and a good case could be made for the statement that it is through the congregational life-style that most adults continue to learn their religion and to develop their faith. The same case could be made for children and youth, but since this essay is related to adults, the focus will remain upon them. It is the life-style of the congregation which socializes in certain ways; it is because the congregation has a peculiar life-style that it provides group experiences such as courses or projects or liturgies or other aspects of the life of a parish.

Nelson describes the process thus:

The community of believers, as we have said, is the group that fosters and gives meaning to faith by the way it worships and lives together. The individual develops his Christian self-identification by his participation in the life of a congregation. The process of self-identification goes on throughout the life span, but it is the adult groups which form and re-form a style of life to which the self is related. Adults in their various roles, especially as parents, communicate the self image that the group forms.[17]

Stages of Faith Development

The concept of faith development is one which is dealt with in some detail elsewhere in this volume, so it will be treated here only by a few observations and the raising of some of the important questions related to this notion. It is included because religious education has accepted so fully the idea of human development in the religious and moral realms that these topics have become a part of almost every book, conference, convention, course, or training program in the field.

Indeed, it is understandable that this should be the case. Since Horace Bushnell proclaimed in his *Christian Nurture*[18] that children should grow up into their religion in much the same way that a flower grows and blossoms, the concept of growth has been a part of the literature and discussion of religious education—at certain times and among some groups a very controversial concept, but never easily discarded. Taking cues from biological growth and development, it seems reasonable to assume that other aspects of the human being have "natural" paths of growth, and that, if these can be discovered, the task of older members of a community is to nurture this process. Of course, this idea has precursors to Bushnell insofar as the world of education and psychology is concerned, but Bushnell was at least one of the most significant figures in applying the idea to the religious (in his case, Christian) development of children. Educators applied the developmental concept to intellectual growth and to social growth, which encouraged the belief that the less-obvious aspects of human nature develop along some continuum in somewhat the same fashion as the physical characteristics.

The ways in which cognition changes over the years from childhood to adolescence seemed to lend themselves to the designation of stages, as seen in the studies by Jean Piaget and others, but the social realm did not lend itself so easily to this developmental theory. The concept of "growth that is natural," or that there are natural developmental patterns, is an idea which seems to be very similar to the Tao of ancient China that there is a "right way to go." In the social sphere, the right way to go is not obvious, nor have the educators and the social scientists figured a means for discovering the usual patterns of change beyond a few very elemental relational behaviors in children and youth. The Social Adjustment series of textbooks for elementary and high school grades was abandoned after considerable criticism arose to the effect that they were geared to the development of conformists.

Another way of working at the same developmental question was to look at the tasks which apparently must be performed at each stage of life. With the recognition that not all persons need to perform these particular tasks at the same age, it was nevertheless possible to work out the developmental tasks using approximate age groups, and Robert Havighurst's *Developmental Tasks*[19] became a standard guide for educators in all fields, religion included. Florence Stratemeyer's "life situation" curriculum,[20] which was very influential in educational circles, was a similar attempt to relate the situations in which persons were located with the tasks common to those situations. Again, with the recognition of the uniquenesses of individuals, these situations could be tied to age groups. Developmental psychology became "the" psychology for religious education.

Nevertheless, by the 1940s, depth psychology—the works of Freud in particular, and Jung, Adler, and Erikson as well—began to be accepted by religious thinkers as compatible with religious ideas. Among other concepts, the idea of stages made an impact, and Erikson's stages especially became known and discussed in religious education, perhaps because they were less sexually oriented than Freud's stages and perhaps because they could be combined with developmental theory rather easily. They seemed congruent with Piaget's stages of cognitive development and not contradictory to the preliminary work he did on moral development. All of this provided a foundation for Lawrence Kohlberg's research to explore whether or not there are stages in the development of moral judgment[21] and James Fowler's stages of faith development.[22]

In most of the research on developmental tasks and developmental psychology, development was traced through childhood and adolescence, but little was done to relate these ideas to the developmental tasks of adults throughout the life-span or to discover the psychological changes of adulthood. The stage theory of Freud and Erikson, however, does put the concept of development into the adult period of life as well as into the younger segments of human existence, and Kohlberg's and Fowler's stages certainly place into the highest stages values which are usually unattainable in childhood and in adolescence. Whether this interest in adult stages has sparked emphasis in the society (and in religion) on the changes in adult life, or whether such factors in the society as the changing ratio of older adults to younger persons, the demands of older persons for rights and a sense of dignity, the development of mid-life and gerontological studies, and the publication of books on the "passages" of adulthood (Gail Sheehy's *Passages*, Daniel J. Levinson's *Seasons of a Man's Life*, for example) have focused attention on possible stages of development in adulthood, it is impossible to say. But it is obvious that increasingly the attention of religious educators has shifted to adults and to stages of faith and moral development. This has recently been climaxed by the creation of the Faith Development in the Adult Life Cycle project of the Religious Education Association, which held a symposium in August 1981, the papers for which are currently being published by William H. Sadlier, Inc.

In spite of all this attention, research, and critical thinking, the question remains whether adults go through identifiable stages or if they simply grow older and at some point move from physical health to a weakened state, from acquisition and outward expansion to retrenchment and simplification, and the like. If there are identifiable stages, does the development of faith (or of religion, if that term is preferred) follow the stages pattern? For all the research and discussion, this is still not clear. This question leads to an examination of some of the problems or questions which scholars have directed at the concept of faith development—questions that have important implications for nurture of adults.

1. There is no uniform definition of *faith*, as is obvious from the discussion of various meanings of the term cited in the "Hypotheses Paper" developed as a basis for the symposium mentioned above of the Faith Development in the Adult Life Cycle project.[23] In that paper definitions by Paul Tillich, Richard McBrien, Avery Dulles, James Fowler, Sam Keen, John Westerhoff, Carl Jung, Thomas Groome, and others are cited, and the section concludes with Fowler's expansion of the many dimensions of faith into a very involved definition:

The process of constitutive knowing

Underlying a person's composition and maintenance of a comprehensive frame (or frames) of meaning

Generated from the person's attachments or commitments to centers of supraordinate value which have power to unify his or her experiences of the world

Thereby endowing the relationships, contexts, and patterns of everyday life, past and future, with significance.[24]

The inference appears to be that this definition might satisfy a majority of persons working in the field and thus provide a satisfactory common definition. When the complexity of the definition is examined, however, many religious educators will have difficulty in relating it to the concept of faith as they have conceived it, and others will see this definition as having little to do with religion.

2. The second problem relates to the meaning of the term *adult*. Moran, in the paper cited above, notes that "we are affected by cultural assumptions concerning connotations of the word *adult*. The cultural pressure leads us to a confusing and inconsistent use of the word *adult/adulthood*."[25] In his book *Education Toward Adulthood*, he explores the nominal and adjectival usages of the term *adult* (to be an adult and to be adult) and sorts out two differing ideals of being adult. He sees these conflicting ideals as "embedded in imagery, language and institutions,"[26] and traces the conflict of these two patterns in educational, religious, social, developmental, and service spheres.[27] Elias discusses the term *adulthood*, rather than *adult*, but couples this discussion with maturity and the attendant questions of what can be identified as maturity and how it is attained.[28] Leon McKenzie is more concerned with defining the contemporary adult than with a general definition of adult or adulthood.[29] Thus, any attempt to define the term *adult* leads into the problems of the various ways in which the term is used, the ideals or characteristics inherent in the highest level of adulthood, and the social context in which adulthood is described by each society. From the scientific point of view, a search for a definition is complicated by the fact that social scientists require an operational definition, whereas religious leaders are more likely to define terms in nonoperational forms.

3. The third problem is the realization that research on stage theory is in a very elemental period, and there is still a real question as to whether or not there are stages. If so, are they hierarchical? Knowles points out two risks in the use of developmental stage theory: first, "to see the stages as hierarchical when they may only be different"; second, "the temptation to use them for stereotyping."[30] This problem becomes increasingly acute with the idea that the stages of faith development may be hierarchical. On the whole religious educators do not want to accept the idea that the higher levels are "better" than the lower stages, and yet the stages are established in a form that puts the values most highly regarded at the top—a universalizing faith (Fowler's highest stage), for example, or justice (as in Kohlberg's stages of the development of moral judgment).

4. There are other problems, but the final one to be discussed here is the concept of the adult life cycle. It is not clear that there is actually such a thing as an "adult life cycle." In its simplest form it seems to mean only that adults move through young, middle, and older adulthood to death. But usually it appears that educators who use this term mean something more complex about adulthood, that there are identifiable stages along this path, and there are "predictable physical, psychological, and social patterns that affect most, if not all, adults as they move through life."[31] One questions whether the concept of cycle is misleading. Is the cycle referring to the whole of life, and is the emphasis upon that segment traversed in adulthood? Is life really a cycle in which adults return to the same state as before birth? Or is there a more adequate metaphor by which to connote life?

To return to the purpose of this brief look at some of the aspects and some of the problems involved in the notion of faith development, it is obvious that if such stages can be identified, and if the needs, interests, and responses of adults in the various stages can be discerned, it is possible for religious educators to take these factors into account as they work in nurture of the religious life; members of a congregation can see themselves and others in terms of their journey along this path in such a way that the religious community can be more truly a nurturing community.

Theoretical Approaches to
Adult Religious Life and Nurture

Since Nelson, Moran, and others called for focusing religious education on adults in the 1960s,[32] attention has turned to a greater concern for theory. Practice is still of importance, especially for the local practitioners as they design and implement programs within the parish, but in the conventions and meetings, as well as in the literature, religious educators are seeking the basic approaches to communication in religion and the theoretical framework which undergirds these approaches. A number of persons have attempted to categorize these theoretical models, and there are some variations among these writers. However, there is a great deal of commonality as well. Elias, for example, uses six theoretical approaches found in philosophy of education[33] and extends those approaches to the field of adult religious education. Thus he presents (1) *adult liberal education in religion* with its emphasis upon "liberal learning, the organization of bodies or disciplines of knowledge, and the development of the rational powers of the mind"[34]; (2) *progressive adult education in religion* which, in the view of George Albert Coe,[35] had "to take account of the natural development of the person in faith, account for human experience in a meaningful manner, and point the way to the solution of social problems"[36]; (3) *socialization-behavioristic theories*, which utilize the findings of psychology and the social sciences to develop a religious education that places "major focus on environmental and cultural factors"[37]; (4) *humanistic adult education in religion*, drawing upon such humanistic psychologists as Carl Rogers and Abraham Maslow and placing as the objective the enabling of adults "to actualize their potentialities to the end that they become more fully liberated as individuals and more fully prepared to participate in bettering the life of the communities to which they belong"[38]; (5) *socio-political adult religious education*, which recognizes that adult religious education is related to the political and social life of a society. Groome is perhaps the best contemporary exemplar of this approach, inasmuch as he clearly recognizes that education and curricular decisions are political activities[39]; and (6) *analytic philosophy of education*, applying "the techniques of traditional logic and contemporary semantics to clarify the meaning of educational language."[40]

One of the problems evident in Elias's approaches is the common problem of typologies. Some religious educators can be discussed under several of these typologies. Moran, for instance, is discussed under three theories. Nevertheless, it is a very useful typology when one is attempting to see an overview of philosophical approaches to the field. From a different perspective, that of the objective of adult religious education, several models are presented here. They are not intended to provide a comprehensive survey of adult religious educational approaches, but rather to focus upon a few of the most visible models in terms of their main objective or practical technique. From this vantage point, the models appear to fall into the following categories: (1) enculturation models, (2) assessment of needs and participation models, (3) group dynamics models, (4) socio-political change models, and (5) ecumenical models.

Enculturation Models

Probably the best-known enculturation model is that of Westerhoff, whose essay "A Socialization Model" in 1972[41] caught the imagination of the religious education community. It represented a reaction from emphasis upon schooling, but it involved also an attempt to take seriously the social sciences, anthropology in particular. Westerhoff focused on three "contexts for learning," as he called them. These three contexts were (1) *ritual*—"meaningful celebration of memory and hope," (2) *experience*—"reflected-upon experience in community," and (3) *action*—"planned-for action around social issues."[42] Since 1972, Westerhoff has worked through many of the implications of these three contexts and discussed them in his later books. In collaboration with Gwen Kennedy Neville, an anthropologist, he has elaborated the role of liturgy in learning in religion. However, the basic pattern established in his earlier works seems to have been retained.

The main theme of this model was expressed by Nelson in 1967, "The main contention is that religion at its deepest levels is located within a person's sentiments and is the result of the way he was socialized by the adults who cared for him as a child."[43] Nelson saw faith as "communicated by a community of believers," and he also saw that "the meaning of faith is developed by its members out of their history, by their interaction with each other, and in relation to the events that take place in their lives."[44] Elias has noted that Marthaler has given socialization theory "a strong theoretical foundation" in his writings and that he "proposes a model of religious socialization that identifies it with the 'catechesis' language of documents of the Roman Catholic Church."[45] How well the process of religious socialization works can be seen by "how well adults are assimilated into the faith community and how closely they identify with it."[46]

This statement by Marthaler was no doubt intended to take the focus off the socialization of children and youth and place it upon adults, but it expresses one of the problems in the theory which has led to a great deal of critical comment; that is, the more effective the religious socialization within a group, the more difficult it becomes for a person to break out of that community of believers when it becomes a rigid, prescriptive community demanding adherence to its rituals, symbols, values, beliefs, and life-styles. How does a religious community provide within its system of values, commitments, and actions the openness that is necessary for individuals to exercise their freedoms? A second problem relates to the role of intentional education within the religious community. Since the enculturation, or socialization, models have emerged out of reaction to schooling, it is not always obvious what directions the planned-for activities might take. Socialization takes place regardless of the efforts of the persons involved, but if it becomes a model for religious education and nurture, then a great deal of attention must be placed on the planned-for experiences. These may include schooling, as Westerhoff says, but the relation between the various activities is not always clear.

Assessment of Needs and Participation Models

Perhaps this approach is not strictly a model, because the assessment of needs can be combined with several other approaches. But there has been sufficient emphasis upon assessment of needs in the past several years that it appears to warrant a category of its own. Adopted from systems theory as it developed in business, government, and education, this theory is built upon participation of adults in their own education. In order for adults to thus participate, it is necessary for them first to assess their needs and interests. The participation must not end at this point, however, and adults must also be involved in the designing and implementing of whatever educational experiences are planned. McKenzie has elaborated such an approach in his recent book, *The Religious Education of Adults*. He took two elements, adult and religion, and looked at them from the perspective of education; that is, he juxtaposed the characteristics of adults as developed from Knowles's idea of andragogy and the mission of the church and derived a propositional theory of adult religious education. This theory includes the following propositions:

1. The initial step of program development (curriculum development) is applied research that gains information from prospective learners about their educational needs and interests. . . .

2. Adults should be involved to help the religious educator plan the educational program. . . .

3. Adults should be invited to help the religious educator implement and administer the educational program. . . .

4. Adults should be invited not only to provide evaluations of the educational program but also be involved, as is feasible, in the planning of program evaluation. . . .

5. In the instructional setting adults must be respected as adults. . . .

6. In the instructional setting adults should be encouraged to be proactive rather than reactive. . . . The instructional climate should be such that adults feel free to initiate discussions, to introduce new topics, and to participate proactively in the educational activity. . . .

7. In the instructional setting, depending on the specific instructional objectives and the content of the instruction, adult learners may be resource persons for learning as well as learners. . . .

8. As regards the explicitly religious message of the church, adults must be given choices and options relating to which aspects of the message interest them. . . .

9. Adult religious education, if it is responsive to adult needs, is a form of service. . . .

10. Adult religious education, if it is responsive to adult interests, can contribute to the formation of community.[47]

The research element of the needs assessment in the first proposition is most important in order to provide an adequate basis for the development of programs, courses, liturgical experiences, and social action.

Gregory Smith approached adult religious education through assessment of needs as well, and most of the theoretical principles which McKenzie mentions are pertinent. However, after adults had carried out the research process assessing their needs and interests, Smith used Avery Dulles's *Models of the Church* with the Christian education councils of a number of Roman Catholic churches in Connecticut to form a basis for program planning and implementation. The council in each church selected the model of the church which most nearly fit its image of their own church: institution, mystical communion, sacrament, herald, servant.[48] With this framework, they were able to go on to develop their own programs. Again, the element of participation on the part of the adults themselves is paramount.

This model has enabled religious educators to draw their boards and committees—those in charge of the administration of the churches and of the training and development of leaders—into an educational process which has been both helpful in their roles as board and committee members and also has provided a nurturing process for the adults in their own faith development.

Group Dynamics Models

Models actually emphasizing the dynamics of groups are found less frequently in religious education today than in the sixties and seventies. Interest in the dynamics of groups shifted the emphasis in the churches from the organization to the people, and relationships became of primary concern. Classes, training programs, and even official boards and committees became encounter groups or began to examine the dynamics at work in their own group experiences. One of the values of this emphasis was that it took attention from formal classes as the form of adult religious education and related education to all groups and activities within the churches. A great many books were published on how to work with church groups, and pastors and parishioners participated in training provided by the National Training Laboratories[49] or similar groups. Among the best known of these movements were the pastoral training programs of Reuel Howe, Episcopal priest and founder and director of the Institute for

Advanced Pastoral Studies in Michigan. His books entitled *Man's Need and God's Action* (with study guide), *The Miracle of Dialogue*, and *Herein Is Love*, among others, expressed the understanding that theology becomes meaningful in an experimental situation, that it is in human relationships that one comes to understand the meaning of God as love, and that "the fruit of dialogue is the reunion of man with himself, with others, and with God who is the source and revealer of all truth, and whose spirit is free to guide when men open themselves to him by turning honestly to one another."[50] Efforts at church renewal included cell groups (Elton Trueblood's *Alternative to Futility*, 1948) and small groups (John Casteel's *Spiritual Renewal Through Personal Groups*, 1957), forming a basis for David J. Ernsberger's approach to adult religious education, *A Philosophy of Adult Religious Education*, 1959. With this influence within the Christian community and with an equally forceful emphasis upon group dynamics in the adult education movement, especially as represented by the Adult Education Association,[51] the growth of small groups in the churches was phenomenal, and much of the theoretical literature in adult religious education centered on the small group as a redemptive fellowship. John Fry, in his critical analysis of adult religious education, called these groups the "Secrets of Jesus Society."[52] The Seabury Series of the Episcopal Church was developed on this theory, probably the most completely group dynamics-oriented curriculum in religious education, the theoretical work being presented by David Hunter in *Christian Education as Engagement*.[53] More recently, the tendency to think of this approach as *the* way to structure adult religious education has moved to a recognition of the human needs of the persons involved, efforts to provide experiences in small groups without losing identification with the entire parish,[54] and concern for the dynamics in every group experience, whether small groups or large. The sense that indeed as one opens up to another human being, one opens to God, permeates much of adult religious education.

Socio-Political Change Models

The concern which George Albert Coe expressed for social issues in religious education in 1917, when his work *A Social Theory of Religious Education* was first published, has waxed and waned and waxed again in religious education. At the height of the civil rights movement in the sixties, it seemed to many leaders in the churches and denominations, and even to many religious educators themselves, that the way to address the critical issues of the time was not to put primary energies into the educational programs which were traditional in the churches but to tackle the problems directly by involvement in social action. In many denominations and councils of churches, community organizers were hired instead of religious educators; urban ministries were developed rather than educational training programs; and religious educators were asking if their profession was obsolete.[55] Nelson, in an address entitled "Is Christian Education Something Particular?" before a joint meeting in 1970 of the Boards of Christian Education of the United Presbyterian Church in the U.S.A. and the Presbyterian Church in the United States, was really speaking to the question of whether social action and Christian education can be equated, not just as a theoretical issue, but because the denominations were moving so rapidly in the direction of equating the two.[56] Nile Harper's study of the churchmen (both clergy and lay) who went to Mississippi in 1964 for the Hattiesburg-McComb voter registration drive and their reflections upon their experiences resulted in a paper[57] drawing implications for adult religious education. On the assumption that adult Christian education "involves training for servanthood, meaning participation in the redemptive work of God in the world,"[58] he constructed hypotheses and raised questions. The hypotheses form a theoretical framework for adult Christian education and social conflict. Harper hypothesizes that adult Christian education takes place at points of social conflict most significantly:

1. when it involves inter-group relationships, living and working together, for a sustained length of time, under circumstances of significant urgency.
2. when elements of action and reflection are combined; there is a specific attempt to interpret action theologically; there is some theological basis which transcends differences; and materials are fashioned to interpret experiences.
3. the focus is outside the local congregation; there are benefits to the local congregation; there is sanction by a regional or other transcendent church or quasi-church body; and there is co-operation with non-church bodies.[59]

By and large these implications have been borne out by other studies, in particular, Jeffrey Hadden and Charles Longino's *Gideon's Gang*, [60] a study of three United Church of Christ churches which were formed to undertake social action. Other religious educators who contributed to development of the socio-political approach in adult religious education included Donald E. Miller and Donald Williams,[61] whereas many of the writings of

Westerhoff evidence this concern, though he is treated here primarily for his emphasis on enculturation, and Groome[62] has developed what he calls a shared praxis approach. All of these educators have been influenced by Freire's work in Third World countries, particularly as expressed in his *Pedagogy of the Oppressed*. Perhaps to a lesser extent, they have been influenced by Ivan Illich's *Deschooling Society*. Freire's concept of conscientization has been particularly fruitful to educators throughout the world. Elias comments that Groome "gives a strong theoretical rationale from Christian and philosophical sources for a shared praxis approach to religious education. He utilizes the Christian symbols of the Kingdom of God, salvation, liberation, and a critical theory of praxis as major elements in his theoretical approach to Christian religious education."[63] Groome has not given as much attention to adult religious education as to children and youth, however, and work remains to be done in developing this model for that population.

The impact of Freire's insights on conscientization, dialogue, education, and knowledge, together with the growth of liberation theologies and the concern for management of conflict, have resulted in works like B. Wren's *Education for Justice: Pedagogical Perspective*, and Thomas Fenton's *Education for Justice*, a resource manual. These works address the issues involved in political and social realities, including the management of conflict, the dynamics and uses of power, and oppression in its various forms. But it is often difficult for the layperson to relate the complexities of the socio-political systems and the risks of involvement with their understandings of their faith. Elias points out the danger if adult religious education does not address these issues:

If adult religious education is to deal seriously with social and political issues, more attention must be given to sociological and political analysis and to strategies for action in these areas. These are precisely the areas where there is greatest complexity and greatest divergence of ideologies and opinions. Yet an adult religious education that does not deal with these issues may easily remain tied to privatistic and institutional concerns.[64]

Ecumenical Models

It might well be argued that there are no real models which could be called ecumenical, and that the prevalence even of efforts to develop such models is minimal. However, the pluralism of our society and the need for a religious education theory that is useful for Jewish religious education, Buddhist religious education,

Muslim religious education, and other faith groups as well as Christian education impel me to include ecumenical models as a developing approach. In his work *Design for Religion*, Moran uses a subtitle: *Toward Ecumenical Education*. Although his more recent works have not stressed the term *ecumenical* as much as this one, his search for an ecumenical model appears to continue. He defines an ecumenical curriculum as "a course for education in religion from birth to grave,"[65] and outlines a sequence which might be used by a Christian who holds certain Christian presuppositions. Although he makes no claims that this sequence will be satisfactory for other faiths, it offers a hypothetical model for others. As obvious from the definition, this is not a model for adult religious education as distinctive from children and youth. During childhood the person is immersed in immediate experience, and ecumenical education at this age "consists in whatever is humanly helpful in his growing up."[66] With the arts forming a synthesis of the two stages, the person moves into the study of history, science, and literature, where linkages to a rather narrow Christianity are discovered. The bridge between the second and third stages is comparative religion, whether studied formally or informally. "There should be admission and appreciation of the fact that there are alternate ways to understand religion."[67] The third, and final, stage is "a study from within one's own religious tradition."[68] Thus the model moves from a rather primitive religion in childhood through a somewhat narrow Christianity to ecumenical religion and the intensive study of Christianity as one's own religious tradition. In describing this approach to religion, Moran says that "ecumenical religion is neither post-Christian nor part Christian, but a religious way of being Christian and a Christian way of being religious."[69]

Experimental Models

In concluding this essay, some mention should be made of the many experimental forms that have been developing in the past two decades in adult religious nurture and education. Some of these forms, because of their informal nature, emphasize the nurturing aspect of working with adults. It is not possible to describe these forms in detail, but only to mention some of the most common. (1) *Intergenerational activities* range from workshops for Advent or other special occasions through study courses to worship experiences. Christian Education: Shared Approaches of Joint Educational Development, for example, has several intergenerational packets for congregational use. (2) *Emphasis on the family, the home, or the primary group*, whatever its makeup. The "family clusters" approach developed by Margaret Sawin, family camps, and home churches, as well as the Marriage Encounter movement and marriage and family enrichment programs, are all part of this thrust. (3) *Future studies* in which adults study alternative futures and make present decisions based upon these scenarios. (4) *Religious education centers* established by several parishes or congregations cooperating together to develop a center with a professionally trained staff. Adults from any of the churches may go to the center for courses, informal activities, individual study, library research, and similar learning experiences.[70] (5) *Religious education of adults in travel experiences*, sometimes consisting of seminars and briefings aboard ship coupled with the visiting of places of religious significance; sometimes on-location lectures by scholars, with planes, trains, or buses providing the transportation; and sometimes single-site visits to museums, cathedrals, churches, synagogues, or other places of religious and historical interest. One of the important aspects of this form of education is the "living together" experience at a time when the focus is upon a spot with religious import.

Perhaps the most encouraging aspect of these experimental forms is the creativity they exhibit. It shows that adults will make use of the many experiences of their lives to grow religiously, and that all of these experiences have potential for helping adults live their religion. The current development of lay ministries within the Roman Catholic Church is another indication that there is openness to growth in religion through many avenues, and that imagination will find many forms in which to nurture the adults in a congregation. The churches are still struggling with the problems of how best to use professional staff, what form of training is needed for working with adults, and how to help adults decide for themselves the directions of their own learning in religion. We are thus reminded once again that everything that takes place within the congregation is making its impact upon the adults and that through the adults the community outside is hearing the message, or messages, which this particular group of people is giving to the world. Learning is lifelong, and the congregational life-style educates.

Notes

1. Joachim Wach, *The Comparative Study of Religion* (New York: Columbia University Press, 1958), 76-77.

2. See C. Ellis Nelson, *Where Faith Begins* (Richmond: John Knox Press, 1967).

3. Ibid.

4. Berard L. Marthaler, *Catechetics in Context* (Huntington, Ind.: Our Sunday Visitor Press, 1973).

5. John H. Westerhoff III, *Will Our Children Have Faith?* (New York: The Seabury Press, 1976); *A Colloquy on Christian Education* (Philadelphia: United Church Press, 1972), 80-90; Gwen Neville and John Westerhoff III, *Generation to Generation* (Philadelphia: The Pilgrim Press, 1974).

6. Studies of preliterate cultures by such anthropologists as Margaret Mead describe these activities; see also such sociological works as Peter L. Berger and Thomas Luckman, *The Social Construction of Reality* (New York: Anchor Books, 1967); H. P. Dreitzel, ed., *Childhood and Socialization* (New York: Macmillan, 1973).

7. Westerhoff, *Will Our Children Have Faith?* See also John H. Westerhoff III, "A Catechetical Way of Doing Theology," in *Religious Education and Theology*, ed. Norma H. Thompson (Birmingham, Ala.: Religious Education Press, 1982), for a discussion of catechesis as "a pastoral activity of intentional Christian socialization."

8. Berard Marthaler, "Socialization as a Model for Catechetics," in *Foundations of Religious Education*, ed. Padraic O'Hare (New York: Paulist Press, 1978), 65.

9. Gabriel Moran, *Interplay: A Theory of Religion and Education* (Winona, Minn.: Saint Mary's Press, 1981), 14.

10. Ralph Linton, *The Cultural Background of Personality* (New York: D. Appleton-Century Co., 1945), 19.

11. John L. Elias, *The Foundations and Practice of Adult Religious Education* (Malabar, Fla.: Robert E. Krieger Publishing Co., 1982), 116.

12. Gabriel Moran, *Education Toward Adulthood: Religion and Lifelong Learning* (New York: Paulist Press, 1979), 106.

13. Elias, *Foundations and Practice*, 116.

14. Ibid.

15. See Paulo Freire, *Pedagogy of the Oppressed* (New York: The Seabury Press, 1970).

16. Elias, *Foundations and Practice*, 116.

17. Nelson, *Where Faith Begins*, 121.

18. Horace Bushnell, *Christian Nurture* (New Haven: Yale University Press, 1967; first published in 1861).

19. Robert J. Havighurst, *Developmental Tasks and Education* (New York: David McKay Co., 1972; first published in 1948).

20. Florence Stratemeyer, *Developing a Curriculum for Modern Living*, 2d ed. (New York: Columbia University Press, 1957).

21. Lawrence Kohlberg, "The Implications of Moral Stages of Adult Education," *Religious Education* 72, no. 2 (1977): 183-201.

22. James W. Fowler, *Stages of Faith* (New York: Harper & Row, 1981).

23. Religious Education Association, Faith Development in the Adult Life Cycle project, "Hypothesis Paper" developed for a symposium (10–14 August 1981, College of St. Thomas, St. Paul, Minnesota), 32.

24. Ibid.

25. Gabriel Moran, Faith Development in the Adult Life Cycle project, "Looking at the Images: The Perspective of Religious Education," 9.

26. Ibid., 10.

27. Ibid., 11.

28. Elias, *Foundations and Practice*, chap. 1.

29. Leon McKenzie, *The Religious Education of Adults* (Birmingham, Ala.: Religious Education Press, 1982), chap. 4.

30. Malcolm Knowles, Faith Development in the Adult Life Cycle project, "An Adult Educator's Reflections on Faith Development in the Adult Life Cycle," 4.

31. Faith Development Project, "Hypothesis Paper," 27.

32. See Nelson, *Where Faith Begins,* and Gabriel Moran, *Vision and Tactics* (New York: Herder & Herder, 1968).
33. Elias, *Foundations and Practice,* chap. 6.
34. Ibid., 157.
35. George Albert Coe, *A Social Theory of Religious Education* (New York: Charles Scribner's Sons, 1917).
36. Elias, *Foundations and Practice,* 162.
37. Ibid., 165.
38. McKenzie, *The Religious Education of Adults,* 13, as quoted in Elias, *Foundations and Practices,* 169.
39. See Thomas H. Groome, *Christian Religious Education: Sharing Our Story and Vision* (San Francisco: Harper & Row, 1980).
40. Elias, *Foundations and Practice,* 154.
41. John H. Westerhoff III, *A Colloquy on Christian Education* (Philadelphia: United Church Press, 1972).
42. Ibid.
43. Nelson, *Where Faith Begins,* 9.
44. Ibid., 10.
45. Elias, *Foundations and Practice,* 166-67.
46. Marthaler, "Socialization as a Model for Catechetics," in *Foundations of Religious Education,* ed. O'Hare, 82.
47. McKenzie, *The Religious Education of Adults,* 129-32.
48. Gregory M. Smith, "Adult Religious Education Needs: Description and Synthesis" (Diss., New York University, 1982).
49. National Training Laboratories, a part of the National Education Association, Washington, D.C., began in Bethel, Maine, in 1947 with a laboratory session on human relations and group processes.
50. Reuel L. Howe, *The Miracle of Dialogue* (New York: The Seabury Press, 1963), cover.
51. See Malcolm Knowles, *Informal Adult Education* (New York: Association Press, 1951).
52. John R. Fry, *A Hard Look at Adult Christian Education* (Philadelphia: The Westminster Press, 1969), 22.
53. David Hunter, *Christian Education as Engagement* (New York: The Seabury Press, 1963).
54. Lawrence O. Richards, *A New Face for the Church* (Grand Rapids: The Zondervan Corp., 1970); Urban T. Holmes III, *The Future Shape of Ministry* (New York: The Seabury Press, 1971).
55. The writer delivered a paper at the annual meeting of the Association of Professors of Christian Education on the Eastern Seaboard in 1965 entitled "Is Christian Education Obsolete?"
56. C. Ellis Nelson, "Is Christian Education Something Particular?" This essay can be found in John H. Westerhoff III, ed., *Who Are We?* (Birmingham, Ala.: Religious Education Press, 1978), chap. 15.
57. Nile Harper, in a paper delivered at the annual meeting of the Association of Professors and Researchers in Religious Education, 1965.
58. Ibid., 16.
59. Ibid., 18.
60. Jeffrey Hadden and Charles Longino, Jr., *Gideon's Gang: A Case Study of the Church in Social Action* (Philadelphia: United Church Press, 1975).
61. Donald E. Miller, "Religious Education and Social Change," a paper delivered at the 1969 annual meeting of APRRE; Donald F. Williams, "Religious Education and Political Socialization," a paper delivered at the same annual meeting.
62. Groome, *Christian Religious Education.*
63. Elias, *Foundations and Practice,* 173.
64. Ibid., 174.

65. Gabriel Moran, *Design for Religion* (New York: Herder & Herder, 1971), 90.
66. Ibid., 92.
67. Ibid., 93.
68. Ibid.
69. Ibid.
70. James R. Schafer, "Update on Adult Education in Churches and Synagogues: Roman Catholicism," *Religious Education* 72 (March-April 1977): 139.

CHAPTER 20

Intergenerational
Religious Education

Charles R. Foster

During the 1970s intergenerational religious education captured the imagination of many people in the life of the church. Influenced by their enthusiasm, many congregations started what they called intergenerational or IG classes or groups. Others followed Margaret Sawin's example and organized in their churches "family clusters," consisting of small groups of four or five families. The movement, if it can be called that, did not originate with some overarching denominational plan. Nor was it inspired by the insights of religious educators who emphasized the interdependence of the generations in the educational process. Instead, the spirit of innovation in worship, education, and mission sweeping the churches of the land during the 1960s and 1970s undoubtedly provided the milieu for creative local church leaders distressed (as George Koehler has observed) by the division of age groups in most church programs.[1] These efforts developed momentum in the mid-1970s with the publication of several descriptions and interpretations of intergenerational religious education.[2]

Perhaps because denominations have, for the most part, blessed rather than incorporated intergenerational religious education into their program designs, the literature in the field continues to come from those who have participated in intergenerational activities in the local church. Two of the most helpful interpreters of the movement are George Koehler and Margaret Sawin, who have explored in some depth the theoretical presuppositions for intergenerational education. The rest of the literature is predominantly programmatic or curricular in character and thereby helpful to persons desiring to introduce intergenerational approaches to education in their own congregations.

In the pages that follow it is my intent to identify and describe certain of the purposes, educational and theological assumptions,

Charles R. Foster is Professor of Christian Education at Scarritt College.

and programmatic characteristics common to the literature, and to ascertain some of the strengths to be reinforced and problems to be examined in future intergenerational approaches to religious education.

The Purposes of Intergenerational Religious Education

The literature describing intergenerational religious education is marked by contrary moods. Most obvious is the optimism and excitement of the writers who have experienced the creative possibilities of intentionally designed activities for people from two or more age groups. More subtle, but just as pervasive, are the themes of frustration and despair over the fragmentation of the family by the social agencies of the community (including the church), the ineffectiveness of the church school as a nurturing community, a general despair over the quality of family life, and a growing awareness of the existence of what sociologists have called the generation gap.

Intergenerational religious education strategies emerged in part as a response to specific and concrete problems and needs in the lives of families in congregations across the nation. The purposes of the movements reflected in the literature consequently tend to be specific rather than comprehensive: (1) to strengthen family life and thereby enrich the possibilities for each individual within the family; (2) to improve communication across the generations both in the home and in the church; (3) to introduce children more fully into congregational life; (4) to make it possible for families to participate in the church as families; and (5) to strengthen the corporate life of the congregation across the age span and among family members.

Although the leaders of intergenerational education events often sense that they are on the creative edge, these purposes are essentially conservative, at times even defensive or protective in nature. They gather people in a quest for experiences associated with memories of the quality of family life in the past, but with a keen awareness that family structures for all appearances, at least, have been radically transformed into a world governed by a "post-modern" mentality.

Common Assumptions

Several common assumptions undergird these purposes and the educational strategies and curricular suggestions designed to embody them. The pervasiveness of these assumptions in the literature does provide coherence and direction for the movement as a whole, even though they are often implicitly rather than explicitly stated.

1. *The church as the body of Christ involves the mutuality and interdependence of persons of all ages.* Among the greatest of the concerns of the intergenerational religious educators are the fragmentation of the family and the corresponding division of people into age group organizations and activities. In contrast, an intergenerational education setting helps "persons experience the colorful spectrum of ages, attitudes, needs, beliefs"; in other words, it helps people "to be the whole church."[3] It affirms the mutuality of children and adults and acknowledges the necessary interdependence of all ages for the enrichment of those persons of each age.

This assumption is rooted in the view that every human being is a child of God to be affirmed and valued as a person of worth whose gifts are to be celebrated. For Sawin the intergenerational approach begins with the assumption that "each human being shares in the life of the Spirit" and as such is to be considered a "child of God" and a member of the "family of God."[4] Since all are equal before God, Sawin contends, age should not be a factor that differentiates the status of persons in the church. Koehler states a similar premise in a more popular idiom. "The old have something to share with the young," and "the young have something to share with the old."[5] For Donald and Patricia Griggs this means that children, youth, and adults participate in a common experience with "equal standing and responsibility."[6]

This perspective may reflect a growing sensitivity to the processes of socialization in which values, commitments, traditions, and rituals transmitted by one generation are subsequently refined and adapted by the next generation for the new situation in which its members find themselves. Certainly John Westerhoff's discussion of religious socialization has given credence to the interest of intergenerational educators in the forces binding the generations and in the power of rites of passage for the lives of people in the life cycle. But it is from the insights of psychologists such as Virginia Satir, author of *Peoplemaking*, that most advocates of intergenerational religious education have drawn their understanding of the mutuality of influence that exists among all members of a group, regardless of age. Satir holds that every person in the family or group has power. Consequently the whole group is affected by the attitudes and behaviors of each person, no matter how young or old. Hence, age should not be construed as a barrier to full participation in the church as the body of Christ.

2. *God enters into the human experience most vividly through persons in actions of reconciliation and healing.* Although it is recognized that God is manifest in many ways, the emphasis in intergenerational strategies of religious education to this point centers on the incarnational character of God's revelation, most fully in Jesus Christ, but through other people in less complete ways. For Koehler, "God seems to come most vividly through other persons, through open dialogue, through a hug, through mutual care with living, breathing human beings."[7] This emphasis provides the impetus for strategies that respond to the general view that the relationships of persons in families and congregations are generally fragmented and that persons experience isolation and alienation much of their lives. It is the restoration of the relational connections between people, and between people and God, that then becomes the focus of intergenerational religious education.

3. *The contemporary American family comes in many forms.* A dominant motif in the literature is the awareness that the structure of the contemporary family is far from monolithic. Although the family is usually viewed as a corporate entity, it comes in a variety of patterns.[8] In contrast to idealistic portrayals of the nuclear family in earlier religious education writings, the view of the interpreters of intergenerational religious education is more descriptive and functional. Hilyard, for example, describes the family as a system of "unique and valued" individual persons who contribute to and have power in that system regardless of age.[9] Sawin's relational concerns are evident in her view that it is in the family that the basic questions of existence are answered, the foundations for relating and responding to life's challenges are laid, and that emotional solace and sustenance are made available.[10] Consequently families may consist of two parents and their children. Just as likely, however, families may involve a single parent with children, a grandparent and grandchildren, or even two or more persons sharing a home—in other words, any structure in which "a person lives in relationship with another, usually under one household."[11]

4. *The contemporary family functions as an "oasis" in a complex and fragmented world.* Margaret Sawin states explicitly what others imply in their quest for an approach to religious education that will strengthen the contemporary family. Sawin observes that in our society the family "must meet all its own needs, including its emotional ones, which can become an insurmountable burden."

Consequently it needs "support from the wider community" if it is to function as an oasis of strength and security.[12]

Intergenerational education, for its adherents, enriches family resources for coping with the issues and problems of family members in communicating their interests, questions, values, and commitments to other members of the family. This emphasis upon "strengthening" is essentially a defensive posture. It conveys the image of a beleaguered people standing over against forces that will not only fragment the family but diminish the potential in each person. It is a protective posture, supporting the isolated and thereby weakened resources of the family in small communities of families who provide mutual care and support. It is also a posture that looks upon withdrawal from the world into "oases" for renewal and revitalization as a necessary requisite for moving back into the pressures of contemporary life.

5. *People grow and change by being nurtured in relationships of trust and love.* Sawin declares what other interpreters of the movement tend to assume. Her "family cluster" model of intergenerational education is a "growth model" facilitating the movement of the individual in actualizing both personal strengths and potential.[13] The sources of this view are located in "humanistic psychology," which centers on the uniqueness of persons and their "ability to change toward more potential and growth." The consequent form of intergenerational educational strategies is experiential in which "reflected experiences become the core of the learning activity, rather than didactic material."[14] Intergenerational religious education to this point consequently involves activities that enhance relationships, provide personal support, encourage exploration and discovery, develop skills to tap personal potential, and celebrate shared meanings and victories. These personally sustaining activities are considered to be essential if people are to move from the helpless self-centered years of infancy into "free, whole, caring, serving maturity."[15]

Characteristics of Intergenerational Religious Education

At least four characteristics may be identified as common to intergenerational religious education. The first is perhaps the most obvious. *Intergenerational education gathers people from at least two and preferably three or more age groups or generations into a teaching-learning process in which all members give and receive from the experience.* Some groups will involve individuals from a number of families. Others, including Margaret Sawin's "family clusters," consist of groups of families. The process in either case tends to emphasize experiential learning to enhance the possibilities for the participation of children in activities shared with adults and to improve the effectiveness of the communicaton between people from different age groups.

The second characteristic is evident in the way *the "school" dominates the organizational imagination of the interpreters of intergenerational religious education.* The programs initially described by both the Griggs and the Rogers involve a multifamily church school class on Sunday morning. Most proposals move away from this traditional church school hour, but the idea of courses or of contract groups that function as short-term courses is still evident. They occur in regularly scheduled times. They have designated leaders. There is usually a curricular resource, often developed by the members of the group (although now church school presses are producing materials for such groups). The stated attempt is often to build "communities" within congregations, but the meaning of community tends to be limited to the fellowship of people in short-term face-to-face groups. These groups, moreover, are gathered primarily into the structures of a class or short-term course.

A third common feature found in intergenerational religious education events is a shared activity that establishes the common ground for all participants. Some focus upon the development of specific communications skills and rely heavily upon the methodologies used in human relations training. Other activities provide the framework for discussion and reflection. In this case role playing, case studies, art, music, audio-visuals, and many other multisensory activities set the stage for the conversation that follows. Topics and themes tend to vary with the interests of the group. In this sense intergenerational religious education looks much like a combination of the best elements in a potluck supper and a creative classroom for children. Otherwise, intergenerational religious education looks for the most part like other educational activities in the church. The procedures for planning found in most contemporary curricular resources are used. Goals are set; leaders are trained; sessions are evaluated. Worship and times for fellowship are included. The major difference is in the presence of persons of diverse ages.

One other characteristic of intergenerational religious education needs to be identified. *The emphasis upon equality, mutuality, reciprocity across the generations has clearly enhanced the status of the child.* Consequently, in contrast to other modes of education in which adult knowledge and ability is the reference point for children, in intergenerational education it is usually the child who tends to function as the reference point for the experience of adults. Although some activities may be planned to accommodate the interests and needs of persons in diverse age groups, most begin with the premise that children should be able to participate in them in ways appropriate to their experience and ability.

Strengths to Be Affirmed

Although intergenerational religious education has been perceived by many as creative and innovative, it is primarily a *conservative* movement in the best sense of that word. In the first place, *its adherents have attempted to reclaim, through intergenerational groupings, the more historical age-inclusive character of church life.* As such, intergenerational religious education stands over against the prevailing wisdom among religious educators for many decades— that the most effective approaches to teaching and learning occur in classes organized by age groups. In the process intergenerational religious education loses some of the orderliness and efficiency of graded courses and resources. And yet it potentially provides greater flexibility for individuals who may not fit general age group expectations, a more significant ratio of adults to children in the teaching-learning environment, and a wider variety of options to be explored in any given issue due to the range of perceptions to be found in a group of people of diverse ages.

A second advantage of intergenerational groups in the church may occur through the *development of networks of support for individuals and families,* who often lack the ties of extended family and close-knit neighborhood. In these networks children find a variety of role models for their lives, and adults without children have the opportunity to influence the future of the race through their relationships with the children of the group. The quality of the communication between persons in these groups may be improved, further heightening self-awareness and sensitivity to others. Skills for negotiating within the family circle may be developed in ways that can build confidence in their use beyond the family. And the affection and care received from others within the group may provide the support people need to face the demands of daily living.

Perhaps the most striking contribution of intergenerational religious education to church life may be traced to *the commitment to equality among the generations.* For the first time children and youth are recognized officially as making a necessary contribution to the nurture of their elders. Consequently, intergenerational patterns contrast with more typical approaches to family education in the church which usually have sought to reach and influence the family through the parents. These latter approaches assume a hierarchical structure in the family rather than an interdependent one. In contrast, intergenerational religious education at its best views each member of the family, as well as each child in the church, as having power and, therefore, influence among the whole. This perspective has made it possible for many youth and at least some children to assume roles of leadership in these groups in relation to their abilities rather than in accord with their own pattern of age-related status.

Issues to Be Explored

In spite of the significance of these contributions, several limitations hinder the potential impact of the movement. In the first place, *intergenerational religious education has for the most part consisted of courses that are added to an already existing educational program in the local church.* As such they tend to be viewed as an extra or a "frill" and end up competing with other educational activities in the church. In the meantime, other occasions in congregational life that are already intergenerational in character are rarely used to their full potential. For example, congregations might explore the usefulness of intergenerational educational approaches in the orientation of new members, in the training of people for the sacraments, in special studies related to the church seasons, for vacation church school, or in any training program for mission or the outreach ministries of the congregation.

The second problem may be located in the concern for inclusiveness. That concern focuses primarily across the age span, but it has not often taken seriously the issues of involving the elderly in cross-generational teaching and learning events. Rarely does it address the issues of inclusiveness across the social divisions within the larger community. Sharee and Jack Rogers and George Koehler allude to the larger social fabric in which intergenerational education may occur, but their emphasis upon the family and the congregation tends to reinforce homogeneous groupings. Consequently the movement has been primarily white and middle class, in spite of the fact that intergenerational groupings may be most common in small as well as in ethnic congregations.

Although Sawin does envision family growth groups as having the potential for religious indoctrination, and many of the curricular suggestions are clearly concerned with exploring the faith and heritage of the church, *the third problem is evident in the lack of attention given to the possibilities in intergenerational religious education for systematic strategies for introducing another generation into the traditions of the faith.* Berard Marthaler illuminates this potential in his observation that it is in the reciprocity of adults and children that the latter "acquire a religious identity by taking on as their own the creedal formulas, rites, the activities and other emblems that symbolize" their solidarity with the larger faith community that encompasses both adult and child.[16]

Needless to say, this process works in reverse as well. As adults encounter in children and youth the actions of appropriating those elements of their common life in their new cultural situation, they participate in the process of a tradition being updated. In this sense children, using the symbols of their common identity, lead their elders into the "new" environments surrounding them. This reciprocity of child and adult is integral to the liveliness of the church's faith and witness through the ages. It is potentially integral to the purposes of intergenerational religious education.

The fourth issue to be addressed by those intrigued with the possibilities of intergenerational religious education is located in *the tendency in the movement to limit the task to strengthening the family unit and nurturing individuals within that unit.* This perspective actually provides a bandage solution to the pain and stress occasioned by the radical transformations occurring in contemporary family life. Gabriel Moran observes that many of the common notions of family prevailing in our American middle-class culture and integral to most of the writers of intergenerational religious education are both nostalgic and inaccurate. Contrast for instance, Moran's insistence that the "family ought not to be the sole source of intimacy, mutuality and socialization"[17] with Sawin's view that it is in the family that the basic questions of existence are answered, that the foundations for relating to and responding to the challenges of life are laid, and that "emotional solace and sustenance are almost solely available."[18] On the other hand, while Moran looks upon the family as one social entity existing with many other nurturing agencies in society, Sawin tends to support Christopher Lasch's thesis that our common view of the family is a "haven in a heartless world."[19] Intergenerational religious education consequently has emphasized the strengthening of family units by merging families into groups for mutual support and care. But the movement, if it is truly to strengthen the family, must help the family both improve its communication skills and learn to negotiate its way through the structures and forces in society that impinge upon family life.

Perhaps the most disturbing facet in the curricular designs for intergenerational religious education is *the tendency to view equality of persons across the age spectrum with uniformity of experience*. As stated earlier, the leaders of intergenerational education events tend to view their plans from the vantage point or angle of vision of the child in the group. To be truly intergenerational, the planning process needs to approach the event from the vantage point of the interests and concerns of all the ages and conditions represented in the group. Perhaps a common experience may illustrate my point. In the family reunions I have attended there is a clear reciprocity of child and adult roles in the larger family structure during the total event. There is a time when the world view of children prevails with its emphasis upon concrete and sensual experience. Often these activities take the form of games. During these times adults enter the activity as "children," suspending adult authority, logic, and strength to the common rules of the shared activity. The reunion, however, also has another time when the older adults forming an inner circle sit around recalling the stories of the family. On occasion a middle-aged adult sitting nearby might enter into the conversation. But those who are younger are on the fringes listening to the stories revealing something of their corporate identity. In this case children enter into the world of their elders, observing the ground rules of authority and place by seniority and experience within the group. Both sets of interactions are crucial to the process of people-making or to the formation of personal identity which always occurs within the solidarity of some corporate identity. Intergenerational education, when effective, must include strategies that embody the connections between generations that link all with both past and future within the circumstances of the present.

Conclusion

Margaret Sawin, Donald and Patricia Griggs, George Koehler, and others have made an important contribution to the way we view the church's educational ministry. They have helped us imagine and experience some of the potential in cross-generational groupings engaged in the activities of teaching and learning. They have begun the task of identifying those theological and educational assumptions that might inform intentional education programs involving several age groups. They have shared their experiences openly that others might build on them. Intergenerational religious education has enlivened the educational ministry in many congregations. Its continuing effectiveness, however, depends upon the extent to which its adherents continue to clarify its theological and educational assumptions and develop strategies that will continue to catch people's imaginations and enrich their educational experience in the church.

Notes

1. George E. Koehler, *Learning Together: A Guide for Intergenerational Education in the Church* (Nashville: Discipleship Resources, 1977), 4-5.
2. Cf. three of the early descriptions of intergenerational religious education. Each grows out of the experience of the authors. Donald Griggs and Patricia Griggs, *Generations Learning Together* (Livermore, Calif.: Griggs Educational Service, 1976); Sharee and Jack Rogers, *The Family Together: Intergenerational Education in the Church School* (Los Angeles: Acton House, 1976); Koehler, *Learning Together*.
3. Koehler, *Learning Together*, 14.
4. Margaret M. Sawin, "Community and Family: Growing in Faith Through Family Clusters," in *Parish Religious Education*, ed. Maria Harris (New York: Paulist Press, 1978), 41.
5. Koehler, *Learning Together*, 11.
6. Griggs, *Generations Learning Together*, 28.
7. Koehler, *Learning Together*, 10.
8. Jane Hilyard, "Family and Intergenerational Education," in *Homegrown Christian Education: Planning & Programming for Christians in the Local Congregation*, ed. David W. Perry (New York: Crossroad, 1979), 105-6.
9. Ibid.
10. Sawin, "Community and Family," 42.
11. Ibid.
12. Ibid., 43.
13. Margaret M. Sawin, *Educating by Family Groups: A New Model for Religious Education* (Rochester, N.Y.: Family Clustering, 1977), 17.
14. Ibid.
15. Koehler, *Learning Together*, 12.
16. Berard L. Marthaler, "Socialization as a Model for Catechetics," in *Foundations of Religious Education*, ed. Padraic O'Hare (New York: Paulist Press, 1978), 82.
17. Gabriel Moran, "Community and Family: The Way We Are: Communal Forms and Church Response," in *Parish Religious Education*, ed. Harris, 30.
18. Sawin, "Community and Family," 42.
19. Christopher Lasch, *Haven in a Heartless World: The Family Besieged* (New York: Basic Books, 1977).

Bibliography

Griggs, Donald, and Jane Griggs. *Generations Learning Together: Learning Activities for Intergenerational Groups in the Church*. Livermore, Calif.: Griggs Educational Service, 1976.

Koehler, George. *Learning Together: A Guide for Intergenerational Education in the Church*. Nashville: Discipleship Resources, 1977.

Rogers, Sharee, and Jack Rogers. *The Family Together: Intergenerational Education in the Church School*. Los Angeles: Acton House, 1976.

Sawin, Margaret M. *Educating by Family Groups: A New Model for Religious Education*. Rochester, N.Y.: Family Clustering, 1977.

————. "Community and Family: Growing in Faith through Family Clusters." In *Parish Religious Education: The People, the Place, the Profession*, edited by Maria Harris. New York: Paulist Press, 1978.

CHAPTER 21

Family Life Experience and Religious Nurture

J. C. Wynn

Beset and besieged, families in the final decades of the twentieth century are struggling against social, political, and economic forces that could threaten their very survival. The continuing high divorce rate, the increase of births to unwed parents, the cohabitation of unmarried couples, the proliferation of one-parent households, the new evidence of violence in our homes: such problems have led some people to assert that family life is dying.

Yet, on the other hand, a number of indicators encourage us to believe that, although the situation appears grim, it is far from hopeless. Families, when threatened from without, tend to turn within; and many are doing just that, finding strength from each other. It is a phenomenon the sociologists call neofamilism. Marriage, after a decade of ridicule as "a mutual suicide pact," "a disaster area," and worse, is back in favor. The decline in the marriage rate has been arrested and is holding steady. Sociological studies[1] discover increased family solidarity, closer marital communication, a reduced generation gap, and lessened mobility. Even the birth rate is again increasing in American families.

Despite the testimony of doomsayers who examine the data and then spread their gloom, there is reason to argue that families are not disappearing but that they are changing. The picture may be grim. But it is not hopeless, and Christians are learning to view the panoply of alternative family styles without the paroxysms of fright they once exhibited. A serious but knowledgeable optimism begins to arise that family life has an astounding capacity to adjust and persist.

John Charles Wynn is Professor of Pastoral Theology at Colgate Rochester Divinity School.

A Changing World and Its Changing Families

Despite a spate of roseate literature about the idea, there probably never has been any golden age for family life. Every age seems to have worried about what was happening to its families. Frightened by new developments and undergirded by the recurrent "myth of the declining family," each period of history tends to mourn what is assumed to have been the loss of ideal family values in some past era. However, instead of some golden age, recent studies in family history offer us a perspective of wider range, illuminating past centuries of child abuse, cynical marital contracts, spousal violence, sexual promiscuity, and gross neglect of even the closest relatives.[2] More recent periods (such as the nineteenth century, with its industrialization that encouraged small and nuclear households) have emphasized a normative domestic privacy, romantic marriage, and parental love, enough to impel us to yearn for more of the positive attributes of familism and also to assume that they existed once long ago in greater stability than at present.

Currently the social psychologists are able to assemble a list of the newer characteristics of contemporary families. The list includes the startling increase in one-parent households; the growing number of women (many of them mothers) in the labor market; a delay in the age at marriage; the acceptance of persons who remain single by choice, as well as voluntary childlessness by married couples; the tolerance for living-together pacts of the unmarried, for high school girls who bear and keep babies although they have no husbands, and for the widespread incidence of divorce.

Statistically, the picture is clear. Some 3.5 million babies are born annually in the United States. Nearly 2.5 million marriages are performed; and close to 1.2 million divorces occur each year.[3] Currently two households out of every hundred are composed of couples living together, another two of communes. One in five households is occupied by a single person living alone. One in six households is inhabited by one parent (usually a mother) living with child or children, a cohort that is increasing noticeably. And although nearly three out of every five households are made up of a conjugal couple, nearly half of these currently have no children in the home.

These inferences are obvious enough. The decline in the birth rate has been stalled, and the nation's population is increasing at a rate of two million each year as the result of the excess of births over deaths. The marriage rate is slightly higher—an indicator, many believe, that although people give up on particular mates they do not give up on the institution of marriage. The divorce rate remains startlingly high, which may mean that spouses are less willing than once they were to put up with unsatisfactory unions. Yet the conjugal family remains as a norm, and most people are able to view changing family styles without panic. Even the demonstrably increased sexual activity of recent history shocks the populace less than it formerly did.

Nevertheless, tribulations in family life in recent years have sparked a deep concern on the part of moralists, scholars, politicians, and just plain folks. The White House Conference on Families, the Family Protection Act, projects of several major church denominations, sex education programs, and even neighborhood associations all bear witness to scattered efforts meant to strengthen families under stress. This mixed bag of organizations, proposals, and hopes illustrates the spectrum of persons and positions to be found among those who wish to stem what is widely viewed as the erosion of family living.

A concerted fear of the many changes in family styles has propelled some unlikely alliances among groups whose goal is to reestablish the nuclear family of father as breadwinner, mother as homemaker, and children in the house. Conservative politicians have recurrently sponsored legislation that would offer federal support for marriage, children, and housing while withholding it from activities they believe undermine the traditional family such as divorce, abortion, homosexual rights, and intervention into more private family problems—child abuse and spouse abuse, for example.

Such is the context, then, of our changing world and its changing families within which religious educators attempt to plan programs and curriculum for and about families. Such also is the setting against which we shall here consider parent education and family nurture, the task of pastoral care and church administration, and some theological clues and problems related to family nurture.

Parent Education and Family Nurture

It is in the family that ultimate questions about the meaning and intention of life are repeatedly raised. There, more than any other place, topics about values, ritual, and purpose get discussed. Children in particular ask searching questions; parents may be hard put to respond to their underlying concerns as well as to the topical details of such queries. Recognizing the simultaneous opportunity and challenge this situation presents to families, church educators have traditionally worked to bring the church into homes to the extent that natural religious education could be advanced there.

The history of family education among the churches is uneven. Off and on through the years, the denominations have mounted programs to foster teaching of the faith directly by parents to their children. Curricula for homes, parent-teacher organizations, publications for families, and promotion of family worship plans are featured in these campaigns. Studies, however, have confirmed that only a tiny minority of parents take on the mantle of teachers at home; fewer still initiate times of worship in the family setting. Denominational officers, realizing the difficulty of this challenge, have tended to cut funds for family religious education, at least until the next surge of neofamilism arrives, at which time a new and revised program may be initiated.

Over the years, churches have frequently patterned their family programming after the example of secular mental health movements. Thus in the forties and fifties when psychologists were emphasizing the shortcomings of mothers and fathers, the churches tended to exploit guilt as motivation for their family curriculum promotion. In the sixties and seventies when the human potential movement flourished, churches emphasized individual development and ministry to the neglected, often at the expense of family programming. More recently, religious leaders have turned to themes of enrichment and wellness, the positive approach; this has redounded to the benefit of family education in the churches.

Enrichment in family education has come to mean the enhancement of relationships for individual family members, couples, parents, entire families, and intergenerational combinations. The emphasis of enrichment in religious education of families has generally featured the teaching of communication skills, experiential education (rather than didactic approaches), methods of conflict resolution, and an emphasis on the ability of persons to change.

Family clustering represents one popular model of the enrichment approach. In a typical church program, a family cluster involves four or five families as well as some single individuals who contract to meet together for some ten weeks. This intergenerational group comes to realize that anyone within it is capable of teaching others regardless of age differences, and that experiential education has a way of leveling out the differences among children and adults. Program plans are evolved one week at a time because each meeting builds upon the previous with its emphases upon mutual support, shared learning, and open communication. Typically, the groups hold two-hour sessions that include manual projects, small-group undertakings, supper, singing and games, and a closing ritual. At the end of the contracted period of weeks, the cluster disbands and others are formed then or later. The cluster concept can be applied through a number of variations, for example, church family nights in which the entire congregation is organized into smaller family-like units; programs within other programs, such as family camping; or special events, such as a cluster night for parents and children in the church school.[4]

The enrichment emphasis also reaches into marriage education. A variety of commendable programs have been developed to strengthen couple relationships. Here again the emphasis is on wellness, that is, to "make good marriages better," rather than upon crisis and an attempt to save marriages in jeopardy. Marriage enrichment is offered through several Marriage Encounter plans that were originally developed under Roman Catholic auspices. Some are sponsored by the Association of Couples for Marriage Enrichment,[5] others by communication laboratories, Transactional Analysis workshops, and the like. Although some critics have questioned the iatrogenic effects of the marriage enrichment events (for example, occasional opening of unrealized tensions, subsequent depression, and even rebellion against the discipline of some of these events), the movement has been gathering momentum and is widespread. Even though the concept has made only gradual headway among the churches, it has become firmly rooted and has a fair chance of becoming the predominant method of marital education in coming years. Numerous ministers are being trained as leaders in these enrichment programs; their commitment indicates something of future program development in parish churches.

Religious leaders frequently adapt educational programs from the secular scene, utilizing those aspects that are appropriate to the church and injecting particular emphases from ecclesiastical traditions that appear to be needed. They have modified Parent Effectiveness Training (PET), Ernest Gordon's popular entry into the enrichment field that brings the enrichment theme to parents and children. Likewise the Adlerian/Dreikurs input of Children the Challenge has received the imprimatur of church advocates for its practical approaches to intergenerational negotiation; it too has been somewhat altered to fit the needs of religious education. More startling is the introduction of "tough love" into the educational work of the churches. This product of the Community Service Foundation stresses firm discipline, organized parent unions, and "coming out of the closet" with an admission of previously unrecognized problems such as drug abuse, runaway teen-agers, and stealing. Yet even this rigorous approach picks up the enrichment theme with its nonblaming attitude, use of mutual support systems, and engagement of mediators. The emphasis here, and present in all the enrichment groups, is on aiding persons to assume responsibility and improve their family relationships.

It is in the instruction of the young that family educators are most adept in our churches; for here they have had long experience. Recognizing that parents are the primary teachers of children, a truism that dates to ancient times (Deut. 6:8; Prov. 22:6), they labor to help parents communicate the faith to their sons and daughters. That this can also be adult education at its best is obvious enough to educators but is often unrealized by the parents themselves. To the extent, however, that they learn how to deal with their children's questions or gain skill in meeting their adolescents where they live and move, parents are doubly served—both as educating and as educated.

The church, indeed, has good reason to be supportive of parents. It is they, as Randolph Crump Miller has suggested, who *are* the church to their children during those early years. Meanwhile it is the church that, through its adults, continues to believe for children until they are old enough to believe for themselves. In such a time, adult Christians keep alive the tradition, pass on the faith, and preserve the liturgy. In its ministry the church reaches out to the minorities, the lonely, the handicapped, the aged, and special persons who are part of the family of God. In so doing, the church needs the administration as well as the ministry of laity, officers, and clergy because an effective family ministry requires the collective support of parish leadership.

Pastoral Care and Church Administration

Pastoral care of families has its beginnings in the pastor's own family life. There the family of origin, spousal relationships (if any), attitudes and contacts with children, and continuing interaction with aging parents lend shape to the ability of a minister to care for pastoral concerns of church families. Nowhere is this more bluntly stated than in I Timothy: "If a man does not know how to manage his own household, how can he care for God's church?" (3:5).

Pastors, however, have astonishing advantages in regard to their ministry to families. They represent what is perhaps the only institution that can maintain continuous contact with a family throughout the lives of its members. They have a ready passport into the homes of the congregation, a privilege that other helping professions frequently envy. And they are the first counselors to whom most people turn, in preference to many other choices in the community, as a number of studies have shown.[6] Family therapy is a part of such pastoral care, a ministry brought into families that are at the time dysfunctional. Although such therapy is not the central duty of pastors, their abilities in this work help families solve problems and forge reconciliations that bring them back to health and understanding.

It is in regard to the family life cycle that pastors have yet another significant advantage. In ministry the church has always had a pastoral obligation to lead its people compassionately through their life pilgrimage. The church had learned to relate to the life cycle of families long before social psychologists had popularized that concept. In loving relation to families at times of birth, growth, crisis, and death, the congregation has an historic obligation. Yet although it has long been realized that church ministry reaches families at dedication/baptism, the Lord's Supper, weddings, maturing, and bereavement, this opportunity is more often "honored in the breach than in the observance." Seminary courses in pastoral care do emphasize these contact stages between families and church ministry; but the possibility of enlisting laity to reach each other in mutual ministry at these times is not realized to the optimum. Those churches that have organized and trained leadership for a ministry to these family life passages report a deepened sense of what it means to be a household of faith.

To take but one example, the pastor's ministry in strengthening marriages within the parish points the direction in which such care might go. Again effectiveness will begin with the pastor's own adjustment to marital status, whatever that is, and proceed from there: preparing couples premaritally for their nuptials, revisiting them after they have been married some months, making contact with them in their first experience of parenthood, opening to them through education the resources of family wellness in enrichment programs and, where need be, offering to them the resources of family therapy when they reach problems they cannot solve.

In such a ministry the pastor lengthens effectiveness through home visits and does some of his or her most influential counseling in the house setting and through the natural contact of calling. That contact is buttressed by the preaching program in the setting of public worship where the family of God is gathered together for prayer and praise.

Sometimes divine worship will be of the contemporary sort that sports balloons and guitars and popcorn. Sometimes it will be of formal liturgy with organ music and stained-glass windows. But the important element is that it be in the presence of the household of God where young and old together proclaim their faith and sing their praises. In the development of special Sundays, of house churches, and of vacation church schools, families can be taught special lessons about the worship of God in Christ. It is in imitation of their elders that children learn reverence. It is by watching their parents at prayer that they learn that God matters to adults. Through their own participation they absorb far more about the liturgy of their church than through courses, blackboard drills, or explanations. This is to say, as John Westerhoff has suggested, that faith and life do not come from the schoolroom model but from the enculturation of the community of faith. It is the *koinonia*, the family of God, that leads households and their young into the company of Christ.

The impressive assets of congregational life come to the fore again and again in the ministry to families. Support groups for the sick and the bereaved, mutual ministry of persons who have similar problems to overcome, such as living with "special children" or working through the grief of a broken marriage, represent such areas. Another positive aspect is the gathering and use of skills available in church members and clergy—skills of healing, counseling, organizing, and sharing. Likewise the church can draw upon the resources of community agencies that assist persons and families and, by means of cooperative service and bartering of help, can increase the effectiveness by which both do their work.

Theological Clues and Theological Problems

Church membership has always implied the concept of a household of faith within the extended family of God. The metaphor is biblical, the model theological. That it has its educational inferences is undeniable. To envision the people of the church as a family, all related to each other because they are first of all related as brothers and sisters of Christ, is not only to understand their congregation as a family but also to train them in their Christian faith as a family unit.

But today's families have become a new mission field. They have been so thoroughly secularized that it is necessary once more to teach them biblical literacy, the faith, and the tradition. Today's churches have the challenge to take the gospel into the homes of the people, and they are finding it to be a difficult task.

It sounds strangely archaic to married couples, for example, that they have a Christian vocation to be a husband, wife, or parent. The Reformation doctrine of vocation is so novel to today's thinking that it will take a major revival in Christianity to bring back that conviction to the central position it once had, and which it deserves for these times. Yet family life is a calling.

It is still in the family, rather than in the church school, that the most profound Christian education takes place. Families exert influence on one another far out of proportion to any other educational institution. The major theological doctrines are better understood within the home than anyplace else. As I have argued elsewhere,[7] we learn to know God and God's truth through our family relationships. Such an assertion admittedly will be unthinkable to those whose homes have fostered earthly hells of battering, abuse, and exploitation. But there are numerous pathways to God, and for many the pathway is in the home.

God's message of revelation has come to us through many contacts, some of them quite ordinary folks who have heard the Word and passed it on. Typically these people have been parents. In the family, the oncoming generation is instructed through a language of relationships, through emotional overtones and undertones among habitual actions and rituals, and in the provision for needs. It is in this matrix, for good or for ill, that we are also grounded in our faith. Parents transmit their convictions in the ways that they talk with their children, walk with them, put them to bed, and greet them in the morning (Deut. 6:7). Much of our theology is devoted toward establishing order out of our broken relationships, many of which are family oriented. The doctrines of sin and of grace both have to be understood relationally. How else could they be conceived? Neither can be experienced apart from other persons, or indeed from the person of God. Unless Christians can begin to conceptualize doctrines such as *redemption* in interpersonal terms, they stand light-years away from conceptualizing them in theological terms. We are not permitted to suppose, of course, that when we understand relationships on a human level that we then, by a cosmic leap, know the mystery of God. In the main, however, all our language about God must necessarily be analogical. To be sure, an analogue about redemption through human friendship will fall short of the full truth about God's redemptive act in Christ; but if we have never known anything about human redemptive experiences, we are even less prepared to apprehend any truth about God's redemption.

Or consider the exchange of *love* between parent and child. The child is taught to love by the example of the parental love. The infant's response, then, comes because a mother has taken the initiative. The baby can love back. This child can someday better comprehend some element of the love of God; we love because he first loved us (I John 4:19). If, however, children are deprived of love when they are infants, they may also be handicapped in their ability to give and receive love later on.

Likewise, children learn what *forgiveness* is by being forgiven. Forgiveness is learned at home if it is learned at all, and there it must be a daily practice in the spirit of love and understanding. Occasionally the pastor receives a confession from some adult parishioner who testifies that he or she cannot feel that God forgives sin. And if the pastor then gently inquires about the home life of that person, it may be discovered that as a child the person never knew forgiveness at home. A mother may have repeatedly used that damnable phrase, "If you do that, Mother won't love you."

Moreover, it is in family relationships that the child will learn what *reconciliation* is. Experiencing broken relations from time to time with members of the family, the child comes to grasp what acceptance and reconciliation are when such splits are healed, and self-esteem is strengthened.

To argue that redemption, love, forgiveness, and reconciliation as practiced in the home will be crucial to understanding these theological doctrines is not to suppose that the human and the divine spheres are identical or that one can take a grand jump from family life to spiritual realms and equally apprehend them both. Rather, it is to argue that God's reconciling the world to himself is a loving act of which our own experience partakes, at least in this small measure. It is to assert that the knowledge of reconciling love and forgiveness in family relationships does prepare one to better understand basic theological teachings. Without analogical experience in our own family relationships, we are handicapped in our abilities to know much of theological truth.

It is in such family life experience that religious faith is nurtured. It is toward such a goal that Christian education, when at its best, is directed.

Notes

1. See, e.g., Theodore Caplow, et al., *Middletown Families* (Minneapolis: University of Minnesota Press, 1982).
2. Edward Shorter, *The Making of The Modern Family* (New York: Basic Books, 1975).
3. "Monthly Vital Statistics Reports," National Center for Health Statistics, U.S. Department of Health and Human Services, 1982.
4. See Margaret Sawin, *Family Enrichment with Family Clusters* (Valley Forge, Penn.: Judson Press, 1979).
5. David and Vera Mace, *Marriage Enrichment in the Church* (Nashville: Broadman Press, 1976).
6. J. C. Wynn, *Family Therapy in Pastoral Ministry* (San Francisco: Harper & Row, 1982), 147.
7. Wynn, *Family Therapy in Pastoral Ministry.*

Bibliography

Anderson, Douglas A. *New Approaches to Family Pastoral Care.* Philadelphia: Fortress Press, 1980.

Greeley, Andrew. *The Family in Crisis or in Transition: A Sociological and Theological Perspective.* New York: The Seabury Press, 1979.

Listening to America's Families: Action for the 80's. A Summary of The Report to The President, Congress, and Families of the Nation. U.S. Government Printing Office, 1980.

Neff, Pauline. *Tough Love: How Parents Can Deal with Drug Abuse.* Nashville: Abingdon Press, 1982.

Sawin, Margaret. *Hope for Families.* New York: William H. Sadlier, 1982.

Tufte, Virginia, and Barbara Myerhoff, eds. *Changing Images of the Family.* New Haven: Yale University Press, 1979.

York, Phyllis, and David and Ted Wachtel. *Toughlove.* Garden City, N.Y.: Doubleday, 1982.

A Selected Bibliography: Since 1973

Compiled by *Marvin J. Taylor*

Current bibliographies have been a feature of these symposia since the Lotz volume published in 1950. The goal has been to provide the reader with a substantial suggested reading list on the several areas which comprise the discipline of religious education. While the purpose has been to be reasonably comprehensive, the discerning reader will note that it is a selected list. Space simply does not permit including everything that has been published.

The date noted above is important. These are recent publications. Each of the bibliographies has by design been limited to those items which have been published since the last bibliography was prepared. Hence, the reader must of necessity consult the earlier books if a genuinely comprehensive coverage of some topic is desired. Older volumes, even when classic in importance, have not been included.

The categories utilized were largely those of the prior bibliographies, adjusted to reflect new emphases and topics. A few subcategories have been dropped, since they have not had enduring value to the discipline. Others have been added as new foci have emerged and been recognized by the appearance of worthy literature. The contributors of the several chapters were involved in these selections indirectly, since their recommendations were taken into account in determining the list. However, the final selection is solely my responsibility, since I often decided to choose from among the volumes cited. Since the list is thus selective, it is obviously personal—the publications which seem to me to be a representative sample. It will be immediately apparent that virtually all denominational publications have been excluded, and this eliminates many fine books. However, since the inclusion of all or even most of these would have made the list too voluminous, it seemed wise to include only a few.

Nature, Principles, and History of Religious Education

Nature, Philosophy, and Principles of Religious Education

Beck, C. *Educational Philosophy and Theory: An Introduction.* Boston: Little, Brown, & Co., 1974.

Boys, Mary C. *Biblical Interpretation in Religious Education.* Birmingham, Ala.: Religious Education Press, 1980.

Brueggemann, Walter. *The Creative Word: Canon as a Model for Biblical Education.* Philadelphia: Fortress Press, 1982.

Burgess, Harold William. *An Invitation to Religious Education.* Mishawaka, Ind.: Religious Education Press, 1975.

Chamberlin, J. Gordon. *The Educating Act: A Phenomenological View.* Washington: University Press of America, 1981.

Cremin, Lawrence. *Public Education.* New York: Basic Books, 1976.

Cully, Iris V., and Kendig B. Cully, eds. *Process and Relationship.* Birmingham, Ala.: Religious Education Press, 1978.

Daniel, Eleanor, John W. Wade, and Charles Gresham. *Introduction to Christian Education.* Cincinnati: Standard Publishing Company, 1980.

Davidson, Robert. *The Bible in Religious Education.* Edinburgh: Handsel Press, 1979.

Duck, Lloyd. *Teaching with Charisma.* Boston: Allyn & Bacon, 1981.

Durka, Gloria, and Joanmarie Smith, eds. *Emerging Issues in Religious Education.* New York: Paulist Press, 1976.

Graendorf, Werner C., ed. *Introduction to Biblical Christian Education.* Chicago: Moody Press, 1981.

Groome, Thomas H. *Christian Religious Education: Sharing Our Story and Vision.* San Francisco: Harper & Row, 1980.

Harper, Norman E. *Making Disciples, the Challenge of Christian Education at the End of the Twentieth Century.* Memphis: Christian Studies Center, 1981.

Harris, Maria, ed. *Parish Religious Education.* New York: Paulist Press, 1978.

Heckman, Shirley J. *On the Wings of a Butterfly, A Guide to Total Christian Education.* Elgin, Ill.: Brethren Press, 1981.

Holley, Raymond. *Religious Education and Religious Understanding.* Boston: Routledge & Kegan Paul Ltd., 1978.

Kelsey, Morton. *Can Christians Be Educated?* Mishawaka, Ind.: Religious Education Press, 1977.

Knox, Ian. *Above or Within: The Supernatural in Religious Education.* Birmingham, Ala.: Religious Education Press, 1976.

Lee, James Michael, ed. *The Religious Education We Need: Toward the Renewal of Christian Education.* Mishawaka, Ind.: Religious Education Press, 1977.

Little, Sara. *To Set One's Heart: Belief and Teaching in the Church.* Atlanta: John Knox Press, 1983.

Manheimer, Ronald J. *Kierkegaard as Educator.* Berkeley: University of California Press, 1977.

Marino, Joseph S. *Biblical Themes in Religious Education.* Birmingham, Ala.: Religious Education Press, 1983.

Miller, Randolph Crump. *The Theory of Christian Education Practice.* Birmingham, Ala.: Religious Education Press, 1980.

Moore, Mary Elizabeth. *Education for Continuity and Change: A New Model for Christian Religious Education.* Nashville: Abingdon Press, 1983.

Moran, Gabriel. *Interplay: A Theory of Religion and Education.* Winona, Minn.: St. Mary's Press, 1981.

———. *Religious Body: Design for a New Reformation.* New York: The Seabury Press, 1974.

Novak, Joseph D. *A Theory of Education.* Ithaca: Cornell University Press, 1977.

O'Hare, Padraic, ed. *Foundations of Religious Education.* New York: Paulist Press, 1978.

———, ed. *Tradition and Transformation in Religious Education.* Birmingham, Ala.: Religious Education Press, 1979.

Perry, David W., ed. *Making Sense of Things: Toward a Philosophy of Homegrown Christian Education.* New York: The Seabury Press, 1981.

Piveteau, Didier-Jacques, and J. T. Dillon. *Resurgence in Religious Instruction.* Notre Dame, Ind.: Religious Education Press, 1977.

Richards, Lawrence O. *A Theology of Christian Education.* Grand Rapids: Zondervan Publishing Corp., 1975.

Russell, Letty M. *The Future of Partnership.* Philadelphia: The Westminster Press, 1979.

Sanner, A. Elwood, A. F. Harper, et al. *Exploring Christian Education.* Grand Rapids: Baker Book House, 1978.

Seymour, Jack L., and Donald E. Miller, eds. *Contemporary Approaches to Christian Education.* Nashville: Abingdon Press, 1982.

Thompson, Norma H., ed. *Religious Education and Theology.* Birmingham, Ala.: Religious Education Press, 1982.

Westerhoff, John H. III. *Tomorrow's Church.* Waco, Tex.: Word, 1976.

———. *Will Our Children Have Faith?* New York: The Seabury Press, 1976.

———, and Gwen Kennedy Neville. *Generation to Generation.* Philadelphia: Pilgrim Press, 1974.

History of Religious Education

Booth, Frank. *Robert Raikes of Gloucester.* Nutfield, Redhill, Surrey: National Christian Education Council, 1980.

Campbell, Eldrich C., Jr. *George Albert Coe and Religious Education.* New York: Carlton Press, 1974.

Chapman, William E. *Roots of Character Education.* Schenectady, N.Y.: Character Research Press, 1977.

Cremin, Lawrence A. *Traditions of American Education.* New York: Basic Books, 1977.

Dobbins, Austin C. *Gaines S. Dobbins: Pioneer in Religious Education.* Nashville: Broadman Press, 1981.

Edwards, O. C., Jr., and John H. Westerhoff III, eds. *A Faithful Church: Issues in the History of Catechesis*. Wilton, Conn.: Morehouse-Barlow Company, 1981.

Gangel, Kenneth O., and Warren S. Benson. *Christian Education: Its History and Philosophy*. Chicago: Moody Press, 1983.

Grassi, Joseph A. *The Teacher in the Primitive Church and the Teacher Today*. Santa Clara: University of Santa Clara Press, 1973.

Greven, Philip. *The Protestant Temperament: Patterns of Child-Rearing, Religious Experience, and the Self in Early America*. New York: Alfred A. Knopf, 1977.

Kathan, Boardman, ed. *Pioneers of Religious Education in the Twentieth Century*. New Haven: Religious Education Association, 1978.

Knoff, Gerald E. *The World Sunday School Movement: The Story of a Broadening Mission*. New York: The Seabury Press, 1979.

LaQueur, Thomas W. *Religion and Respectability: Sunday Schools and the Working Class Culture, 1780-1850*. New Haven: Yale University Press, 1976.

Lynn, Robert W., and Elliott Wright. *The Big Little School: Two Hundred Years of the Sunday School*. Rev. ed. Birmingham, Ala.: Religious Education Press and Nashville: Abingdon Press, 1980.

Morrison, Theodore. *Chautauqua: A Center for Education, Religion, and the Arts in America*. Chicago: University of Chicago Press, 1974.

Parker, Inez Moore. *The Rise and Decline of the Program of Education for Black Presbyterians of the United Presbyterian Church, U.S.A., 1865-1970*. San Antonio: Trinity University Press, 1977.

Perkinson, Henry J. *Two Hundred Years of American Educational Thought*. New York: David McKay Co., 1976.

Peters, R. S. *Essays on Educators*. London: George Allen & Unwin, 1981.

Schmidt, Stephen A. *History of the Religious Education Association*. Birmingam, Ala.: Religious Education Press, 1983.

Seymour, Jack L. *From Sunday School to Church School: Continuities in Protestant Church Education*. Washington: University Press of America, 1982.

Smart, Ninian, and Donald Horder, eds. *New Movements in Religious Education*. London: Temple Smith Ltd., 1975.

Smith, David L. *Symbolism and Growth: The Religious Thought of Horace Bushnell*. Chico, Calif.: Scholars Press, 1981.

Towns, Elmer L., ed. *A History of Religious Educators*. Grand Rapids: Baker Book House, 1975.

Tyms, James D. *The Rise of Religious Education Among Negro Baptists*. Washington: University Press of America, 1979.

Warren, Michael, ed. *Sourcebook for Modern Catechetics*. Winona, Minn.: St. Mary's Press, 1983.

Westerhoff, John H. III. *McGuffey and His Readers: Piety, Morality, and Education in Nineteenth-Century America*. Nashville: Abingdon Press, 1978.

Wills, Wesley R. *200 Years—and Still Counting: Past, Present, and Future of the Sunday School.* Wheaton, Ill.: Victor Books, 1979.

Liberation Themes and Religious Education

Barker, Kenneth. *Religious Education, Catechesis, and Freedom.* Birmingham, Ala.: Religious Education Press, 1981.

Collins, Davis. *Paulo Freire: His Life, Work, and Thought.* New York: Paulist Press, 1977.

Elias, John L. *Conscientization and DeSchooling: Freire's and Illich's Proposals for Reshaping Society.* Philadelphia: Westminster Press, 1976.

Elizondo, Virgilio, and Norbert Greinacher, eds. *Women in a Man's Church.* New York: The Seabury Press, 1980.

Freire, Paulo. *Pedagogy in Process: The Letters to Guinea-Bissau.* New York: The Seabury Press, 1978.

Harding, Vincent. *There Is a River: The Black Struggle for Freedom in America.* New York: Harcourt Brace Jovanovich, 1981.

Lerner, Gerda. *The Majority Finds Its Past: Placing Women in History.* New York: Oxford University Press, 1979.

O'Hare, Padraic, ed. *Education for Peace and Justice.* San Francisco: Harper & Row, 1983.

Russell, Letty M. *Growth in Partnership.* Philadelphia: The Westminster Press, 1981.

———. *Human Liberation in a Feminist Perspective.* Philadelphia: The Westminster Press, 1974.

Sawicki, Marianne. *Faith and Sexism: Guidelines for Religious Educators.* New York: The Seabury Press, 1979.

Warford, Malcolm L. *The Necessary Illusion: Church Culture and Educational Change.* Philadelphia: Pilgrim Press, 1976.

Wilmore, Gayraud S., and James Cone, eds. *Black Theology: A Documentary History, 1966-1979.* New York: Orbis Books, 1979.

Wren, Brian. *Education for Justice: Pedagogical Principles.* Maryknoll, N.Y.: Orbis Books, 1977.

Religious Growth and the Teaching-Learning Process

Moral and Religious Growth

Bringuier, Jean-Claude. *Conversations with Jean Piaget.* Chicago: University of Chicago Press, 1980.

Bronfenbrenner, Urie. *The Ecology of Human Development.* Cambridge: Harvard University Press, 1979.

Brusselmans, Christiane, ed. *Toward Moral and Religious Maturity.* Morristown, N.J.: Silver Burdett Company, 1980.

Bufford, Rodger K. *The Human Reflex: Behavioral Psychology in Biblical Perspective.* San Francisco: Harper & Row, 1981.

Cochrane, D. B., C. M. Hamm, and A. C. Kazepides, eds. *The Domain of Moral Education*. New York: Paulist Press, 1979.

Conn, Walter E. *Conscience: Development and Self-Transcendence*. Birmingham, Ala.: Religious Education Press, 1981.

Cully, Iris V. *Christian Child Development*. San Francisco: Harper & Row, 1979.

Damon, William, ed. *Moral Development*. San Francisco: Jossey-Bass, 1978.

DeBenedittis, Suzanne M. *Teaching Faith and Morals: Toward Personal and Parish Renewal*. Minneapolis: Winston Press, 1981.

DePalma, D. J., and J. M. Foley, eds. *Moral Development: Current Theory and Research*. Hillsdale, N.J.: Lawrence Erlbaum Associates, 1975.

Duska, Ronald, and Mariellen Whelan. *Moral Development: A Guide to Piaget and Kohlberg*. Paramus, N.J.: Paulist Press, 1975.

Dykstra, Craig. *Vision and Character: A Christian Educator's Alternative to Kohlberg*. New York: Paulist Press, 1981.

Elkind, David. *The Child's Reality: Three Developmental Themes*. New York: John Wiley and Sons, 1978.

Faber, Heije. *Psychology of Religion*. Philadelphia: The Westminster Press, 1975.

Fleck, J. Roland, and John D. Carter, eds. *Psychology and Christianity: Integrative Readings*. Nashville: Abingdon Press, 1981.

Fowler, James W. *Stages of Faith: The Psychology of Human Development and the Quest for Meaning*. San Francisco: Harper & Row, 1981.

———, et al. *Trajectories in Faith*. Nashville: Abingdon Press, 1980.

Hall, Brian P. *The Development of Consciousness*. New York: Paulist Press, 1976.

Hall, Robert T. *Moral Education: A Handbook for Educators*. Minneapolis: Winston Press, 1979.

Hennessy, Thomas C., ed. *Values and Moral Development*. New York: Paulist Press, 1976.

———. *Values/Moral Education: Schools and Teachers*. Ramsey, N.J.: Paulist Press, 1979.

Joy, Donald M., ed. *Moral Development Foundations: Judeo-Christian Alternatives to Piaget/Kohlberg*. Nashville: Abingdon Press, 1983.

Kohlberg, Lawrence. *Essays in Moral Development. Volume One: The Philosophy of Moral Development*. San Francisco: Harper & Row, 1981.

Lickona, T., ed. *Moral Development and Behavior*. New York: Holt, Rinehart & Winston, 1976.

Loder, James E. *The Transforming Moment: Understanding Convictional Experiences*. San Francisco: Harper & Row, 1981.

Miller, Donald E. *The Wing-Footed Wanderer: Conscience and Transcendence*. Nashville: Abingdon Press, 1977.

Munsey, Brenda, ed. *Moral Development, Moral Education, and Kohlberg*. Birmingham, Ala.: Religious Education Press, 1980.

Murray, Frank B., ed. *The Impact of Piagetian Theory on Education, Philosophy, Psychiatry, and Psychology*. Baltimore: University Park Press, 1979.

Myers, David G. *The Human Puzzle: Psychological Research and Christian Belief*. San Francisco: Harper & Row, 1978.

Nelson, C. Ellis. *Don't Let Your Conscience Be Your Guide*. New York: Paulist Press, 1978.

Peatling, John H. *Religious Education in a Psychological Key*. Birmingham, Ala.: Religious Education Press, 1981.

Rizzuto, Ana-Maria. *The Birth of the Living God*. Chicago: University of Chicago Press, 1979.

Scharf, Peter, et al, eds. *Readings in Moral Education*. Minneapolis: Winston Press, 1978.

Stokes, Kenneth, ed. *Faith Development in the Adult Life Cycle*. New York: William H. Sadlier, 1982.

Sullivan, Edmund V. *Moral Learning*. New York: Paulist Press, 1975.

Ulanov, Ann, and Barry Ulanov. *Religion and the Unconscious*. Philadelphia: The Westminster Press, 1975.

Wilcox, Mary M. *Developmental Journey*. Nashville: Abingdon Press, 1979.

Wilson, John, and Barbara Cowell. *Dialogues on Moral Education*. Birmingham, Ala.: Religious Education Press, 1983.

Youniss, James. *Parents and Peers in Social Development: A Sullivan-Piaget Perspective*. Chicago: University of Chicago Press, 1980.

The Teaching-Learning Process

Bowman, Locke, E., Jr. *Teaching Today*. Philadelphia: The Westminster Press, 1980.

Chadwick, Ronald A. *Teaching and Learning: An Integrated Approach to Christian Education*. Old Tappan, N.J.: Fleming H. Revell Co., 1982.

Foster, Charles R. *Teaching in the Community of Faith*. Nashville: Abingdon Press, 1982.

Kohl, Herbert. *On Teaching*. New York: Schocken Books, 1976.

McBride, Alfred A. *Creative Teaching in Christian Education*. Boston: Allyn & Bacon, 1978.

Reichert, Richard. *A Learning Process for Religious Education*. Dayton, Ohio: Pflaum Publishing Co., 1975.

Rogers, Donald B. *In Praise of Learning*. Nashville: Abingdon Press, 1980.

Wolterstorff, Nicholas P. *Educating for Responsible Action*. Grand Rapids: Wm. B. Eerdmans Publishing Co., 1980.

Wynn, J. C. *Christian Education for Liberation*. Nashville: Abingdon Press, 1977.

Organization and Administration for Religious Education

Church Educational Patterns

Anderson, Clifford V. *Count on Me!* Wheaton, Ill.: Victor Books, 1980.

Anderson, James D., and Ezra Earl Jones. *The Management of Ministry*. San Francisco: Harper & Row, 1978.

Argyris, Chris. *Increasing Leadership Effectiveness*. New York: John Wiley and Sons, 1976.

Bossart, Donald E. *Creative Conflicts in Religious Education and Church Administration*. Birmingham, Ala.: Religious Education Press, 1980.

Byrne, Herbert W. *Improving Church Education*. Birmingham, Ala.: Religious Education Press, 1979.

Campbell, Thomas C., and Gary B. Reierson. *The Gift of Administration: Theological Bases for Ministry*. Philadelphia: The Westminster Press, 1981.

Cully, Iris V. *New Life for Your Sunday School*. New York: Hawthorn Books, 1976.

Furnish, Dorothy Jean. *DRE/DCE—The History of a Profession*. Nashville: Christian Educators Fellowship, 1976.

Gangel, Kenneth O. *Building Leaders for Church Education*. Chicago: Moody Press, 1981.

Gilbert, E. Kent, ed. *The Shaping of the Parish for the Future*. Philadelphia: Parish Life Press, 1975.

Harris, Maria. *The D. R. E. Book*. New York: Paulist Press, 1976.

———, ed. *The D. R. E. Reader: A Sourcebook in Education and Ministry*. Winona, Minn.: St. Mary's Press, 1980.

Olson, Richard A., ed. *The Pastor's Role in Educational Ministry*. Philadelphia: Fortress Press, 1974.

Powers, Bruce P., ed. *Christian Education Handbook*. Nashville: Broadman Press, 1981.

Richards, Lawrence O., and Clyde Hoeldtke. *A Theology of Church Leadership*. Grand Rapids: Zondervan Publishing Corp., 1980.

Towns, Elmer. *The Successful Sunday School and the Teachers Guidebook*. Carol Stream, Ill.: Creation House, 1976.

Worley, Robert C. *A Gathering of Strangers: Understanding the Life of Your Church*. Philadelphia: The Westminster Press, 1976.

Religion and the Schools: Public and Private

Abernathy, M. Glenn. *Civil Liberties Under the Constitution*. New York: Harper & Row, 1977.

Barr, David, and Nicholas Piediscalzi, eds. *The Bible in American Education*. Chico, Calif.: Scholars Press, 1982.

Bellah, Robert N. *The Broken Covenant: American Civil Religion in Time of Trial*. New York: The Seabury Press, 1975.

Engel, David E., ed. *Religion in Public Education*. New York: Paulist Press, 1974.

Gaffney, Edward McGlynn, Jr., ed. *Private Schools and the Public Good: Policy Alternatives for the Eighties*. Notre Dame, Ind.: University of Notre Dame Press, 1981.

Holm, Jean L. *Teaching Religion in School*. London: Oxford University Press, 1975.

Hull, John M., ed. *New Directions in Religious Education*. Barcombe, Lewes, Sussex: The Falmer Press, 1982.

Hulmes, Edward. *Commitment and Neutrality in Religious Education*. London: Chapman, 1979.

McCarthy, Rockne, et al. *Society, State, and Schools*. Grand Rapids: Wm. B. Eerdmans Publishing Co., 1981.

O'Neil, Robert M. *Classrooms in the Crossfire: The Rights and Interests of Students, Parents, Teachers, Administrators, Librarians, and the Community*. Bloomington, Ind.: Indiana University Press, 1981.

Piediscalzi, Nicholas, and William E. Collie, eds. *Teaching About Religion in Public Schools*. Niles, Ill.: Argus Communications, 1977.

Taylor, Lynn. *Religion and Culture in Education: Open Door for the Fourth R*. Lawrence, Kan.: University of Kansas Press, 1977.

Warsaw, Thayer S. *Religion, Education, and the Supreme Court*. Nashville: Abingdon Press, 1979.

Weinstein, Joshua. *When Religion Comes to School*. Washington, D.C.: University Press of America, 1979.

Will, Paul J., ed. *Public Education Religion Studies: An Overview*. Chico, Calif.: Scholars Press, 1981.

Roman Catholic Religious Education

Boys, Mary C., ed. *Ministry and Education in Conversation*. Winona, Minn.: St. Mary's Press, 1981.

Dyer, George J., ed. *An American Catholic Catechism*. New York: The Seabury Press, 1975.

Hofinger, Johannes. *Evangelization and Catechesis*. New York: Paulist Press, 1976.

Marthaler, Berard, and M. Sawicki, eds. *Catechesis: Realities and Visions*. Washington: United States Catholic Conference, 1977.

Murphy, Elly, Marisa Guerin, John Roberto, and Margaret Wilson Brown, eds. *Hope for the Decade: A Look at the Issues Facing Catholic Youth Ministry*. Washington: National Catholic Youth Organization Federation, 1980.

Religion and Higher Education

Betz, Hans Dieter, ed. *The Bible as a Document of the University*. Chico, Calif.: Scholars Press, 1981.

Rankin, Robert, ed. *The Recovery of Spirit in Higher Education*. New York: The Seabury Press, 1980.

Westerhoff, John H. III, ed. *The Church's Ministry in Higher Education*. New York: United Ministries in Higher Education, 1978.

The Curriculum of Religious Education

Anderson, Digby C. *Evaluating Curriculum Proposals*. New York: John Wiley and Sons, 1981.

Colson, Howard P., and Raymond M. Rigdon. *Understanding Your Church's Curriculum*. Nashville: Broadman Press, 1981.

Cully, Iris V. *Planning and Selecting Curriculum for Christian Education*. Valley Forge, Penn.: Judson Press, 1983.

Guide to Curriculum Choice. Elgin, Ill.: Brethren Press, 1981.

Pinar, William, ed. *Curriculum Theorizing*. San Francisco: McCutchan, 1975.

Stoughton, C. R. *Issues in Curriculum Theory*. Washington, D.C.: University Press of America, 1981.

Methods and Age Level Religious Education Materials

General Considerations of Method

Bissonier, Henri. *The Pedagogy of Resurrection: The Religious Formation and Christian Education of the Handicapped and Maladjusted*. Ramsey, N.J.: Paulist Press, 1979.

Koehler, George E. *Learning Together: A Guide to Intergenerational Education in the Church*. Nashville: Discipleship Resources, 1977.

Rogers, Sharee, and Jack Rogers. *The Family Together: Intergenerational Education in the Church School*. Los Angeles: Acton House, 1976.

Russell, Letty M. *The Liberating Word*. Philadelphia: The Westminster Press, 1976.

Weil, Marsha, and Bruce Joyce. *Models of Teaching*. Englewood Cliffs, N.J.: Prentice-Hall, 1978.

Religious Education of Children

Applebee, Arthur N. *The Child's Concept of Story: Ages Two to Seventeen*. Chicago: University of Chicago Press, 1978.

Barber, Lucie W. *Celebrating the Second Year of Life*. Birmingham, Ala.: Religious Education Press, 1978.

———. *The Religious Education of PreSchool Children*. Birmingham, Ala.: Religious Education Press, 1981.

Coons, John, and Stephen Sugarman. *Education by Choice: The Case for Family Control*. Berkeley: University of California Press, 1977.

Crow, Gary A. *Children at Risk: A Handbook of the Signs and Symptoms of Early Childhood Difficulties*. New York: Schocken Books, 1978.

Griggs, Patricia. *Using Storytelling in Christian Education*. Nashville: Abingdon Press, 1981.

Koulomzin, Sophie. *Our Church and Our Children*. Crestwood, N.Y.: St. Vladimir's Seminary Press, 1975.

Lema, Anza A. *Child Development and Educational Planning*. Geneva: Lutheran World Federation, 1981.

Perske, Robert. *Hope for the Families: New Directions for Parents of Persons with Retardation or Other Disabilities*. Nashville: Abingdon Press, 1981.

Robinson, Edward. *The Original Vision: A Study of the Religious Experience of Childhood*. New York: The Seabury Press, 1983.

Westerhoff, John H. III. *Bringing Up Children in the Christian Faith*. Minneapolis: Winston Press, 1980.

Zuck, Roy B., and Robert E. Clark, eds. *Childhood Education in The Church*. Chicago: Moody Press, 1975.

Religious Education of Youth

Brake, Michael. *The Sociology of Youth Culture and Youth Subcultures.* London: Routledge & Kegan Paul, 1980.

Coleman, James S., ed. *Youth: Transition to Adulthood.* Chicago: University of Chicago Press, 1974.

Doherty, Sister M. Michael. *Spiritual Dimensions in Teaching High School Religion.* New York: Alba House, 1976.

Hargrove, Barbara. *Religion for a Dislocated Generation.* Valley Forge, Penn.: Judson Press, 1980.

Harris, Maria. *Portrait of Youth Ministry.* New York: Paulist Press, 1981.

Holmes, Urban T. III. *Confirmation: The Celebration of Maturity in Christ.* New York: The Seabury Press, 1975.

Kett, Joseph F. *Rites of Passage: Adolescence in America, 1790 to the Present.* New York: Basic Books, 1977.

Roadcup, David, ed. *Ministering to Youth: A Strategy for the 80's.* Cincinnati: Standard Publishing Company, 1980.

Sparkman, G. Temp, ed. *Knowing and Helping Youth.* Nashville: Broadman Press, 1977.

Toward Adolescence: The Middle School Years. Seventy-ninth Yearbook of the National Society for the Study of Education. Part I. Chicago: National Society for the Study of Education.

Warren, Michael. *A Future for Youth Catechesis.* New York: Paulist Press, 1975.

————. *Youth and the Future of the Church: Ministry with Youth and Young Adults.* New York: Seabury Press, 1982.

————, ed. *Youth Ministry: A Book of Readings.* New York: Paulist Press, 1977.

Wyckoff, D. Campbell, and Don Richter. *Religious Education Ministry with Youth.* Birmingham, Ala.: Religious Education Press, 1982.

Religious Education of Adults

Agnew, Marie. *Future Shapes of Adult Religious Education.* New York: Paulist Press, 1976.

Clements, William M., ed. *Ministry with the Aging: Design, Challenges, Foundations.* San Francisco: Harper & Row, 1981.

Cross, K. Patricia. *Adults as Learners.* San Francisco: Jossey-Bass, Publishers, 1981.

Elias, John L. *The Foundations and Practice of Adult Religious Education.* Melbourne, Fla.: Krieger Publishing Co., 1982.

————, and Sharan Merriam. *Philosophical Foundations of Adult Education.* New York: Krieger Publishing Co., 1980.

Lovell, R. Bernard. *Adult Learning.* New York: Halsted Press, 1980.

McKenzie, Leon. *Adult Education and the Burden of the Future.* Washington, D.C.: University Press of America, 1979.

————. *The Religious Education of Adults*. Birmingham, Ala.: Religious Education Press, 1982.

Moran, Gabriel. *Education Toward Adulthood: Religion and Lifelong Learning*. New York: Paulist Press, 1979.

Murray, Richard T. *Strengthening the Adult Sunday School Class*. Nashville: Abingdon Press, 1981.

Families and Religious Education

Anderson, Douglas A. *New Approaches to Family Pastoral Care*. Philadelphia: Fortress Press, 1980.

Durka, Gloria, and Joanmarie Smith, eds. *Family Ministry*. Minneapolis: Winston Press, 1980.

Greeley, Andrew. *The Family in Crisis or in Transition: A Sociological and Theological Perspective*. New York: The Seabury Press, 1979.

Kaye, Evelyn. *Cross Currents: Children, Families, and Religion*. New York: Clarkson N. Potter/Publisher, 1980.

Lasch, Christopher. *Haven in a Heartless World: The Family Besieged*. New York: Basic Books, 1977.

Leichter, Hope Jensen, ed. *The Family as Educator*. New York: Teachers College Press, 1974.

Poster, Mark. *Critical Theory of the Family*. New York: The Seabury Press, 1978.

Sawin, Margaret M. *Family Enrichment with Family Clusters*. Valley Forge, Penn.: Judson Press, 1979.

————, ed. *Hope for Families*. New York: William H. Sadlier, 1982.

Sell, Charles M. *Family Ministry*. Grand Rapids: Zondervan Publishing Corp., 1981.

Shorter, Edward. *The Making of the Modern Family*. New York: Basic Books, 1975.

Wynn, J. C. *Family Therapy in Pastoral Ministry*. San Francisco: Harper & Row, 1982.

Religious Education, the Arts, and Worship

Durka, Gloria, and Joanmarie Smith. *Aesthetic Dimensions of Religious Education*. New York: Paulist Press, 1979.

Gobbel, A. Roger, and Phillip C. Huber. *Creative Designs with Children at Worship*. Atlanta: John Knox Press, 1981.

Neville, Gwen Kennedy, and John H. Westerhoff III. *Learning Through Liturgy*. New York: The Seabury Press, 1978.

Ng, David, and Virginia Thomas. *Children in the Worshipping Community*. Atlanta: John Knox Press, 1981.

Index